INFORMATION TECHNOLOGY AND ARBITRATION

A PRACTITIONER'S GUIDE

INFORMATION TECHNOLOGY AND ARBITRATION

A PRACTITIONER'S GUIDE

By
Thomas Schultz

With a Foreword by
Gabrielle Kaufmann-Kohler

KLUWER LAW
INTERNATIONAL

A C.I.P. catalogue record for this book is available from the Library of Congress.

ISBN 90 411 2515 9

Published by:
Kluwer Law International
P.O. Box 316
2400 AH Alphen aan den Rijn
The Netherlands

Sold and distributed in North, Central and South America by:
Aspen Publishers, Inc.
7201 McKinney Circle
Frederick, MD 21704
United States of America

Sold and distributed in all other countries by:
Turpin Distribution Services Ltd
Stratton Business Park
Pegasus Drive
Biggleswade
Bedfordshire SG18 8TQ
United Kingdom

Printed on acid-free paper

CONTENTS

ABBREVIATIONS

AAA	American Arbitration Association
ACJ	America's Cup Jury
ADR	Alternative Dispute Resolution
AIBA	International Boxing Association
ALR	Australian Law Reports
Am Rev Int'l Arb	American Review of International Arbitration
Am U Int'l L Rev	American University International Law Review
AmLaw Tech	The American Lawyer's supplement on IT and the law
App	Application
ASA	Association Suisse d'Arbitrage
ASA Bull	Bulletin of the Swiss Arbitration Association
ascii	American Standard Code for Information Interchange
B U J Sci & Tech L	Boston University Journal of Science and Technology Law
bcc	Blind carbon copy
bmp	Bitmap format
Bus Law	Business Lawyer
CA	Court of Appeal or Certification authority
CAS	Court of Arbitration for Sports
cc	Carbon copy
CEPANI	Belgian Center for Arbitration and Mediation
CIETAC	China International Economic and Trade Arbitration Commission
Chi J Int'l L	Chicago Journal of International Law
Cir.	US Circuit Court
Com Ct	Commercial Court within the Queen's Bench Division
CPU	Central processing unit
Croat Arbit Yearb	Croatian Arbitration Yearbook
DDC	District of D.C.
D Del	District of Delaware
doc	Microsoft Word document format
EC	European Communities
ECAF	Electronic Case Facility (WIPO)
ECHR	European Convention for the Protection of Human Rights and Fundamental Freedoms 1953
ed, eds	Editor, Editors
edn	Edition
EHRR	European Human Rights Reports
EWHC	England & Wales High Court (reporter)
Fed Cir	Federal Circuit
FISA	International Rowing Federation

FRD	US Federal Rules Decisions
ftp	File Transfer Protocol
gif	Graphics Interchange Format
GnuPG	Gnu's Not Unix Privacy Guard
GPRS	General Packet Radio Service
html	Hypertext Markup Language
http	Hypertext Transmission Protocol
https	Hypertext Transmission Protocol secure
HUP	Harvard University Press
ICAC	International Commercial Arbitration Court at the Chamber of Commerce and Industry of the Russian Federation
ICANN	Internet Corporation for Assigned Names and Numbers
ICC	International Chamber of Commerce
ICC Bull	ICC International Court of Arbitration Bulletin
ID	Identity
Int A L R	International Arbitration Law Review
Int'l Arb Rep	Mealey's International Arbitration Report
IOC	International Olympic Committee
IP	Internet Protocol
IRC	Internet Relay Chat
ISDN	Integrated Services Digital Network
ISP	Internet Service Provider
IT	Information Technology
J Disp Resol	Journal of Dispute Resolution
J Int Arb	Journal of International Arbitration
J Int'l Econ L	Journal of International Economic Law
J Marshall J Computer & Info L	John Marshall Journal of Computer & Information Law
JCAA	Japan Commercial Arbitration Association
jpg / jpeg	Joint Picture Group / Joint Picture Expert Group format
Kbps	Kilobits per second
LCIA	London Court of International Arbitration
LGDJ	Librairie Générale de Droit et Jurisprudence
Lloyd's Rep	Lloyd's Report
MHz	Megahertz
MIT	Massachusetts Institute for Technology
N Ky L Rev	Northern Kentucky University Law Review
N M L Rev	New Mexico Law Review
NAFTA	North American Free Trade Agreement
NC J L & Tech	North Carolina Journal of Law & Technology
NCAIR	National Center for Automated Information Research
NYC	New York Convention on the Recognition and Enforcement of Foreign Arbitral Awards
ODR	Online Dispute Resolution
Ohio St J on Disp Resol	Ohio State Journal on Dispute Resolution
pdf	Portable Document Format
Personnel J	Personnel Journal
PGP	Pretty Good Privacy protocol
PIL	Private International Law

QB	Queen's Bench (Law reports)
RDTI	Revue du droit des technologies de l'information
Rev Arb	Revue de l'Arbitrage
RO	Official Reporter of the Swiss Supreme Court
rtf	Rich Text Format
RTMP(T)(S)	Real-Time Message Protocol, and variants
Rutgers Computer & Tech L J	Rutgers Computer and Technology Law Journal
RWS	Recht Wirtschaft Steuern Verlag
SC L Rev	South Carolina Law Review
SCC	Stockholm Chamber of Commerce
Series A	Publications of the European Court of Human Rights; Judgments and Decisions
smtp	Simple Mail Transfer Protocol
SSL	Secure Sockets Layer
Stan L Rev	Stanford Law Review
Stetson L Rev	Stetson Law Review
Swiss PIL Act	Swiss Private International Law Act
TCP/IP	Transmission Control Protocol/Internet Protocol
Tex Int'l L J	Texas International Law Journal
Tiff	Tag Image File Format
U Mich JL Ref	University of Michigan Journal of Law Reform
UCITA	US Uniform Computer Information Transaction Act
UCLA L Rev	UCLA Law Review
UDRP	Uniform Domain Name Dispute Resolution Policy
UETA	US Uniform Electronic Transactions Act
UMass	University of Massachusetts
UMTS	Universal Mobile Telecommunications System
UNCC	United Nations Compensation Commission (Iraq compensation program)
UNCITRAL	United Nations Commission on International Trade Law
UNCTAD	United Nations Conference on Trade and Development
url	Uniform Resource Locator (Internet address)
USB	Universal Serial Bus
VoIP	Voice over IP
VPN	Virtual Private Network
WBR	Dutch Wetboek van Burgerlijke Rechtsvordering
WiFi	Wireless Fidelity
WIPO	World Intellectual Property Organization
WL	WestLaw
WLR	Weekly Law Reports
xml	Extensible Mark-up Language
Yale J of L & Tech	Yale Journal of Law and Technology
Yearbook Comm. Arb'n	ICCA Yearbook Commercial Arbitration
ZPO	German Zivilprozessordnung

FOREWORD

by

Gabrielle KAUFMANN-KOHLER
Professor at Geneva University Law School

Richard Susskind, one of the earliest and most visionary scholars in the field of information technology (IT) and the law, predicted some ten years ago that lawyers would regularly use e-mails to communicate with clients.[1] Time proved him right, but, according to his own recollection, at the time the legal community thought he was 'nuts' and simply dismissed the idea.[2] Ten years later, the author's opinion on the influence of IT on legal practice has become even stronger. He writes:[3]

> The next ten years should [...] bring more rapid and far-reaching change for lawyers than the last. [...] Technology will alter the very fabric of legal life. [...] The foundations of dispute resolution will be rocked by a combination of electronic disclosure, e-filing in the courts and online dispute resolution. [T]he working relationships between lawyers and their clients will mutate beyond recognition, as they come under the one virtual roof and operate under a new order of online collaboration and communication.

The present book, authored by a recognized expert in online dispute resolution, explores a field where the impact of technology on 'the foundations of dispute resolution' is widely expected. With a resolutely practical approach, it examines the main applications of technology in arbitration, a field in which progress is likely to take place particularly rapidly due to the flexibility of the legal framework that governs arbitration.

This work fills a gap: it is the first handbook on what is likely to become one of tomorrow's incontrovertible topics in the field of arbitration, namely, increasing the efficiency of arbitral procedures with IT solutions. The evolution towards a better integration of technology in arbitral procedures is unstoppable. The extensive use of computers already permeates every aspect of contemporary business life, and arbitration is no exception to this trend. Nevertheless, arbitration practitioners frequently appear to be struggling with IT tools, either refusing to use them to any significant extent or facing technical and organizational problems, thereby missing significant opportunities to reduce costs and accelerate the arbitral process or at least their own work. Surprisingly, but maybe for reasons similar to those that triggered the legal community's contempt for e-mail ten years

1 R. Susskind, *The Future of Law* (Oxford, OUP, 1996).
2 R. Susskind, 'Hold on to your seats, change is getting faster', *The Times*, 24 January 2006.
3 Ibid.

ago, the topic of IT in arbitration has received limited attention so far. To date, the most important work on the use of technological tools in arbitral procedures is the 2004 guidelines of the International Chamber of Commerce Task Force on IT in Arbitration.[4] However, many practitioners find them too technical and complex to be really helpful in practice. This book thus comes as a welcome contribution to the relationship between IT and arbitration.

It must be distinguished from publications on online dispute resolution (ODR). ODR is a topic that has already been the subject of much scholarly and practice-oriented writing. As the author explains, there are significant differences between ODR and what this book refers to as 'the use of IT in arbitration'. The differences are primarily the types of disputes resolved (small ones in the former, larger ones in the latter), the contexts (niche contexts in the first case, ordinary commercial arbitrations in the second), the practitioners and academics composing the field, and their understanding of the role of technology in dispute resolution and of the way IT operates. In this book, the author bring his knowledge and experience of ODR to 'the use of IT in arbitration', thereby allowing the reader to understand a set of reflections which have become relatively common in ODR but remain largely ignored in the field of arbitration. As this book shows, arbitration can undoubtedly learn from ODR.

One of the main advantages of this work is that it is accessible to persons with a limited knowledge of technology. Thomas Schultz made a deliberate effort to take the reader by the hand and lead him or her on a journey starting with simple explanations of the reasons to use IT and its practicalities, the choices made by the prevalent arbitration institutions in this regard, and the legal limits to the use of such technologies. The journey ends with a summary of these findings in the form of practice guidelines, drafting suggestions for arbitrators or parties wishing to use IT, as well as checklists and reminders to be used in practice.

The author has drafted this handbook in a style that avoids the pitfall of the dry language affecting most practitioners' guides. Anecdotes, vividly depicted examples, and interesting background information make this book an astonishingly pleasant read for a rather arduous topic.

Some may deplore the relatively narrow scope of the book. It encompasses only a specific number of technologies and a limited set of issues related to their use. The reader will not find a comprehensive guide on how to equip a law office with IT solutions for arbitration, or a manual on the use of the IT platforms of, for example, the International Chamber of Commerce or the American Arbitration Association. This limitation is a logical consequence of the approach chosen for this book, which has its own advantages. As much as possible, the approach seeks to avoid giving advice on ways to use technology that are eminently dependent on each practitioner's conception of his or her work and the ways of organizing it. The book thus largely steers clear of recommendations that

4 'Operating Standards for Using IT in Arbitration' [2004] ICC Bull, special supplement on 'Using Technology to Resolve Business Disputes'.

merely reflect personal preferences and opinions and are of limited general interest. The author is mindful that there are no rules about how to use IT in arbitration, so rather than attempting to articulate any rules, he provides a *focused* insight into the IT toolbox available for arbitration. In the toolbox, the reader will find descriptions and recommendations on case management websites, videoconferencing, live notes, ODR platforms as ready-to-use solutions, and e-mail. The recommendations are remarkably accessible and easy to understand.

In sum, Thomas Schultz does an outstanding job of providing the arbitration practitioner with good reasons to resort to IT solutions, while offering sufficient advice for everyone to make up his or her own mind about which type of technology to use in a given situation and providing useful considerations on the way to use them.

This book is the product of a research project conducted at Geneva University Law School that I had the pleasure of directing in collaboration with Professor Nadia Magnenat-Thalmann, Director of MIRALab, the University of Geneva's center for virtual reality and computer science. Thomas Schultz's contribution to this project, and to this book in particular, was significant enough for him to appear as the sole author of this publication. It must be acknowledged, however, that an entire team contributed to the research.

This book is mainly for arbitration practitioners, be they arbitrators or counsel. But the well informed general public with an interest in how technology continues to shape the practice of law should also greet it with acclaim, for they will enjoy it and learn much. And there is little doubt that time, as it did for Richard Susskind, will prove the author right about the importance of the matters addressed here.

PREFACE

Since the publication of my first book, authored with Gabrielle Kaufmann-Kohler, *Online Dispute Resolution: Challenges for Contemporary Justice*, in 2004, many arbitration practitioners have contacted me to request advice on whether resorting to 'online dispute resolution' would be useful for some major upcoming arbitration in which they were going to be involved. They ask, in other words, if they should give technology a real try – and usually they also wish to know whether the effort of reading the book would be rewarded with a definite answer to their question. *Online Dispute Resolution*, the book, is not an answer to this question, but the present book hopefully is.

One may wonder what the difference is between online dispute resolution (ODR) and what forms the substance of this book. ODR refers to dispute resolution processes which take place exclusively or at least essentially online; such processes are in principle reserved for small and medium size disputes, most of which originate in e-commerce transactions. Moreover, ODR usually takes the form of computer-assisted negotiation, online mediation, and online non-binding arbitration. True arbitration, in the context of ODR, is infrequent. It is even more infrequent when large disputes are involved. This does not mean, however, that information technology (IT) is not used for large arbitrations, but it is used differently there. Such use of IT for large arbitrations is what forms the substance of the present book; it addresses various IT solutions which may be put to use in traditional arbitral proceedings. ODR and the use of IT in traditional arbitral proceedings are two different fields, which differ (up to now at least) with respect to the main types of disputes resolved, the dominant methods of dispute resolution, the principal institutional actors, the people who make up the field, and, to a certain extent, the demands made on technology.

In other words, this book is not meant for specific niches of dispute resolution, but for standard procedures. It is not about ODR, but about how various IT solutions may be put to good use in traditional arbitral proceedings. It seeks to chart progress not of online arbitration, but of the use of IT in offline arbitration.

More precisely, this work addresses the following basic questions: why use IT in arbitration? Which forms of IT (which tools or technologies) are available for use in arbitration? How should they be used? How can they be set up technically and legally? What are the main concerns related to their use, in terms of security and efficiency, but also in relation to the procedural rights of the parties?

This book is practice-oriented, and thus includes practice guidelines, provides standard forms for the use of IT, and presents the services currently offered by major arbitral institutions.

It is addressed to 'ordinary' lawyers, not to lawyers who are computer buffs in search of the latest trends in workflow technologies. It is not meant for particularly computer-literate counsel or arbitrators, but for practitioners with a standard understanding of IT. Hence, its subject matter is centered on a discussion of the more commonplace IT solutions – for example online filing, case management websites, videoconferencing, and even e-mails – and not on exotic, sophisticated and rarely used technologies. This book is not addressed either, a fortiori, to computer scientists. Therefore, the explanations and categories may not follow the traditional divisions used in computer science: rather, they seek to present the current technologies most commonly used in arbitration, addressed in a manner easily understandable to arbitration practitioners.

This work is one of the products on an interdisciplinary research project conducted at the Private International Law Department of Geneva University Law School, in collaboration with MIRALab, a center for computer science of the same university specialized in virtual reality. The project was financed by the Swiss National Research Fund, for a period lasting from late 2003 to late 2005. It gave rise, in addition to various articles,[5] to a work-in-progress publication of the present manuscript, released in a December 2005 issue of the Swiss law review JusLetter. The present text is a substantial revision of that earlier version.[6]

The project was directed by Gabrielle Kaufmann-Kohler, who practices international commercial arbitration and researches and teaches international dispute resolution at Geneva Law School and other universities. It was co-directed by Nadia Magnenat-Thalmann, Director of MIRALab and Vice-Rector of Geneva University. The research fellows associated with the project over the years were, in addition to the author, Victor Bonnin, Eleanor Loukass and Vanessa Manarin, of Geneva University Law School, and HyungSeok Kim and Dimitris Protopsaltou, of MIRALab.

A number of people have provided valuable guidance, information, and support, which proved indispensable for the completion of this book. First of all, it owes much to Gabrielle Kaufmann-Kohler, who has provided continuing support for this work and has enriched it through her academic knowledge as well as her seemingly limitless practical experience. (Nevertheless, as the formula goes, any errors remaining are unfortunately my own.) She is the most faithful and reliable director of research one may hope for and has thus naturally become a dear friend over the years. Gabrielle – thanks for your time, and thanks for providing me with the opportunity to write this book.

Many of the solutions recommended in this book were tested with arbitration practitioners, academics, and friends, who kindly offered their time and advice, agreed to share their experience, expressed their enthusiasm and doubts, and thereby helped to iron out

5 For a list of these other publications, see <www.online-adr.org>.

6 G. Kaufmann-Kohler and T. Schultz, with the collaboration of E. Loukass, V. Bonnin, D. Protopsaltou, and H. Kim, 'The Use of Information Technology in Arbitration' [2005] *JusLetter* <www.weblaw.ch/jusletter/Artikel.asp?ArticleNr=4410&Language=1>.

many practical inconsistencies; they included Christine Chappuis (Geneva University Law School), Pierre-Yves Gunter (Python Schifferli Peter), Laurent Hirsch (Hirsch Kobel), Brian Hutchinson (University College Dublin), Pierre Kobel (Hirsch Kobel), Juan-Carlos Landrove (Lausanne University Law School), Lorine Meylan (Lalive and Partners), Antonio Rigozzi (Schellenberg Wittmer and Neuchatel University), Silja Schaffstein (Queen Mary, University of London), Matthias Scherrer (Lalive and Partners), and Michael E. Schneider (Lalive and Partners). Their help is gratefully acknowledged here.

Among them, Pierre-Yves Gunter and Michael E. Schneider deserve special consideration, having agreed to review, and to provide insightful comments on, the drafting suggestions of the procedural order and other forms included in this book.

Many thanks also go to Eleanor Loukass for reviewing the English of this book; if it were not for her, there would be many more mistakes and stylistic infelicities in the English than in fact remain.

Further acknowledgements are addressed to the arbitration institutions that have granted copyright permission for screenshots reproduced in this book, and have provided occasional corrections of the descriptions of the services they provide. These institutions are: the International Chamber of Commerce Court of International Arbitration, in particular Ms Mirèze Philippe, for its NetCase system (Figures 24–26); the American Arbitration Association, in particular Ms Debi Miller-Moore, for its WebFile system (Figures 4–16); and the World Intellectual Property Organization, in particular Mr Erik Wilbers and Ms Eun-Joo Min, for its ECAF system (Figures 17–23).

Thomas Schultz
Cambridge
March 2006

INTRODUCTION

'We are stuck with technology when what we really want is just stuff that works. How do you recognize something that is still technology? A good clue is if it comes with a manual.

[...]

I've come up with a set of rules that describe our reactions to technologies:

1. Anything that is in the world when you're born is normal and ordinary and is just a natural part of the way the world works.
2. Anything that's invented between when you're 15 and 35 is new and exciting and revolutionary and you can probably get a career in it.
3. Anything invented after you're 35 is against the natural order of things.'

(Douglas Adams, *The Salmon of Doubt*, 2002)

A new society has arisen from the displacement of so many of our daily activities by technology. It is a society governed, to an unprecedented extent, by speed, globalism, and constraints on costs in every economic sector. The sharp increase in international commerce, i.e., globalization, is one of the most essential expressions of these changes. And globalization is occurring because of technology: technology strongly contributed to bringing down the walls between the East and the West by allowing information to spread and weaken propaganda; technology largely promotes foreign investments by facilitating information transmissions between remote places; technology has greatly accelerated international transfers of funds; technology has made the world market more open with stronger competition and thus more cost constraints. Indeed, international commerce feeds on technology, and technology fundamentally shapes international commerce; it is a ubiquitous element that brings about new challenges, along with new possibilities and expectations. Arbitration, as a key element of international commerce, cannot escape these changes. Technology also addresses new challenges and offers new possibilities to arbitration, thereby yielding new expectations from its users. Understanding how to use information technology (IT), in business, in international commerce, and thus in arbitration as well, seems crucial in remaining an actor in today's society.

More concretely, disputes submitted to arbitration are becoming more international, more complex, and increasingly include multiparty proceedings and mass claims, while cost constraints remain stringent and demands for speedy resolution intensify. And it may be recalled that, in the international arena, the large majority of complex disputes, many of which include state parties, are settled through arbitration. Complaints about the excessive duration and costs of the administration of justice are commonplace nowadays. IT tools can help address these complaints by accelerating and facilitating arbitration. Indeed, IT tools can reduce costs and time radically, thereby maintaining a necessary level of access to justice, in international commerce in particular, as well as in other business areas.

In spite of its obvious advantages, many practitioners are still reluctant to use IT in arbitration. Because arbitration is a quasi-judicial process, it must comply with procedural guarantees, which impose certain constraints on the process. In addition, in the last two decades, arbitration has evolved towards more antagonism, becoming an increasingly formalistic, court-like procedure – a manifestation of the so-called 'judicialization' or 'legalization' of international arbitration. Hence, parties and arbitrators fear that resorting to IT may jeopardize procedural rights and create grounds for useless procedural complications or even the annulment of arbitral awards.

Despite these reservations, it appears inevitable that the emergence and development of IT tools for dispute resolution will change the conduct of international commercial arbitration proceedings. The actors in international commerce expect their disputes to be resolved according to the same standards under which they carry out the transactions giving rise to such disputes. Arbitration's current tendency towards more formalistic procedures often results in procedural incidents, slowing down the general process and further widening the gap with the pace of international commerce. IT tools can significantly alleviate this problem by accelerating the arbitral process, while safeguarding procedural guarantees and maintaining the quality of justice.

IT is indeed a very powerful toolbox for international arbitration. In addition to helping accelerate the dispute resolution process, it may also facilitate the handling of the increasingly voluminous records that characterize present-day arbitrations. It is likely to significantly improve the administration of justice in complex, multiparty, or mass claims disputes. And IT can render arbitration more accessible, for instance making it possible for parties with less economic power to save certain costs that would otherwise put them at a disadvantage.

Today, the use of IT in the arbitral process is in its infancy, although it is gathering strong momentum. Indeed, major arbitral institutions like the International Chamber of Commerce (ICC), the American Arbitration Association (AAA), and the World Intellectual Property Organization (WIPO) have recently launched IT systems offering case management websites, virtual case rooms, extranets, and other IT tools allowing multiparty communications.

To understand the phenomenon of IT usage in arbitration, what the precise advantages of specific technologies are, and how such technologies should be used, it is preferable to start with a few general explanations and reminders on the use of IT in general. Why should IT be used? When should it be used? How should it be resorted to and what are the main stumbling blocks that should be avoided? These questions, along with a brief reminder of the general evolution of IT usage in dispute resolution, form the substance of the first chapter of the book.

Chapter 2 then critically reviews the most significant information technologies for arbitration. For this purpose, emphasis will be placed on electronic communication means, in other words IT tools used to transmit information, as opposed to purely local data management applications. The latter applications, of which examples are legal thesauri and glossaries, databases of legal texts and Internet websites, time-sheet software, voice recognition capabilities, and deadline reminders, are the matter of ordinary contemporary work organization choices and, hence, do not deserve special treatment in this book. Instead Chapter 2 will focus on case management websites and videoconferencing, and will touch upon live notes applications used by court reporters and global online dispute resolution platforms. 3D shared virtual workspaces, as a possible future development of IT usage in arbitration, will also be mentioned.

Thereafter the book discusses the current practice of IT usage at three of the world's most prominent arbitration institutions, namely the International Court of Arbitration of the ICC, the AAA, and the Arbitration and Mediation Center of WIPO. Their IT systems, mentioned above, are presented in detail with screenshots of their user interfaces. Further on the practice at the ICC, Chapter 3 also reviews its guidelines on the use of IT, taking into consideration both a preliminary report which sets out the rough lines of IT requirements in arbitration and more practical guidelines which provide responses to such requirements.

After this presentation of the IT solutions that may be resorted to in arbitration, suggestions are provided as to the way such solutions should be used. These suggestions are based on legal requirements, specified in Chapter 4, and on practical and technical constraints, of which an account is given in Chapter 5 in the form of concrete practice guidelines.

Chapter 6 takes an even more practical approach and sets forth recommendations regarding the drafting of arbitration agreements providing for IT solutions and procedural orders. It also offers an initiation form, to be used by either the parties or the arbitral tribunal to suggest IT usage, and an incident form, to be filled in if a technical failure occurs which must be reported to the other participants in the proceedings.

In its last part, the book seeks to summarize much of the contents of the preceding chapters in the form of checklists, reminders, and charts, which are meant as convenient tools for practical reference.

CHAPTER 1

SETTING THE STAGE

Introductory considerations on the use of IT

Judex non calculat, goes the saying; lawyers are not at home in mathematics. The same, unfortunately, often holds true in relation to the machines that calculate for us: computers. For many very diverse reasons, the use of information technology in the legal context is still very much below its potential. It is misunderstood, mistrusted, misused, and generally considered to be someone else's problem – with the noticeable exception of specific niches like e-commerce law and related matters.

Nevertheless, technological changes have already profoundly affected legal practice. They have changed how legal information is created, how it is spread, and how it is accessed. Simple technologies like e-mail have also transformed the way people interact, and thus what people expect from each other – including what clients expect from their counsel and what parties expect from the arbitrators appointed to their case. Consequently, whatever the reason not to gain serious insight into information technology (lack of time, lack of interest, traditions, general delegation of tasks, past successes without computers, etc.), most members of the legal community would be well-advised to take the necessary steps to enter the information age.

Hence, this first chapter seeks to put IT usage in perspective. It provides a global introduction on information technology, giving an overview on standard technologies and global developments, discussing the use of IT in general, and offering some first basic recommendations.

This chapter starts by telling the story of information technology, law, and dispute resolution: how they interact and how IT has progressively become part and parcel of the manner in which law is practiced today (Section I). It provides a perspective on where we are and where we may take it from there.

After that, Section II discusses why IT should be used. For this purpose, it first reviews the general benefits that may be gained from electronic communication technologies and then considers a list of functions IT may fulfill in relation to arbitration, i.e., the kinds of uses it may have.

Section III moves from these introductory points towards pragmatic considerations, addressing the question when, concretely, the benefits and functions identified in the preceding section may be realized. In answer to this question, this section suggests a list of situations in which arbitral proceedings call for such technologies.

After thus addressing why and when IT should be used, Section IV focuses on the most fundamental aspects of how such technologies should be used. In this regard, it recalls two golden rules that must be kept in mind when planning to use any IT tool.

Finally, Section V briefly presents five basic communication technologies that constitute either quantitatively important technical tools, or qualitatively significant components of more complex sets of communication systems.

I. DEVELOPMENTS OF IT IN DISPUTE RESOLUTION

Computers, since their early development after World War II following Alan Turing's work, have gradually changed the way we approach law, the way we practice it, the way we do business and, at the crossroads of these trends, computers have begun to change the way we resolve disputes. Setting up arbitration procedures that rely heavily on IT is in this regard not a spontaneous innovation, but merely a logical next step in the history of how computers penetrate the law. It simply follows the movement started some 20 years ago by the arrival of computers in offices.

Consequently, before turning to a pragmatic approach of the use of IT in arbitration, a perspective that will be kept for most of this book, some considerations on the origin and development of the role of information technology in law and dispute resolution, in other words some theoretical background, are in order. Such considerations may help understand the past failures and achievements of IT in arbitration, i.e., the lessons that can be drawn from its evolution, its current capabilities, the variety of its potential uses and objectives, as well as the likely directions it may take in the future. The developments discussed below have shaped the context of the use of IT in arbitration.

Computers

Beyond mere text editing, chronologically, attention was first focused on the effects computers have on the law, how independent or unconnected computers changed our relationship to legal materials. The main topics of interest, at the time, were information management and artificial intelligence.[7] These topics, despite still being the subject of much development in theory and practice, do not deserve a more detailed analysis here, as they do not relate to the subject matter of the present work beyond a chronological connection.

Networks

The second relationship between information technology and the law dealt with the effects of networked computers, and in particular the Internet, on the circulation of information. The newly unrestrained, instantaneous, and global movement of information revolutionized all forms of information transformation, bringing nearer people and

[7] See, for example, B.G. Buchanan and T.E. Headrick, 'Some Speculations About Artificial Intelligence and Legal Reasoning' (1970) 23 Stan L Rev 40, R. Susskind, *Expert Systems in Law* (Oxford, OUP, 1987), R. Susskind, *Essays on law and artificial intelligence* (Oslo, Tano, 1993), and P. Capper and R. Susskind, *Latent Damage Law – The Expert System. A Study of Computers in Legal Problem Solving* (London, Butterworths, 1988).

centers of activities throughout the world in MacLuhan's paradigmatic 'global village'.[8] The Internet, born out of the mere interconnection of computers, is now a central driving factor of economic globalization.[9] It has had at least three types of effects on law and dispute resolution. First, it increased the geographical scale of disputes, as distant transactions became increasingly common, some of which necessarily gave rise to disputes. Second, it caused legal information to flow differently, the clearest examples being online legal databases such as Lexis or WestLaw, accessible from any computer, irrespective of its geographical location.[10] Third, this form of globalization increased the globalization of the law – e.g., the harmonization of legal regimes and an escalation of extraterritorial effects – and of dispute resolution processes.

Online dispute resolution

The globalization of dispute resolution processes led to one epitomic movement: online dispute resolution (ODR).[11] ODR represents the third main relationship between IT and the law, because of both its quantitative importance and its qualitative specificity. In fact, it probably embodies the heaviest reliance of legal processes on IT. The salient characteristic of ODR is the ease of its access, which is ubiquitous, and consequently the relatively low costs generated by the procedures. However, an important finding in the ODR field is that it is almost exclusively usable for small and medium size disputes raising factually simple issues. Large international disputes are still solved essentially by offline processes of dispute resolution.

The ODR movement nonetheless remains a reference phenomenon for the use of information technologies in arbitral proceedings and has taught us many lessons on this subject. IT usage in offline arbitration is for a good part an offshoot of the ODR movement, ODR having recently gone through a series of phases that led to its extension to more complex and more economically significant disputes, and thus to primarily offline arbitral proceedings. The following quickly reviews the phases that lead to the combination of ODR and offline arbitration.

The first reason for the ODR movement was the lack of confidence that characterizes e-commerce. Internet shoppers need a dispute resolution system that relies on the same

---

8 M. McLuhan, *Explorations in Communication* (Boston, Beacon Press, 1960).

9 T. Friedman, *The Lexus and the Olive Tree* (HarperCollins, Glasgow, 2000) p. xvi ('this globalization system is also characterized by a single word : the *Web*').

10 For a detailed analysis of the Internet's influence of the circulation of legal information, see e.g., O. Rabinovich-Einy, 'Balancing the Scales: The Ford-Firestone Case, the Internet, and the Future Dispute Resolution Landscape' (2004) 6 Yale J of L & Tech 2. See also R. Susskind, *Transforming the Law* (Oxford, OUP, 2000), p. 85 et seq. and E. Katsh, *The Electronic Media and the Transformation of Law* (Oxford, OUP, 1989).

11 Online dispute resolution covers all dispute resolution methods whose essential elements of procedure take place using electronic means of communication. See G. Kaufmann-Kohler and T. Schultz, *Online Dispute Resolution: Challenges for Contemporary Justice* (The Hague, Kluwer Law International, 2004), p. 7.

form of communication that was used to conclude the transaction in the first place: electronic means of communication. The electronic accessibility of the procedures allows these consumers to be provided with points of reference, landmarks of justice in cyberspace: they may return to the place where the transaction was concluded – and thus where the dispute arose – and find a link to a dispute resolution process specifically adapted to their dispute.[12] After this first impulse related to consumer protection concerns, it was soon realized that the advantages of ODR could also be used to facilitate – and sometimes actually permit – access to justice for all small disputes, especially when they involve rather large distances between the parties, or even different countries of residence. It was then clearly recognized that ODR is not merely a by-product of e-commerce, or even a set of tools that belongs to the broader field of cyberspace law, but a change with potentially profound implications for the entire field of dispute resolution. Indeed, electronic communication means, and information technology in general, if used correctly, facilitate almost any form of resolution of almost any dispute. IT, if used correctly, improves the effectiveness of dispute resolution processes by simplifying information transmission and generally accelerating the proceedings. IT also improves efficiency, i.e., it reduces the costs of dispute resolution processes, in particular by limiting the need for travel.

IT as the 'fourth party'

The fourth – and probably the most important – relationship between information technology and the law was also triggered by the ODR movement: this time, the focus was on the effects IT can have on the work of mediators and negotiators. It all started during the final period of the war in Yugoslavia. As the difficult negotiations between Bosnian Serb, Croat, and Muslim ethnic factions seemed to have stalled, the United States brought in a clever and innovative IT solution to help the negotiators and the mediator reach an agreement.[13] They simply gathered the different factions around a digital map of the territories at stake in the negotiations. This very detailed map was interactive, thereby allowing the negotiators to work with realistic and graspable analyses of construction feasibility, minefield clearance operations, and boundary marking. Other examples are computer-assisted negotiation systems from afar, where the computer automatically carries out some of the tasks a human third party would usually have to do – such as sending reminders, proposing action plans, and suggesting standard settlement

[12] See, for example, T. Schultz, 'Does online dispute resolution need governmental intervention? The case for architectures of control and trust' (2004) 6 NC J L & Tech 71, pp. 84-87. See also T. Schultz, *Réguler le commerce électronique par la résolution des litiges en ligne* (Brussels, Bruylant, 2005), pp. 198–250 and E. Katsh, 'Adding Trust Systems to Transaction Systems: The Role of Online Dispute Resolution', paper presented at the first Forum on Online Dispute Resolution of the United Nations Economic Commission for Europe, Geneva, 6–7 June 2002, <www.ombuds.org/un/unece_june2002.doc>, p. 4.

[13] R.G. Johnson, 'Negotiating the Dayton Peace Accords Through Digital Maps', (2000) 8 *Virtual Diplomacy Report Series* <www.usip.org/vdi/vdr/rjohnsonISA99.html>.

terms.[14] Drawing on this example, Ethan Katsh and Janet Rifkin developed the concept of the 'fourth party',[15] as

> 'something that is an influence on the process of communication and negotiation, something that adds value to the third party [i.e., the mediator or the arbitrator], something that typically does not replace the third party but can displace her, in the sense that the third party operates with an ally or assistant alongside'.[16]

This fourth party further takes the form of 'applications that enhance the expertise of the third party and thus do more than simply deliver the expertise of the human third party across the network'.[17] In other words, the third party, be it the mediator or the arbitrator, is there to help the parties solve their dispute[18] and the fourth party does exactly the same: it is not only an ally to the *third party*, but also an assistant – next to the third party – to the two *disputing parties*.

The technology that the fourth party represents is globally developing along two main lines.[19] First, very simple tools are being used, such as red flags, emoticons, images or sounds whose goal may be compared to that of pens and flipcharts in traditional offline dispute resolution methods, i.e., to help clearly convey a message or to attract attention. Such tools also serve other, though similar functions by virtue of their automation: they may for instance help automatically remind participants of deadlines.[20] On the other

---

14 For concrete examples of such tools being used, see, for example, SmartSettle <www.smartsettle.com> and The Claim Room <www.theclaimroom.com>. For a description of the former One Accord, see, for example, E.M. Thiessen and J.P. McMahon, 'Beyond Win-Win in Cyberspace' (2000) 15 Ohio St J on Disp Resol 643. See also the consumer filing forms proposed by many ODR providers (e.g., ECODIR and SquareTrade), and T. Schultz, 'Connecting complaint filing processes to online resolution systems' (2003) 10 *Commercial Law Practitioner* 307.

15 E. Katsh and J. Rifkin, *Online Dispute Resolution. Resolving Conflicts in Cyberspace* (San Francisco, Jossey-Bass, 2001), p. 93 and E. Katsh, 'Online Dispute Resolution: The Next Phase' (2002) 7-2 *Lex Electronica* <www.lex-electronica.org/articles/v7-2/katsh.htm>.

16 E. Katsh, 'Online Dispute Resolution: The Next Phase', n. 15 above, para. 16.

17 Ibid, para. 18.

18 For an overview of the role of the third party, see generally M.J. Mustill, 'Arbitration: History and Background' (1989) 6 J Int'l Arb 43; B. Yngvesson and L. Mather, 'Courts, Moots, and the Disputing Process' in *Empirical Theories About Courts*, K.O. Boyum and L. Mather (eds) (New York, Longman, 1983); L.M. Friedmann, 'Courts Over Time: A Survey of Theories and Research' in ibid; R.L. Abel, 'Western Courts in Non-Western Settings: Patterns of Court use in Colonial and Neo-Colonial Africa' in *The Imposition of Law*, S.B. Burman et B.E. Harell-Bond (eds) (New York, Academic Press, 1979).

19 On these two lines of development, see E. Katsh and A. Gaitenby, 'Introduction: Technology as the "Fourth Party"' in *Online Dispute Resolution (ODR): Technology as the 'Fourth Party' Papers and Proceedings of the 2003 United Nations Forum on ODR*, E. Katsh and D. Choi (eds) (UMass, Amherst and United Nations, Geneva 2003) <www.odr.info/unece2003/-pdf/Intro.pdf>.

20 See E. Katsh, 'Online Dispute Resolution: The Next Phase', n. 15 above, para. 23.

hand, complex and sophisticated technological tools and platforms are being experimented with and sometimes implemented. This use of high technology aims at a much more intense exploitation of the tools that electronic communication technology offers. Virtual workspaces are one example – and in many respects an extreme one – of such complex and sophisticated tools.[21] In between these two extremes of simplicity and complexity, a whole range of technologies exist, the best known being extranets and virtual case-rooms, case management websites, and videoconferencing. At this stage, it must be remembered that the fourth party is not limited to ODR nor to processes that take place essentially online;[22] it can also be used in all types of dispute resolution processes.[23] As suggested above, much of the experience gathered in ODR is actually being exploited in the context of offline arbitration – the role of IT as a fourth party is one such lesson of ODR.

IT at arbitration institutions

The fifth and last relationship between information technology and the law, which follows from all the above, is the effects IT can have on arbitration procedures. The most prestigious arbitration institutions are currently experimenting with IT tools: the International Chamber of Commerce (ICC) with its NetCase program,[24] the American Arbitration Association (AAA) with its WebFile scheme,[25] and the World Intellectual Property Organization (WIPO) with ECAF.[26] Private ventures are developing hardware and software and trying to sell them to the arbitration world,[27] not to mention the various online

---

21 See D. Protopsaltou, T. Schultz, and N. Magnenat-Thalmann, 'Taking the Fourth Party Further? Considering a shared virtual workspace for arbitration' [2006] *Information and Communication Technology Law*, special issue on the virtualization of justice, in press.

22 For a definition of ODR, see, for example, G. Kaufmann-Kohler and T. Schultz, *Online Dispute Resolution*, n. 11 above, p. 7 and American Bar Association Task Force on Electronic Commerce and Alternative Dispute Resolution and Shidler Center for Law, Commerce and Technology, University of Washington, 'Addressing Disputes in Electronic Commerce : Final Recommendations and Report' (2002) 58 Bus Law 415, p. 419.

23 For a more developed discussion of this concept of a 'fourth party', see D. Protopsaltou, T. Schultz, and N. Magnenat-Thalmann, 'Taking the Fourth Party Further?', n. 21 above.

24 See Chapter 3, Section I. State of practice, C. ICC – NetCase, p. 93 below.

25 See Chapter 3, Section I. State of practice, A. AAA – WebFile, p. 76 below.

26 See Chapter 3, Section I. State of practice, B. WIPO – ECAF, p. 85 below.

27 IT tools for offline arbitration are provided by the following ventures: the American Bar Association, see <www.abanet.org/tech/ltrc/home.html> and <www.elawyering.org>; NetTech, see < www.nettechinc.com/lawtech.htm>; CaseCentral, see <www.casecentral.com/cc/home>; Documentum, see <www.documentum.com/eroom>; iManage, see <www.imanage.com>; LegalFiles, see <www.legalfiles.com/main.htm>, NetDocuments, see <www.netdocuments.-com>; EliteManager, see <www.eliteis.com/solutions/prod_casemanager.asp>; CaseShare, see <www.caseshare.com>; Eversheds, see <www.eversheds.com>; and Allen & Overy, see <www.newchange.com>.

arbitration programs developed by the Chartered Institute of Arbitrators.[28] Legal commentators have also started to embrace this topic.[29]

In summary, the idea of using IT in arbitration is a burgeoning theme, which follows from experiments related to global electronic information management, the circulation of information in an increasingly globalized and borderless world, the online dispute resolution movement (which led, more specifically, to lessons regarding procedural setups and dispute resolution techniques using IT), the idea that IT may displace or on some occasions even replace the neutral third party in dispute resolution, and the gradual introduction of IT tools into everyday business and legal practice.

II. WHY IT?

It is generally agreed that information technology yields tremendous advantages for office work. IT is systematically sold as the way to get rid of bulky cabinets and pesky folders, do away with paper spilling over every surface, and thus make work more

---

28 See G. Kaufmann-Kohler and T. Schultz, *Online Dispute Resolution*, n. 11 above, pp. 253, 295–301.

29 See, for example, E. Schäfer, 'Der Einsatz von Informationstechnologie in der Handelschiedsgerichtsbarkeit', <www.dis-arb.de/materialien/DIS_Vortr_ITuARB.pdf>, 10 April 2002; E-Arbitration-T Consortium, 'Online Arbitration: What Technology can do for Arbitral Institutions', <www.e-arbitration-t.com/papersadr/ubrun_seminar_content.pdf>, 20 January 2003; M. Klang, 'Improving Arbitration with Information Technology' in *Proceedings of the 21st Information Systems Research Seminar in Scandinavia (IRIS)*, 'Information Systems Research in Collaboration with Industry', 8–11 August, H.J. Buch and others (ed.), Sæby Søbad, Denmark, Department of Computer Science, Aalborg University; E. Rholl, 'Web-enabled ADR and extranets', *National Law Journal* <www.nlj.com>, 2 December 2002; International Chamber of Commerce, Commission on Arbitration, 'Report by the Section on Information Technology on Special IT Requirements in International Arbitration', Doc. 420/21-005, 18 March 2002; E. Katsh, 'Online Dispute Resolution: Some Lessons from the E-Commerce Revolution' (2001) 28 N Ky L Rev 810. See also the empirical research carried out by the E-Arbitration-T consortium on the effects of IT on arbitration, with respect to rapidity, costs and over quality of justice, report available at <www.brunel.ac.uk/~csstade/eat/ubrun-2046-1/index.-html>. See further the numerous articles published in the related field of IT in court proceedings, for example, M.D. Roth, 'Laissez-Faire Videoconferencing: Remote Witness Testimony and Adversarial Truth' (2000) 48 UCLA L Rev 185; R.D. Friedman, 'Remote testimony' (2002) 35 U Mich JL Ref 695; P. Raburn-Remfry, 'Due Process Concerns In Video Production Of Defendants' (1994) 23 Stetson L Rev 805; S. Nauss Exon, 'The Internet Meets Obi-Wan Kenobi In The Court Of Next Resort' (2002) 8 B U J Sci & Tech L 1; J. Crowell, 'The Electronic Courtroom' (1997) 4 B U J Sci & Tech L 10; L. Helland, 'Remote Testimony – A Prosecutor's Perspective' (2002) 35 U Mich JL Ref 719; F.I. Lederer, 'The Road to the Virtual Courtroom? A Consideration of Today's – and Tomorrow's – High-Technology Courtrooms' (1999) 50 SC L Rev 799.

productive. There is also a consensus that the same advantages apply to arbitration. This section seeks to substantiate this general assumption, to examine just why IT usage is useful in arbitration, what its definite advantages are, and thus how it can advance legal practice.

It should be specified that this section only provides a general introduction of the advantages IT can offer for arbitration; the respective advantages (and disadvantages) of specific tools or technologies will be addressed in Chapter 2.

For the purpose of such an introduction, this section proceeds in two steps. It first reviews the various benefits of IT, if correctly used, for the practice of arbitration. As a second step, this section lists the main functions IT may fulfill in relation to arbitration, i.e., the kinds of uses it may have.

A. Benefits of IT Usage

The purposes of using IT in work environments are basically always the same, regardless of the context in which these types of technologies are used. Such technologies allow tasks to be accomplished at lesser cost, more rapidly, and more easily. In other words, they pursue the properties of efficiency, effectiveness, and convenience. The question here is how IT, in general, can achieve these properties in the context of arbitration. The answer to this question forms the substance of the following paragraphs, which examine these three properties in turn.

1. Efficiency

The most apparent and acclaimed reason why IT should be used in arbitration is that it provides opportunities to reduce costs and time. The main items of cost and time savings relate to travel, document handling, and the workflow related to a case.[30]

Travel

Travel costs can be reduced when online meetings replace face-to-face meetings. In such situations, IT can provide significant cost savings: in addition to out-of-pocket expenses (flight tickets, accommodation, rental of conference rooms, etc.), costs savings also include lost working time (including productivity diminution due to jetlag). Such travel-related costs concern all the participants in the arbitration, including the arbitrators, the parties and their counsel, witnesses and experts.

Admittedly, situations where online meetings replace face-to-face meetings are not very frequent yet. The online dispute resolution experience has largely shown that, in

[30] See also T. Schultz, *Réguler le commerce électronique par la résolution des litiges en ligne*, n. 12 above, pp. 257–260.

large cases, the cost savings generated by avoiding travel are not sufficient to lead the parties to renounce in-person meetings altogether; the parties will in principle want to meet face-to-face and be heard orally to maximize the quality of justice they receive.[31] However, not all meetings have the same importance and the less important ones – which may for example be purely procedural in nature – do not necessarily call for in-person presence. It is in those instances that videoconferencing should be resorted to and that travel costs can be saved. This is discussed in further detail in Chapter 2.[32]

Document handling

Document handling also generates costs that can be reduced by resorting to IT. Such cost reduction possibilities may be classified in the three following categories:

- *Document reproduction.* As opposed to photocopies, digital copies cost virtually nothing. This is especially beneficial for larger cases with numerous lengthy documents.
- *Document storage.* Digital copies of documents reduce the need for storage space, as a standard CD or DVD can contain thousands of files.
- *Document shipment.* Transmitting files in electronic format, whether by e-mail or stored on a CD or DVD, rather than sending by mail or special courier (if not small van-loads) of printed material around the globe can save significant shipping costs.

In terms of time savings, IT-related benefits concern the following areas:

- *Time for the realization of tasks.* General tasks, such as transferring documents, but also more specific ones like hearings and other forms of meetings, can be undertaken more rapidly when appropriate technologies are used. Such technologies are for instance simple electronic communication means like e-mails for a limited number of relatively small files, but they can also be more sophisticated tools such as case management websites with powerful mass uploading and downloading facilities for larger or more numerous files, or videoconferencing for hearings and other meetings such as deliberations.
- *Time between tasks.* IT can also save time in between specific tasks, in the sense that if travel or shipping times can be reduced or suppressed entirely, more tasks can be carried out in a shorter time space and it also becomes easier for all participants to find common available periods. Consequently, the procedure will be accelerated. The same holds true for the waiting periods due to shipping, whose suppression allows

31 See, for instance, G. Kaufmann-Kohler and T. Schultz, *Online Dispute Resolution*, n. 11 above, p. 294.

32 See Chapter 2, Section II.C. Uses and advantages (of videoconferencing), p. 50 below. See also Chapter 5, Section III.A. To videoconference or not to videoconference, p. 168 below.

more seamless workflows, thereby increasing productivity and potentially shortening procedures.

Workflow

Cost and time reductions can also be obtained through a form of automation and standardization of certain aspects of an arbitral procedure, achieved through information technologies. These elements primarily relate to the case intake, which can be organized on the basis of online forms that automatically classify and transmit the information submitted, or more generally on a series of online interactive Web pages guiding the parties through the process of filing.[33]

Although the situations that can benefit most clearly from such systems are procedures handling a large number of relatively small cases (because the amount of formalities is proportionally higher),[34] a simplification of formalities, global acceleration and cost savings can be achieved for all procedures not individually customized, through the standardization of the different steps of a procedure.

2. Effectiveness

In addition to accelerating the proceedings, reducing costs, and improving the productivity of the various people involved in an arbitration, IT can also increase the effectiveness of certain aspects of an arbitral procedure. (Efficiency is achieving the same result with less resources, effectiveness is achieving better absolute results.)

In some situations, this means that tasks can be undertaken – or goals can be reached – in a way that may not have been practicable without IT. For example, in the absence of IT availability, costs and time constraints may lead to renouncing certain actions, like hearing a witness or an expert who may not be quickly available, especially in fast-track procedures. This is for instance why witnesses and experts were heard using videoconferences during arbitrations at the Olympics, where time constraints would have prevented their testimony if they had had to be physically present.[35]

In other, less radical situations, IT can improve the quality of some actions. For instance, videoconferencing allows a richer information transfer as it conveys a more detailed message than teleconferencing, and research in the field of online dispute resolu-

---

33 For concrete examples of such online forms and interactive guidance, see Chapter 3, Section I. State of practice, p. 75 below. For a discussion of the contents of such filing forms, see, for example, T. Schultz, 'Connecting Complaint Filing Processes to Online Resolution Systems', n. 14 above.

34 See further paragraph Mass claims, p. 19 below.

35 See generally G. Kaufmann-Kohler, *Arbitration at the Olympics: Issues of Fast-Track Dispute Resolution and Sports Law* (The Hague, Kluwer Law International, 2001).

tion has shown that, in general, richer communications have a higher potential to lead to satisfactory results.[36]

Drawing on this distinction between efficiency and effectiveness, it may be suggested that videoconferencing should not only be compared with face-to-face meetings, but also (and even more so) with teleconferencing. The basis of this argument is that the sense of reality conveyed by videoconferencing is midway between teleconferencing and face-to-face meetings. On the one hand, videoconferencing may replace *teleconferencing* with advantages related to the quality of the discussion – achieving better results, a matter of effectiveness. On the other hand, it may replace *face-to-face* meetings, either on those occasions where the level of detail of the discussion is less important (the advantage of resorting to IT would then essentially be related to speed and costs, a question of efficiency) or when an in-person meeting is not a practicable solution at all, in which case the advantages would be a matter of effectiveness.[37]

3. Convenience

Finally, IT may facilitate certain actions related to arbitral procedures in a way that does not concern speed, costs, or the quality of certain tasks, but that simply makes some processes more convenient. For instance, electronic documents can be searched easily using the 'find' function available in all word processors, which saves much time and allows a user to ascertain whether a given word or phrase exists in a document. Text passages can also be copy-pasted from one document into another – for instance from the parties' submissions into the arbitral award when quoting the argument of one of the parties.

It should be kept in mind, though, that this obviously requires the documents to be in a format where the text is recognized as such, which notably excludes documents that are scanned, for instance in pdf or jpg format, without recourse to a text recognition function and a subsequent check of the recognized text. (Although scanning briefs in image format for subsequent transmission to the arbitral tribunal makes little sense, it is not unheard of.)

Other advantages on the front of convenience that were already mentioned above are for example the possibility of archiving documents easily and the ability to carry an enormous amount of files to a hearing without any consideration of their physical weight.

---

36 See further G. Kaufmann-Kohler and T. Schultz, *Online Dispute Resolution*, n. 11 above, p. 61.

37 Such comparisons of videoconferencing, teleconferences, and in-person meetings are addressed in further detail in Chapter 2, Section II.C. Uses and advantages (of videoconferencing), p. 50 below and Chapter 5, Section III.A. To videoconference or not to videoconference, p. 168 below.

B. Functions of IT for Arbitration

In its most comprehensive sense, information technology encompasses any use one can make of computers. Indeed, every time one uses a computer, one handles information through technology. Hence, speaking of IT usage in arbitration may in fact cover a large variety of radically different actions, which collectively cover – and go beyond – the daily work of most lawyers. Such recourse to technology ranges from the use of handheld devices (such as personal digital assistants or smart phones), to simple word processing, online legal research, billing software, shared calendaring, automated interest calculation, automated conflict of interest checking, e-mailing, videoconferencing, and more exotic technologies like 3D virtual reality.

It is not the purpose of the present book to comment on all these IT uses; this is not a treaty on legal software and hardware. Instead, the focus will be on issues that involve data transmission, i.e., electronic communication means that can be used in the context of arbitral procedures. Individual data management, i.e., situations in which data is handled but not transmitted over electronic networks, will in principle be left aside, except for occasional examples, illustrations, or explanations.

Nevertheless, in this chapter's context of a general introduction to IT in arbitration, it seems worthwhile to briefly list, from a global perspective, the main purposes of technology in this field, even if these purposes relate exclusively to data handling. And indeed, on some occasions, the tools that are further analyzed in this book are mere extensions of more traditional data handling technologies, pertaining for example to document management or digital presentations. Such technologies form the basis of collaborative electronic environments or more generally of technologies used in situations where data is transmitted, e.g., case management websites or digital presentations during videoconferences. Hence, a brief overview of the variety of uses of IT in arbitration may help understand the general technological environment in which the more advanced tools are being developed.

The following provides a general overview of the basic types of IT uses in arbitration; most other IT functions (legal research aside) can be considered to be derivatives or combinations thereof.

Transmitting messages and files

One of the most obvious uses of information technology – beyond text editing – is the transmission of messages and documents using electronic networks. Usual technologies for this purpose are e-mails and Web-based means such as Web interfaces and bulletin boards.

Meeting from afar

A thin line separates the idea of transmitting messages and files, which can be considered to take place in asynchronous fashion, from something closer to an actual meeting online. Meetings of this kind are based on technologies such as chat rooms and videoconferences, which imply synchronous communications.

Handling documents

Documents can be handled (in the sense that their content is interacted with) using IT with some notable benefits. For instance, the ability to rapidly search for occurrences of specific words largely increases access to the information contained in a document – and may consequently increase the probability that the point gets through to the recipient. The possibility of copying and pasting entire sections of documents is another obvious and often-used advantage. In addition, documents can be linked to each other through hyperlinks.

Creating documents

IT also facilitates the production of new documents. As suggested above, tools like 'copy-paste' accelerate the process of production. Typically, in the context of arbitration, the drafting of an award involves many instances of 'copy-pastes' from the parties' briefs and from documentary evidence. IT has also generated a new way of producing documents, since it is no longer uncommon that people in different parts of the world collaborate in the drafting of documents.

Managing documents

Using documents in electronic form further facilitates their management, i.e., the interaction with the files as information carriers, as opposed to their content. Their storage can for instance be facilitated, and searching and finding a document can be significantly accelerated if the naming of the files follows a clear policy.

Managing cases

Information technology can also be used to improve the management of cases, for instance by using progress tracking software, which shows at which stage a given case is, what the upcoming actions are, which participant is expected to act next, and when a specific deadline is. It may also graphically show the relationships between the various actors of the case.

Visually presenting arguments and facts

IT solutions such as digital slideshows, video depositions and presentations are increasingly being used during arbitral hearings, because visual presentations, and especially graphic ones, are more memorable and clearer than purely oral presentations.

Tracking

IT has, to put it simply, an amazing memory. IT allows us to track everything that occurs on our (virtual) desktop and, with the collaboration of others, on their desktops. IT may indeed be used to record and store not only documents, but also presentations, oral statements, and videoconferencing exchanges. The advantage (and sometimes the danger) of this is that such data can be reproduced by anyone gaining access to it with perfect accuracy and at any time.

III. WHEN TO USE IT?

Having considered the various uses of IT for arbitration and their different advantages, it remains to be seen in which specific situations these benefits may be put to use. The discussion above on the various functions of IT and which general advantages it may have if used correctly shows that *some* recourse to *some form* of IT appears useful in almost any situation. However, in certain specific cases, the benefits of using IT are particularly clear. This section focuses on those cases to illustrate the main factors that should trigger a particular interest in the use of IT.

A precise and circumstantial answer on the appropriateness of using IT in a given situation depends on the specific IT tool one is considering. However, the purpose of the present chapter is not to provide such an answer, but instead to serve merely as an introduction on information technology in arbitration. Consequently, the following simply lists general considerations regarding the situations in which a rather heavy reliance on IT may be of particular interest.

Time constraints

Resorting to IT is most evidently of interest in time-driven procedures, or particularly time-constrained aspects of an arbitral procedure. In such situations, when time becomes paramount, any solution that contributes to accelerating the proceedings without creating a serious reduction of the quality of the procedure appears useful.

More precisely, such time-sensitive situations could include:

- *Hearings on provisional measures*. The very nature of provisional measures requires proceeding quickly. Hence, even though a videoconferencing session may not yield results that are as good as in an in-person hearing, it will certainly be preferable to no hearing at all or to the absence of provisional measures.
- *Fast-track arbitrations*. The rationale of expedited proceedings (which are available at most major arbitration institutions) is to respond to a real need for urgency; arbitrators are available on very short notice to hear the case as soon as the parties are ready, only the indispensable minimum of formalities is contended with, and the award is rendered within a very short time frame. It is in the spirit of such arbitrations to resort to any reasonable means that may accelerate the proceedings – IT tools for example. This is precisely the modus operandi of what may be considered the epitome of fast-track procedures: the Olympics arbitration scheme administered by the ad hoc Division of the Court of Arbitration for Sports, where awards are rendered within 24 hours of filing. Because of the very tight schedule of the Olympics, hearing witnesses or experts in person is often impossible, and therefore the ad hoc Division often resorts to videoconferencing.[38]

[38] See generally G. Kaufmann-Kohler, *Arbitration at the Olympics*, n. 35 above.

Cost constraints

Low-cost procedures constitute the second type of situation for which IT can provide particularly useful advantages. Consumer dispute resolution is probably the best known example of such situations. The cost-saving potential of resorting to IT was in fact one of the main factors of development of the online dispute resolution movement in the first place – although, as the experience in this field has shown, the development costs may be quite high; it is the marginal costs related to the use of the system that are low.[39] More generally, all disputes where cost constraints are a major consideration may in fact benefit from cost savings through IT.

Short meetings of secondary importance

As was suggested above, a relatively clear occasion for resorting to IT is the replacement of face-to-face meetings by some form of online meeting in situations where the sense of reality and the ability to feel each other's state of mind is not indispensable.[40] Such replacement of face-to-face meetings may be achieved, depending on the actual situation and the desired level of presence, by videoconferencing, chat rooms, or bulletin boards. It may be specified that videoconferencing, especially for participants not used to this technology, is more adapted to short meetings, because of the extra attention its special environment requires.[41]

Mass claims

Technology is particularly useful when a high number of claimants bring relatively similar cases before the same arbitration institution. The usefulness of technology in such situations is that it can contribute to simplifying the process. Such simplification can for instance be achieved by streamlining the submission phase using electronic forms.

This was done, for example, in the context of the Iraq compensation program of the United Nations Compensation Commission (UNCC), whose mandate was to process claims for damage suffered as a direct result of the invasion and occupation of Kuwait – which repeatedly involved similar issues.[42]

The online assisted negotiation and online mediation programs used for eBay disputes are another example of technology simplifying the administration of mass claims. SquareTrade, the Californian online dispute resolution institution providing these programs for eBay,[43] has resolved over two million disputes in the last five years, and this

---

39 T. Schultz, *Réguler le commerce électronique par la résolution des litiges en ligne*, n. 12 above, pp. 259–260.

40 See paragraph Travel, p. 12 above and Section 2. Effectiveness, p. 14 above.

41 See further Chapter 2, Section II.C. Uses and advantages (of videoconferencing), p. 50 below and Chapter 5, Section III.A. To videoconference or not to videoconference, p. 168 below.

42 See <www2.unog.ch/uncc> and, for a presentation of this procedure, N. Wühler, 'The United Nations Compensation Commission: A new contribution to the process of international claims resolution' (1999) 2 J Int'l Econ L 249.

43 See <www.squaretrade.com>.

number is growing each year. Most of these disputes originated on eBay. The case intake and the first steps of resolution are entirely automated using interactive electronic forms.[44]

Drawing on these examples, it may be expected that IT will play a growing role in class actions, which in the U.S. are increasingly brought to arbitration.[45]

Multiparty disputes

A dispute involving many parties leads to a second situation, aside from mass claims, of particular interest for IT usage: the more numerous the participants in a single arbitration, the more benefits may be reaped from the use of technology. The rationale for resorting to IT in this context is that it makes almost no difference whether one or a very large number of copies are made of a file in electronic format. Its distribution also takes roughly the same amount of time whether the file is addressed to one or many recipients.[46]

A good illustration of this situation is provided by the multiparty arbitrations of the America's Cup, which in principle involve all 12 teams as well as the official bodies of the Cup. Understanding the benefits to be gained from technology, the America's Cup Jury (i.e., the arbitral tribunal of the Cup) has recently started to use an electronic case management system accessible on the Web. This system, called the America's Cup Jury Electronic Case Facility (ACJ ECAF), was specifically developed for the sailing event by

---

44 See also paragraph Workflow, p. 14 above. For a discussion of these dispute resolution mechanisms for eBay, see, for example, E. Katsh, J. Rifkin, and A. Gaitenby, 'E-Commerce, E-Disputes, and E-Dispute Resolution: In the Shadow of eBay Law' (2000) 15 Ohio St J on Disp Res 705; T. Schultz, 'eBay: un système juridique en formation' (2005) 22 RDTI 27 and T. Schultz, 'Connecting Complaint Filing Processes to Online Resolution Systems', n 14 above.

45 See, for example, A. Lockridge, 'The Silent Treatment: Removing the Class Action From the Plaintiff's Toolbox Without Ever Saying a Word' [2003] J Disp Resol 255.

46 The same idea has been experimented in the context of online mediation, in the well-publicized Frankfurt airport mediation. Frankfurt airport, one of the world's largest airports, had gone through a series of extensions in the 1980's, much against the public opinion. As a result, strong social pressure had built up against any further addition of new runways. But in 1998, Lufthansa claimed that the airport had reached its maximal capacity and that delays and unsatisfactory transport conditions through Frankfurt were now to be expected. Lufthansa threatened to withdraw completely its operations from this airport, which until then had been its 'hub', i.e., its home base. In reaction, the local government set up a wide-ranging, multiparty mediation between nearby residents, economic stakeholders, and government representatives, on the question of whether, where, and when a new runway should be built. The mediation, which involved an extremely large number of participants, was partly held online through discussion forums. This was considered to be the most appropriate way to provide everyone with a voice and thus to allow state authorities to understand the variety of issues that the airport's extension would raise. This example showed how a dispute resolution process can be organized with a number of participants exceeding what would be feasible offline. See <www.mediationflug-hafen.de> and <www.gew-frankfurt.de/index.php?id=91&backPID=91&tt_news=88>.

the Arbitration and Mediation Center of the World Intellectual Property Organization, which has experience in this matter as it was one of the first arbitration institution to offer such electronic facilities for the procedures conducted under its auspices.[47] It may be noted that the America's Cup Jury is also contemplating the use of videoconferencing.[48]

IV. HOW TO USE IT?

For many people, information technologies and computers in general still have some sort of magical appeal, and are considered to be different in nature than mere pen and paper. They are sometimes viewed as something that, if mastered, may provide their bearer with some kind of special power. Hence, they are treated differently than traditional work tools in the sense that some believe, often unconsciously, that, on the one hand, the more IT, the better, and, on the other hand, the more important the situation, the more 'powerful' the technology should be. This attitude leads to two misuses that may totally defeat the purpose of IT: first, general overuse and, second, recourse to technology as if it were a trump card to be played in particularly important situations only. These two misuses call for the two following fundamental caveats and recommendations.

A. Creeping featurism: the more IT, the better?

Many people can be classified in one of two categories: those who dislike and distrust technology, and those who love it. The people of the first category often suffer the consequences of being every day a bit further behind the pack, in terms of work organization and productivity. Those of the second category run a different risk: creeping featurism. This is the tendency to try to develop a process (typically software, but the concept is also used in relation to manufacturing or general administration) on the basis of one, exclusive, rationale: adding features. The result is that the process being thus modified develops in a patchwork pattern, without a global plan and to the detriment of other, in principle prevailing rationales, such as simplicity and usefulness. The users of Microsoft Word and Windows will know what I mean. The fundamental flaw of creeping featurism is that features, which are so many tools, are never a goal in and of themselves. Tools are only a means to an end.

On this basis, it should be recalled that the basic rule governing all uses of IT, in all situations, is that technology is not a goal in and of itself and should only be resorted to if it actually improves the process for which it is used.

---

[47] See Chapter 3, Section I. State of practice, B. WIPO – ECAF, p. 85 below.

[48] On the use of IT at the America's Cup, see Chapter 3, Section I. State of practice, B.2. America's Cup arbitration and domain names dispute resolution, p. 92 below.

As was suggested above,[49] three main criteria may be retained to assess the actuality of this improvement by technology: does recourse to technology make the process more effective, i.e., is the quality of the outcome of the task improved? Does it make the process more efficient, i.e., does technology allow reaching a comparable outcome but at a lower cost or in less time? And does IT usage improve convenience, i.e., may the task be handled in a more convenient way with the help of technology?

In a number of circumstances, none of these three criteria will be met. Hence, 'e-everything', understood as resorting to as much technology as possible regardless whether it is actually sensible of not, must strictly be avoided.

It should also be remembered that increased technological complexity on the end user side requires exponentially increased time for familiarization with the technology and its integration into one's work habits. As was just said, the price paid when decreasing user-friendliness in exchange for enhanced technological capabilities (i.e., additional features) should not be underestimated. But even if both user-friendliness and technological capabilities *are* improved by a technological change, the familiarization with the new technology and the modification of work habits should always be weighed in the balance – oftentimes they are annoyingly time consuming. The popular so-called 'KISS principle' ('keep it super simple', 'keep it simple and straightforward', or 'keep it simple and stupid') may be an over-simplified reaction to this issue, but it has the advantage of clearly expressing the intuitive rule that investments in terms of time, money, and effort in new software or hardware will only be made reluctantly by the vast majority of people. This is particularly true of professionals with well-developed working habits and time restrictions, which is in principle the case of arbitrators and counsel in arbitration.

Simplified, the recommendation may be summarized in the three following, partly overlapping rules:

(a) Do not overdo it.
(b) Use only a little IT, but use it well.
(c) Do not be a geek – IT is not an end in itself: it should never be used just because it is fun; it is only an instrument that must be mastered to take advantage of the functions it provides.

B. Lack of Experience: IT as a Trump Card?

It often happens, not just in relation to the use of information technology but in life in general, that we have in mind some innovative solution or technique, thought to be extraordinary or at least particularly impressive, but have never had the time to try it out. Then, one day we are faced with a particularly important event and, keen to impress, decide the time has come for using our secret weapon of sorts. This leads to try new ways

[49] See Section A. Benefits of IT usage, p. 12 above.

of making a presentation at a major conference, a new rhetoric during a crucial discussion, or new tricks thought to be particularly shrewd during a critical negotiation. The result is that these 'trump cards' often fail quite spectacularly because we are in fact mere beginners at these new, previously untested solutions or techniques.

Why we have a tendency to do this may only be guessed – probably some sort of mix of an intuition that we are not up to the task and a form of organization that makes us believe that only urgent matters are really important, thereby repeatedly postponing tasks that do not have an immediate result, and all this combined with the general tension generated by the importance of the occasion. The fact is that many people do indeed use techniques before having taken the time to master them.

The use of IT is no exception. For instance, lawyers soon having a major case seek to use some relatively complex IT solution without having the time to try the system – to *play* with it, really – before this major occasion. The result is unlikely to be a frank and easy success.

Hence, the second golden rule in relation to the use of IT is: do not try new tools when things are getting serious or, in other words, master an IT solution before using it!

V. FUNDAMENTAL COMMUNICATION TECHNOLOGIES

Having thus discussed why, when, and how IT may be beneficially resorted to in relation to arbitral procedures, it is now necessary to start explaining what this IT actually consists of. Hence, as the goal of this chapter is merely to set the stage and to provide a general introduction, this section will briefly present some standard communication technologies. The technologies addressed here are either directly used in the context of arbitration, or they constitute parts or even the basis of other means of communication that are relevant to arbitration.

In addition, such a basic presentation also appears important because it helps understanding in rough terms how these technologies work from a technical point of view, which then facilitates the understanding of the pros and cons they imply, and of the opportunities and issues they raise.

The following will thus provide a brief overview of e-mails and discussion lists; chats; bulletin boards (often called Internet forums); designated community websites; and Wikis.

A. DISCUSSION LISTS

Discussion lists are based on e-mail messages, as opposed to online forums, which play the same role but are based on a Web page. Both promote geographically independent discussions on either professional or popular topics. Discussion lists can be public or private lists (the private ones being by far the most numerous), and can be moderated or not. Moderation ensures control of membership and that content is maintained. It can, however, be used to stifle discussion. In general, though, moderated lists are the more effective communication spaces.

B. Chats

Text chat, more commonly known as 'instant messaging', is a roughly simplified form of e-mailing for short messages. Its most popular non-commercial system is the Internet Relay Chat (IRC).

One of the main characteristics (and advantages) of instant messaging is that it almost provides synchronicity. Even though e-mails can also be used as a real-time, synchronous communication means, the layout, configuration, addressing system, and general organization of instant messaging make it much more adapted to synchronicity. A further characteristic of instant messaging is its usual dedication to a specific discussion. Indeed, chat systems support virtual environments that can be configured to establish chat rooms (also called channels) around particular topics, interests, or real and virtual groups. For these two reasons, chat systems can be compared to analogue CB radio, while e-mailing is comparable to a telephone with voicemail.

Chat systems are often integrated into more sophisticated means of communication that may be used in arbitration, such as case management websites and videoconferencing. In these contexts, their purpose is primarily to constitute a fallback solution should other, more fragile, channels of communication (video and audio transmission, for instance) cease to work.

To use instant messaging, it is first necessary to install a client program, which connects to one of a number of interconnected servers. These last years, the most widely deployed IRC clients were mIRC267 for Windows and Ircle for MacOS.

C. Bulletin boards

In their traditional sense, electronic bulletin boards were most commonly used in the eighties, before the World Wide Web (i.e., the graphical interface between an end user and a remote server, which takes the form of Web pages) became popular. Such traditional bulletin boards allowed users, just as today, to check the notices on the board and post their own messages. But to do this, the users had to dial in and log on to a remote computer. In many instances it was possible to exchange messages in real time with other users who were logged on simultaneously. Such bulletin boards offered the users a sense of control and interactivity – unlike discussion lists, where they received every message, bulletin boards provided for better selectivity, through topical threads. Participants had access to all the available information, but they could choose what they wished to access. Such bulletin boards operated on the same technology that forms the basis of chat systems.

Since that time, technology has evolved and bulletin boards in this traditional sense are barely used nowadays. Since the mid-nineties, the term 'bulletin board' is increasingly used in the sense of 'Internet forums' (they are also termed 'Web forums', 'message boards', 'discussion boards', 'discussion groups', or simply, 'forums'). In this sense, they refer to applications providing for threaded discussions on a specified Web page, organized according to topics and date of posting.

In contrast to chat systems, bulletin boards are more asynchronous in nature, because chats are used for immediate reactions, often within a few seconds (hence their name of 'instant messaging'), and are usually not recorded somewhere, whereas bulletin boards generate slower reactions and the various posts are in principle recorded by the server and stay online for quite some time.

In the context of arbitration, bulletin boards are for instance used in virtual case-rooms to record briefs and other documents filed or to organize procedural matters.

D. Designated community websites

The development of Web technologies has moved many bulletin boards or IRC-type activities to broader community websites, whose open character allows people to make new connections and to add other features to their primary means of communication (bulletin board or instant messaging).[50] Such designated community websites typically include private messaging facilities, an events calendar, a message board, home pages and profiles, and a contact management system – all of which may profitably be used in arbitration. And indeed, case management websites are precisely built on this concept; the various participants in an arbitration proceeding constitute, after all, a designated community. In this sense, the communication technologies used in arbitration are a means to enhance collaboration within a community.

E. Wikis

A Wiki is defined by its inventor Ward Cunningham as 'the simplest online database that could possibly work',[51] and takes the form of a collaboratively edited website which can be altered either by any user or only by specific users. In other words, a Wiki is a website on which individuals can add contents as on an Internet forum, but this content can then be edited by other users: it is a collaborative writing tool accessible directly through a Web browser. 'WikiZens', as the people editing Wikis are known, contribute to the development of their contents by adding to or editing the work of their fellow authors. The most significant work achieved so far by WikiZens is Wikipedia, a multilingual

---

50 Ryze, for instance, was built with the special purpose of helping to create and extend business networks; it supports over 150 networks with very different sizes and communication intensities: see <www.ryze.com>

51 See <wiki.org/wiki.cgi?WhatIsWiki>

Web-based and Wiki-based free-content encyclopedia, authored collaboratively by any Internet user who volunteers. In order to avoid malevolent or involuntary deletion (and incompetent editing as well), most Wikis have a rollback system that allows the recovery of all precedent versions of a Wiki entry and facilities for blocking the IP addresses of Wiki offenders.

In the legal context, one of the most famous recent uses of a Wiki is the collaborative writing of the second edition of Lawrence Lessig's book *Code and other Laws of Cyberspace*, whose actual text is open to editing by any Internet user until a specific date, after which it will be revised by the main author and published in paper form.[52]

This technology provides particularly useful advantages when a team is working at the same time on the same text, as it avoids working with numerous versions of the same document annotated and corrected by different people.

[52] See <codebook.jot.com/WikiHome>.

CHAPTER 2

INFORMATION TECHNOLOGIES FOR ARBITRATION

What technologies the practitioner may consider using

In Chapter 1, we have seen how IT, generally speaking, may contribute to improving the conduct of arbitral proceedings. We have seen that IT may save time and expenses, that on some occasions it may permit certain actions that would not have been possible without technology – such as hearing a witness from afar in situations of particularly severe time constraints – and that it could, if used correctly, make our lives easier, not more complex. Accordingly, suggestions have been made as to how IT differs from the analogical world we are used to and how we should consequently adapt some of our actions to avoid the pitfalls of technology-enabled solutions, and take advantage of as much of their potential as possible. These general considerations must now be translated into more concrete examples, and applied to specific technologies of interest to arbitration.

Needless to say, IT has spread through the daily lives of lawyers, and the current market offers so many tools, virtually thousands of applications that may be used in relation to arbitration, from programs converting speech into text and allowing users to write a brief simply by dictation, to sophisticated applications supporting oral presentations, automatic time-sheet drafters, programs teaching typing skills, and legal thesauri and dictionaries, etc. But this book's purpose is not to review these applications to provide practitioners with a ready-to-go list of legal applications to acquire in order to upgrade one's law firm to the current standards. This has been done elsewhere, in a format that allows the necessary constant updating.[53] Instead, this book will focus on the most fundamental technological developments, and the opportunities and challenges they

[53] See, for example, the American Bar Association's Legal Technology Resource Center, <www.-abanet.org/tech/ltrc/home.html>; FindLaw's Law Practice and Technology Magazine, <prac-tice.findlaw.com>; FindLaw for Corporate Counsel Market Center, rubrics Legal software <marketcenter.findlaw.com/software.html> and Legal technology <marketcenter.findlaw.com/-hardware_technology.html>; NetTech, <www.nettechinc.com/lawtech.htm>; Brett Burney's columns for LLRX <www.llrx.com/cgi-bin/llrx.cgi?function=browseauth2&id=265>; Legal Technology Online, <www.digital-lawyer.com/digital-lawyer/index.html>; the downloads (many of which are free) from Law.com's LegalTechnology downloads directory <www.law.-com/jsp/ltn/download.jsp>; the white papers, explaining how to use technology, from Law.com's LegalTechnology white papers directory <www.law.com/jsp/ltn/whitepapers.jsp>; and the pay per view Law Office Computing magazine <www.lawofficecomputing.com/EDC/home/home.php>.

entail for the practice of arbitration, as well as the way they may globally modify legal practice in the context of arbitration.

The most fundamental technological developments for arbitration are case management websites and videoconferencing. The former profoundly affect document and information management; the latter help bridge distances by permitting a new form of presence in situations where the physical presence of all participants – which is never completely replaced through technology – is not indispensable. Amongst these technologies, the emphasis is placed on videoconferencing, which raises many more questions than case management websites. If the latter is relatively complex to set up from a technological point of view (a topic beyond the scope of the present study), it is easier to use.

In addition to case management websites and videoconferencing, this chapter also reviews two further uses of technology: live notes and online dispute resolution platforms. Live notes are transcripts taken by court reporters during a hearing using a system which allows a complete reproduction of all verbal exchanges made during the hearing to be immediately accessible on the computer screens of all participants, in real time. They often prove to be particularly useful during arbitrations which involve hearing witnesses on complex situations of fact. Online dispute resolution platforms do not, as such, constitute a specific technology. However, they represent a special use of technology, consistent with the idea that IT management may profitably be externalized altogether to organizations which have a thorough experience in such dealings; online dispute resolution providers no doubt have the most experience in such matters because of the number of disputes they solve.

For purposes of monitoring technological development, this chapter also presents an innovative technology: shared virtual environments, which are not currently used, but may constitute a future direction for the use of IT in arbitration.

For each of these technologies, this chapter describes the technology and, if applicable and not addressed elsewhere in this book, discusses specific uses or experiments made of the technology. Thereafter, the use of these technologies is assessed and compared to other ways to communicate and interact in the context of arbitral proceedings. Finally, certain recurring issues and concerns are discussed and solutions put forward.

It must finally be specified that this chapter does not address the exchange of files on data carriers, i.e., CDs and DVDs. Admittedly, these have some of the typical advantages of IT tools, such as lower costs of transmitting data, portability, and the ease of arranging files or linking them using hyperlinks between documents or specific locations in such documents – physical data carriers even have an advantage over the electronic transmission of documents, as hyperlinks pointing to files stored on a hard disk easily become unusable when transmitted from one computer to another. This matter, however, does not deserve special consideration here, as it does not raise any particular legal issue. For an introduction to the advantages of using data carriers, the reader may revert to the general considerations addressed in Chapter 1.

I. CASE MANAGEMENT WEBSITES

What arbitration practitioners are mostly in need of, in terms of technology, are communication technologies that allow the management and transmission of a large number of long, interrelated documents, in a convenient and efficient way. E-mails do not provide a satisfactory response to this – or at least they do not constitute the best solution considering what is available today. Hence, different forms of applications specifically developed for such purposes have been imported and adapted from other business contexts into the arbitration world.

In substance, all these applications consist of a sophisticated website allowing users to upload, store, organize, and retrieve documents and other files. As additional features, they usually include tools that provide for posting messages and sharing electronic agendas, in order to facilitate the resolution of minor procedural issues. They also generally facilitate access to and the overview of all information related to a specific case, such as the contact details of all participants, financial aspects, and a rundown of past and upcoming events.

These technologies, alternatively called extranets, case management websites, and virtual case rooms, may be either institutionally implemented (as in the cases of WeFile,[54] ECAF,[55] and NetCase[56]) or provided for ad hoc, by referring either to a virtual case room provider,[57] or to one of the existing self-service collaborative workspaces not specifically designed for legal matters but more generally for secure communication, collaboration, and coordination.[58] Simplified versions of such technologies have already been used by some law firms for several years.[59] Whether institutional or ad hoc, they fundamentally share the same pros and cons, and raise the same issues. They will thus be addressed without distinction in the following.

This section first sets out this general technology in more detail, explaining its operations and uses. It then reviews the reasons for its use, i.e., the properties it offers and functions it fulfills, and finally discusses the main issues and concerns it raises. The latter part includes aspects requiring special attention when utilizing this technology, as well as limitations imposed in order to respect procedural rights.

---

54 See Chapter 3, Section I. State of practice, A. AAA – WebFile, p. 76 below.

55 See Chapter 3, Section I. State of practice, B. WIPO – ECAF, p. 85 below.

56 See Chapter 3, Section I. State of practice, C. ICC – NetCase, p. 93 below.

57 See n. 27 above.

58 To refer only to one such shared workspace application, one may mention Lotus QuickPlace, which has been tested and found adequately useful for the sort of file transmission and organization that most arbitrations would require.

59 An example is Allen Overy in London, see <www.allenovery.com/asp/ProductsServices.asp>. For a presentation of these services, see, for example, W.R. Leibowitz, 'The Wired World of Marketing Legal Services: There's a New Standard in Netting, Knowing and Keeping Clients' (2001) 27 *Law Practice Management* 28.

A. What is a Case Management Website?

The concept of a case management website may best be explained with reference to two closely related electronic communication means: extranets on the one hand, virtual case rooms on the other. The difference between these three technologies is essentially a question of degree or of specification of use; case management websites are, so to speak, the 'middle' concept. Consequently, the balance of this book will use only the term 'case management website', thereby possibly referring to technological configurations that rather pertain to one of the two other notions addressed here. For the moment, however, specifying their respective nature and their differences sheds a useful light on what this type of technology can be used for.

Extranets

Extranets are basically private segments of the Internet or private spheres of cyberspace. They are 'Web spaces' with secure aspects, which means they include firewall server management, means of user authentication such as passwords or digital certificates, and message encryption. They may also rely on virtual private networks or VPN, which are specific and exclusive connections that tunnel through the public network. For the rest, they use the same networks as those that constitute the Internet (i.e., the public telecommunications system) and the same protocol for exchanging information (i.e., the Transmission Control Protocol/Internet Protocol, or TCP/IP).

From a functionality perspective, one may simply say that an extranet is used as a common repository of shared data to which all authorized members have access over the Internet. More precisely, the purpose of an extranet is to share, in a private fashion, part of an organization's information and operations with its members, as well as with its suppliers, customers, and partners. This extension of the authorized members to individuals external to the company or entity or project (the suppliers, customers, and partners) is what differentiates an extranet from an intranet.

The access to such shared data has in principle two goals: document management and scheduling. Document management includes retrieving and reviewing the latest version of documents from remote locations and, conversely, publishing documents firm-, project-, or client-wide. Scheduling consists of online calendaring and includes setting deadlines and posting reminders, scheduling meetings with lists of attendees, and monitoring the status of projects.

Case management websites

Case management websites are extranets that are specifically designed for the management of a legal case. They serve two main purposes:

(a) providing a universally accessible, but password-protected, platform for document repository, and
(b) constituting a Web-based interface that allows users to communicate rapidly and securely.

These purposes may translate into functionalities such as information sharing, claims screening, matter tracking, discovery management, patent/trademark management, and contract tracking.

Typically, such websites are accessible to the parties, counsel, arbitrators, arbitral institution, and possibly, with restrictions, to witnesses and experts. Access is typically protected by passwords, but additional security can also be sought from any of the additional technologies just mentioned for extranets (VPN against data interception, firewalls against intrusion, digital certificates for authentication).

Typical uses of case management websites – before the technology was acquired by the major arbitration institutions, which extended this technology to all types of cases[60] – were mass claims and multiparty proceedings, because automation and standardization through electronic workflow are most obviously efficient in situations involving a large number of plaintiffs.[61]

Virtual case rooms

Virtual case rooms are case management websites that are more specifically dedicated to the actual resolution of a case. Other case management websites are generally designed to assist with the global management of the case, but not its actual resolution. Consequently, virtual case rooms may include more sophisticated means of communication including for instance more developed bulletin boards, telephone conferencing facilities, or video-conferencing software.

Examples of case management websites are reproduced in Chapter 3, in the review of the practice of the AAA, WIPO, and the ICC.[62]

B. Uses and advantages

As we have seen, case management websites are basically a sophisticated online repository for electronic documents, with some additional features. As such, they offer a number of advantages, in terms of efficiency, effectiveness, and convenience,[63] for tasks that are typically undertaken during arbitration proceedings. These advantages and uses are listed below.

Voluminous document transmission

E-mails allow users to send only a limited amount of information at a time. The first reason for this is volume restrictions set by Internet service providers. But even if special

---

60 See Chapter 3, Section I. State of practice, p. 75 below.

61 This was discussed in Chapter 1, Section III. When to use IT?, p. 18 above.

62 See Chapter 3, Section I. State of practice, p. 75 below.

63 These three types of advantages of IT have been discussed in Chapter 1, Section II. Why IT?, A. Benefits of IT-usage, p. 12 above.

arrangements are made to increase significantly the maximal allowed size of e-mails, transmitting numerous documents, e.g., hundreds of files as is regularly the case in larger arbitration cases, is troublesome using e-mails.

The advantage of case management websites is that they often allow the uploading and/or downloading of entire folders at a time, with no limitation regarding the volume or number of documents. This simple difference has important practical consequences; it saves time, reduces the risk that a file is forgotten, and simplifies the whole process.

Security and confidentiality

Setting up secure, encrypted e-mails is not a difficult task.[64] Nevertheless, the vast majority of practitioners have not done it, with the consequence that their communications with their clients, the arbitral tribunal, the other party, and all other participants in an arbitration could be intercepted by a third party, using a technique that probably several million individuals master.[65] Hence, a security solution that requires no special action from its users should be welcomed. Case management websites are such a solution.

Typically, all communications and documents traveling between the user's browser and the case management website are encrypted. Documents are automatically checked for viruses before being posted, and any infected document is refused. Access to the website is also protected by user names, passwords, and possibly a security certificate. Additional security measures include those discussed above, in relation to the presentation of extranets, case management, and virtual case rooms. The participants thus communicate in an environment that is clearly more secure than the exchange of unprotected e-mails.

Access to submissions can also be restricted to certain participants as appropriate. The platform may for instance be opened to witnesses and experts in such fashion that they have access only to the shared calendar. It may happen that a document is placed in a given section of the website by mistake, making it available to a participant who is not an intended recipient. In such a case, the advantage of case management websites over an e-mail sent to an unintended recipient is that the website provides a chance to change access rights or to remove the misplaced document before the unintended recipient accesses it. Conversely, a sent e-mail cannot be cancelled. It may be added that the fact that someone has indeed accessed a document can easily be tracked electronically, as this person would have had to identify herself on the website.

Accessibility and speed

Case management websites are accessible anywhere and at anytime, immediately, just as any other website. If well designed, they operate whatever the browser and operating system being used, and are thus accessible regardless of the computer being used. The acces-

---

64 For a description of how to set up and use secure and encrypted e-mails, see Chapter 5, Section II.D. Encrypting and digitally signing e-mail, p. 158 below.

65 Further on data interception, see Chapter 5, Section I.A.1. Interception, p. 133 below.

sibility of the information posted and the speed of the data transmission process is further ensured by the fact that each uploading of a file or posting of a message on the message board generates an automatic notification, by e-mail, to all interested parties. Case management websites are thus as fast as e-mails, as accessible as webmails (i.e., Web-based e-mail interfaces), and provide for enhanced organization and more convenience, as discussed in the next point.

Organization and convenience

On case management websites, all information and documents are in principle organized in a uniform manner and are 'searchable'. Such websites often label automatically each document with the person who has uploaded it and the time at which it was done, or they require the users submitting the files to do so. Hence, the origin of the documents is easily identifiable.

Also, all submissions and exchanges are in principle tracked to show the chronology of a case, which makes document retrieval much easier than if e-mails or (considering the usual organization of a lawyer) hanging folders and ring binders are used.

It may also be reminded that the information contained in the documents is more easily accessible and retrievable than it would be on paper, as electronic documents lend themselves to fast searches for keywords or specific text passages. Cross-document searches may also identify within seconds what part of which document, submitted by which party at what time, contains a specific word, reference, or sentence, corresponding to a given argument, reference to a certain exhibit, or request for a particular action of the arbitral tribunal, one or both of the parties or any other participant.

Financial information can also be tracked, and a complete account of arbitration costs may be accessed at any time. Other features may include an 'address book' with the contact details of all participants; a general overview of the case; a calendar of the proceedings; and guidelines for the use of the website.

Cost savings

It may finally be recalled that, compared to working with hard copies of documents, case management websites allow significant costs savings, as the costs of preparing, handling, and sending hard copies are greatly reduced. The smaller the arbitration, the higher these savings will be proportionally.

C. Caveats

Case management websites raise no legal issues that are of either particular nature or significant importance.[66] Nevertheless, their use must not be an occasion to disregard the

---

66 This book specifically excludes issues of liability for security breaches and for damages caused by inoperative technology (which are in principle exclusively governed by the respective

usual requirements deriving from the parties' procedural rights. Hence, some simple caveats relating to the use of this technology will be reviewed here briefly. These caveats will be addressed in further detail in Chapter 4, which analyzes the general legal framework that governs IT usage in arbitration.

The right to be heard in an adversary proceeding
A party has the right to be heard in an adversary procedure, which includes at least one opportunity for a party to present its allegations of facts and legal arguments, and the right to tender pertinent evidence on relevant facts, as well as the right to rebut the opponent's case, which implies equal access to the record and that the arbitral tribunal does not have ex parte communications with any party.

Equal treatment
The parties must be treated equally from a procedural point of view. In the present context, this requirement implies that the website be easily accessible to users with different levels of computer literacy. The filing processes should be simple and assistance should be available, whenever possible.

Transparency of the process
A clear description of the process should be available, including any specific costs generated by the use of the website, and any substantive and procedural rules. The publication of any outcomes or statistics must be clearly disclosed. Any information given must not only be complete, but also easy to access and understand.

II. VIDEOCONFERENCING

Next to managing and transmitting documents, the second most important organizational aspect of an arbitration is gathering people, for hearings, discussions with co-counsels or co-arbitrators, and other types of meetings. But in some situations, traveling to a meeting is not a suitable solution; it may be impracticable due to time or cost constraints, or more simply travel may be an excessive burden in view of the lack of significance of the meeting. Such situations are often handled by telephone conferences. But on some such occasions, a telephone conference is not completely satisfactory, or perhaps even totally inadequate. Technology's response to the need that emerges from such circumstances is videoconferencing. Videoconferencing may thus be considered the second electronic communication technology of most interest to the arbitration practitioner.

In substance, videoconferencing (sometimes known as a 'video teleconference') is an IT-based solution that enables meetings among persons using telephony and closed circuit television technologies simultaneously. It allows two or more participants located in

---

applicable national law). Such issues are beyond the scope of this book, because they do not relate directly to the relationship between the conduct of arbitral proceedings and IT-usage.

different places to communicate with almost no consideration for geographic distance, sharing images, sound, and possibly software applications.

In the past, videoconferencing required relatively sophisticated and expensive technical equipment, and its quality was relatively poor. This, however, has largely become untrue during the last years. The criticism videoconferencing receives, being rejected out of hand as an impracticable solution, is nowadays largely based on a lack of recent experience on the part of its critics. On the one hand, low-cost, user-friendly systems can now deliver a reasonably good quality of sound and image transmission. Such systems have recently been developed in the wake of new compression technologies and protocols allowing the transmission of video data over IP, i.e., simply connecting to the Internet through a Web page. On the other hand, high-end equipment is also available, at much higher costs but with a near-perfect rendering of image and sound. Both of these systems are of interest to arbitration. The simple ones for less important online meetings or smaller arbitrations; the more sophisticated ones when cost constraints are less important. In between, a whole range of videoconferencing solutions exist, which may be adapted to different arbitration needs. This section is about those needs and the corresponding videoconferencing solutions.

The first part of this section describes the technologies that constitute the different forms of videoconferencing currently available, in order to get a basic technical understanding of how this tool works and which forms it may take. This section then presents a videoconferencing experiment carried out at the University of Geneva with arbitration practitioners. Most of these practitioners were inexperienced with videoconferencing, and their reactions reveal enjoyment, concerns, and limitations that are likely to match those of other arbitration practitioners inexperienced with this means of communication. The third part of this section then reviews the actual uses and advantages of videoconferencing. Finally, some caveats are provided.

A. VIDEOCONFERENCING TECHNOLOGIES

Before presenting the various uses of videoconferencing, it seems necessary to delve shortly into some technical aspects of this tool, in order to understand the main current types of technologies and the current evolutionary trends. Tremendous progress has indeed been made since the radio-frequency-based systems used by NASA during the first manned flights, which simply resorted to two closed-circuit television systems, operating on standard, analog television technologies.

1. THE EVOLUTION OF CODECS

The main technological point of videoconferencing worth understanding is that its most challenging feature is the digital compression technology – which must operate in real time – of the audio and video data transmitted. This compression is operated by software called a coder/decoder protocol (or codec). Current decoders achieve compression rates of up to 1:500, which means that the information transmitted is globally 500 times smaller that what is in principle necessary to deliver the image, sound, and possibly the software operations that the user creates or witnesses. In other words, a codec twice as efficient requires a bandwidth twice as narrow to support the same videoconferencing. The other components of a videoconferencing system, such as the video camera, video display device, microphone, and speakers or headset also influence the quality and costs of an online meeting, but their importance is globally marginal in comparison with the codecs.

Due to the rapid evolution of codecs throughout the nineties, videoconferencing systems have evolved from requiring highly expensive proprietary equipment, software, and network to standards-based technology that is readily available to the general public at a reasonable cost. The best equipment one could get ten years ago would probably be outclassed by most of today's free Web-based systems.

Nowadays, there are fundamentally two kinds of videoconferencing systems, which correspond to two different technologies and two different types of codecs: dedicated systems and IP-based systems.

2. DEDICATED VIDEOCONFERENCING

Dedicated videoconferencing systems rely on a technical standard called H.320, which is the standard for public switched telephone networks or for ISDN videoconferencing. Such systems usually come as a global package, which include all required components in a single console. They often, but not necessarily, take the form of particularly high-end solutions, including for instance very high quality conferencing microphones, extra-large screens or very powerful projectors, and cameras that could be controlled in pan, tilt, and zoom from afar. Most importantly, such systems rely on dedicated connections, which could be land lines or even satellite-based networks. The fact that the connection lines are dedicated means that the speed of transmission can be better controlled (as no one else shares the lines) and is in principle much higher than the fastest commonly available broadband Internet connections.

Traditionally the use of videoconferencing in arbitration and in legal processes relied on such high-end solutions. Business, government, and the military still predominantly – though not exclusively – use dedicated videoconferencing systems.

Typical videoconferencing hardware equipment of this type costs approximately USD 10,000–15,000.[67] They allow, however, particularly high quality audio and video transmission.

Such systems are best left to professional companies. Indeed, in addition to requiring a significant financial investment, such high-end IT solutions may be quite complex to use,

[67] For examples, see e.g., <www.kilchenmann.ch/de/telematik/videoconferencing/produkte-anwendung/einzelplatz>.

for instance because they require non-standard equipment, which may use different transmission protocols and be complicated to install. As a result, for such high-end solutions, it is best to resort to professional videoconferencing service providers, i.e., private companies that provide videoconferencing equipment, rooms, and technical assistance.[68]

To those who have had some experience with such dedicated videoconferencing systems, it may finally be pointed out that most uses of video linkups in dispute resolution contexts have been point-to-point connections. Most uses indeed included only two terminal stations, usually one for the arbitral tribunal and the parties who convene in a conference room, and one on the other side for the witness or expert who for some reason could not join the hearing in person.[69] But videoconferencing can actually be used in more sophisticated configurations, e.g., connecting a higher number of individuals. Such multiple connections may best be achieved using IP videoconferencing.

3. IP VIDEOCONFERENCING

Described in simple terms, IP-based videoconferencing systems communicate over the Internet using common communication protocols and everyday equipment, connecting generally through an ordinary website. The user simply switches on a standard desktop computer, connects equipment that can be bought at any computer shop for less than USD 100, opens Internet Explorer or any other Web browser, goes to a website, logs in, and starts a discussion with image and sound, and may even share documents through this website.

Put more technically, IP videoconferencing relies on a different technical standard than dedicated videoconferencing, called H.323, developed in the late nineties for Internet telephony – also called Voice over IP or VoIP. This is the technology that Skype and Google Talk use, for example. IP videoconferencing is fundamentally Skype or Google Talk with image in the bargain. This new standard of data compression is radically more powerful than what existed before and has allowed the development of videoconferencing systems working with fairly basic terminal equipment (the equipment each end user must have on its side of the connection). Videoconferencing sessions have thus become accessible to anyone with a good broadband Internet connection, a webcam, a microphone, and speakers or headphones, as well as a reasonably powerful computer. In addition to reducing the costs involved, the radical simplification of the required terminal equipment also largely facilitates the organization and use of such software.

IP videoconferencing has developed along two lines. On the one hand, free services and software have emerged, among which one may count Yahoo Messenger,[70]

---

68 See, for example, E. Schäfer, 'Videoconferencing in arbitration' (2003) 14:1 ICC Bull 35, p. 36. For an example of such videoconferencing service providers, see <www.demorum.com>

69 Ibid.

70 See <messenger.yahoo.com/messenger/superwebcam>.

NetMeeting,[71] and MSN Messenger.[72] Most of these systems are of relatively low quality, although they are making remarkable progress from year to year. Above all, they often do not support multipoint conferencing, i.e., a videoconference involving more than two participants at a time, which is technologically much more complicated to operate. On the other hand, systems for professional use have also developed. They are based on the same technology and require the same hardware, but involve more powerful software and servers. Consequently, the quality of the transmitted image and sound is better and multipoint conferencing is possible. Some of the best examples of such professional IP videoconferencing systems are ClickToMeet[73] and Macromedia Breeze.[74]

Although IP videoconferencing has often been dismissed as not sufficiently sophisticated for arbitration,[75] an experiment carried out at the University of Geneva seems to indicate that this could change soon. This experiment is described in the next section. At any rate, one should remember, in this situation just as in any other situation where recourse to IT is made, that the simplest solution that provides the intended result should in principle be preferred; it is generally the most robust and the easiest to implement and to use.

B. The Geneva experiment

In the spring and summer of 2005, we conducted, at Geneva University Law School, an experiment on the practicability of videoconferencing in arbitration, in collaboration with MIRALab, the Geneva University computer-science research center specialized in virtual environments. The purpose of the experiment was to assess whether videoconferencing in arbitration could be done using basic, everyday computer equipment worth less than USD 100 per participant – in addition to the standard desktop and laptop computers that were used. The result was quite clear: it can be done. This section reports on the experiment.

First, the experiment itself is described in more detail, including who participated, which software application was used, how it was organized, and what the global result was. Thereafter, this section features the arbitration scenario according to which the experiment was conducted. Based on a real case that took place during the 2000 Sydney Olympics, it formed the rough lines of the script of the replies by the parties, the arbitrator, and the witness. The third part describes the technology that we used. The last part then presents the results of the experiment.

---

71 See description in Chapter 5, Section III.C Examples of videoconferencing software, p. 173 below.

72 MSN Messenger version 7.0 and later. See <messenger.msn.com/Xp/Default.aspx>.

73 See <www.clicktomeet.com>.

74 See <www.macromedia.com/software/breeze>. Breeze offers a free trial version which we recommend for a full-scale test of videoconferencing.

75 E.g., E. Schäfer, 'Videoconferencing in arbitration', n. 68 above.

1. GENERAL DESCRIPTION

The experiment was conducted with arbitration practitioners[76] as well as faculty members from both the Law School[77] and MIRALab,[78] so that it could be assessed from the perspectives of both legal practice and computer science. The participants connected mainly from computers housed in the Law Faculty, although there were also connections from abroad, including from Ireland and South Korea.

The experiment used a commercial software application, ClickToMeet,[79] configured so as to be best able to meet typical arbitration requirements. This application provides a videoconferencing platform featuring various online collaborative tools, such as document presentation and application sharing. It works on a standard PC.

The test sessions started with a short technical explanation, which was quite limited as one goal was to see if the system could be used almost intuitively. Thereafter followed an oral hearing on the simulated case, which included referring to and viewing several exhibits in the form of pictures, affidavits, and expert opinions. On some occasions, a witness was also heard and a secretary-technician assisted the arbitrator.

The general result was that, despite several critical comments and specific improvements suggested, almost all participants concluded that the system was definitely usable in practice, and some even inquired when this system might be ready for use in actual cases. An upgraded version of this system was actually used, a few months later, in a real arbitration by one of the practitioners who had participated in the experiment.

2. SCENARIO

The scenario of the experiment was based on a real case administered by the ad hoc Division of the Court of Arbitration for Sports during the 2000 Olympic Games in Sydney.[80] The case involved a single sculls rower, Ms Rumyana Neykova, who contested

---

[76] The following arbitration practitioners participated in the experiment: Michael E. Schneider (Lalive and Partners), Pierre-Yves Gunter (Python Schifferli Peter), Matthias Scherrer (Lalive and Partners), Dr Antonio Rigozzi (Schellenberg Wittmer), Pierre Kobel (Hirsch Kobel), Laurent Hirsch (Hirsch Kobel), and Lorine Meylan (Lalive and Partners).

[77] The experiment involved the following faculty members of Geneva University Law School: Prof. Christine Chappuis, Juan-Carlos Landrove, and Silja Schaffstein. Brian Hutchinson, of University College Dublin, also agreed to participate.

[78] Two fellows from MIRALab participated: Dimitris Protopsaltou and HungSeok Kim, who connected from South Korea.

[79] See n. 73 above and, for more details, Section 3. The technology, p. 44 below.

[80] CAS OG 00/012, reported in *CAS Awards - Sydney 2000. The decisions delivered by the ad hoc Division of the Court of Arbitration for Sport during the 2000 Olympic Games in Sydney* (Lausanne, CAS, 2000), pp. 123–130.

the photo finish on the basis of which the judges had awarded her the silver medal, on the grounds of an alleged defect of the official timing and recording equipment.

After a recapitulation of the main relevant information, such as the parties and the subject matters at issue, the following paragraphs set out the dialogue of the simulation hearing in bullet point format, as it was provided to all participants to the test; this format was used to leave room for some improvisation.

RUMYANA DIMITROVA NEYKOVA *v.* INTERNATIONAL ROWING FEDERATION AND INTERNATIONAL OLYMPIC COMMITTEE

ad hoc Division of the Court of Arbitration for Sports, 2000
(adapted for the purposes of the experiment)

a. Background

Summary

Ms Rumyana Neykova, a rowing athlete, finished second at the final of the Sydney Olympics, behind Ms Ekaterina Karsten, from Belarus. The time difference was approximately one hundredth of a second.

The official photo and timing system, supplied by Swatch, showed Ms Karsten in first place. The Sydney Olympic Broadcasting Organisation's video recording equipment, set up for the purpose of providing footage for TV audiences and not part of the official recording system, showed Ms Neykova in first place.

Ms Neykova claims that the official Swatch recording system is defective.

Parties
- Claimant: Rumyana Dimitrova Neykova
- Respondent: International Rowing Federation (FISA) and International Olympic Committee (IOC)

Participants
- Counsel for claimant
- Counsel for respondents
- Arbitrator

Subject matters
- Rowing regatta
- Appeal against a decision of FISA
- Accuracy of technical equipment
- Olympics gold medal attribution and ranking modification

Exhibits
- Exhibit no 1: Photo of the Swatch recording system
- Exhibit no 2: Photo of the Sydney Olympic Broadcasting Organization's video recording equipment
- Exhibit no 3: Expert opinion by Mr Stein on the accuracy of digital and analog cameras
- Exhibit no 4: Affidavit by Mr Bauman, a Swatch official, regarding the position of the Swatch camera and the TV camera

b. Script

INTRODUCTION

Arbitrator
- Introduces the case.
- Reminds parties that proceedings are conducted under rule for expedited arbitration, that no witnesses nor experts will be heard, that arbitral tribunal will rule immediately on its jurisdiction, and that award is rendered immediately after the end of the hearing, with a written decision containing the reasons to be issued shortly thereafter.
- Asks the parties to introduce themselves.

ON JURISDICTION

Arbitrator
- Reminds parties that defendant notified intention to challenge jurisdiction.
- Opens the floor, first respondent, then claimant.

Respondent
- Issue involves field of play rules: i.e., dispute not arbitrable.[81] Technical decisions by sports officials made during sporting events cannot be submitted to arbitration. Refers to M. v. AIBA (CAS ad hoc division, Atlanta, OG 96/006): 'Traditionally, doctrine and judicial practice have always deemed that game rules in the strict sense of the term, should not be subject to the control of judges, based on the idea that "the game must not be constantly interrupted by appeals to the judge"'.

---

[81] The arbitrability issues raised by this case are discussed in G. Kaufmann-Kohler, *Arbitration at the Olympics – Issues of Fast Track Dispute Resolution and Sports Law* (The Hague, Kluwer Law International, 2001), p. 25 *et seq.* and A. Rigozzi, *L'arbitrage international en matière de sport* (Basle, Helbing & Lichtenhahn, 2005), p. 364 *et seq.*

Claimant

- Admits that this corresponds to most precedents.
- But field of play rules theory should be revisited, and this is an occasion to do it.
- Field of play rules theory is in reality not a question of arbitrability. Arbitrability is in Switzerland (seat of the arbitral tribunal) determined by art. 177 Swiss PIL act, which reads: 'All pecuniary claims may be submitted to arbitration'. Many sports decisions, and the present one is no different, have substantial direct pecuniary implications. Hence, they are arbitrable.
- What the field of play rules theory in fact seeks to achieve is, as respondent suggested, to avoid 'constant interruption of the game by the judge or the arbitrator'. It is in reality a question of scope of consent given to arbitration. In principle, consent does not cover field of play rules, precisely because the parties do not want interruptions of the game. But in this case, it is different.
- In this case, it is a question of the accuracy of technical equipment. Sanctioning such inaccuracy would not lead to any interruption of the game. In addition, this issue is fundamental enough to the competition that one may assume that the parties intended to allow a decision on equipment to be revised before an arbitrator. This dispute is arbitrable.

Arbitrator

- Makes ruling on jurisdiction: dispute arbitrable.
- Case proceeds.

ON THE MERITS

Arbitrator

- Reminds parties that the question is the validity of the official photography, which determines the winner.
- Reminds parties of the relief requested by claimant (ranking reconsidered; she be awarded co-gold medal; the race a tie between Neykova and Karsten, current gold medalist).
- Specifies that, according to the rules, one opportunity for each to make the case, and possibly short reply to each other's arguments.
- Opens the floor.

Claimant

- Mechanical error, or at least inaccuracy in the photo finish, i.e., picture not taken at the right time. Shows exhibits 1 and 2, i.e., the two pictures of the finish, one showing Karsten in first place, the other one showing Neykova.
- On Australian television, based on the Sydney Olympic Broadcasting Organisation's video recording equipment, Neykova won the race.
- On official cameras, Karsten won the race.
- Time difference only one hundredth of a second.

- If two cameras show different results, means that recording equipment cannot be accurate enough to single out a winner by one hundredth of a second.
- Unfair to proclaim a single winner with such a precision, as the technical equipment is manifestly unable to provide such accuracy.
- Arbitral tribunal should declare the race a tie between Neykova and Karsten. Neykova deserves co-gold medal.

Respondent
- *First argument*: TV recording less reliable technology than the one used by Swatch.
- Swatch is digital, uses digital technology, stores electronic data which can later be used to create image like photographic image but more precise.
- Video tapes, which were used by Olympic Broadcasting Organization, produce less accurate images, as tape needs to be moved across the camera's lens to create an image on tape; this makes recording much slower and offsets an image in time by several milliseconds at least.
- Refers to expert opinion by Mr Stein, a video engineer. Shows exhibit no 3.
- *Second argument*: TV camera was located 10 centimeters in front of finish.
- Swatch camera exactly on line.
- When 10 centimeters projected across 200 meter width of course, perspective different. Shows exhibit 4.
- Camera located exactly on line should prevail.
- *Conclusion*: Official camera perfectly accurate, to the hundredth of a second.
- Other camera poorly located and uses a much less precise technology.
- Other camera should not be taken into consideration.
- Gold medal should stay with Karsten and with Karsten alone.

Arbitrator
- Thanks for arguments.
- Reminds parties that he will now give conclusions and the decision orally, which will be followed by a written award.
- Conclusion and decision: deficiency of mechanical operation of official photo finish equipment not established; ranking case will not be revised; Ms Neykova remains second.

3. The technology

The software application used for the Geneva experiment was ClickToMeet, an IP-based multipoint videoconferencing application quite typical of what the market currently offers. The following details its main technological aspects.

a. Features

ClickToMeet has a number of features, which may be adapted for different uses. For the experiment, we found the following to be the most useful.

- *Videoconferencing*: up to 16 participants can be shown at the same time on the platform while in videoconferencing-only mode, as opposed to videoconferencing plus document presentation or application sharing, where the maximal number of participants showing on the screen is limited to five. These numbers only relate to 'video-actors', i.e., participants who send video and audio data. This restriction to 16 or to five video-actors is essentially due to screen size, although the amount of information transmitted, which increases exponentially with every additional video-actor, is also a limiting factor. The more information is transmitted, the more powerful the central server must be and the faster the Internet connections must be. However, several hundred participants who only watch and listen in the background (i.e., 'spectators') can log on to a session. In addition to video-actors and spectators, other participants may also connect to the platform using a standard telephone or an IP phone; it this case, videoconferencing and teleconferencing are combined in the same virtual conference room.
- *Document presentation*: the platform permits the uploading of a document of almost any format, which is then converted into a new format specific to the platform for faster viewing. Such documents can be uploaded in advance to the server of the platform, and accessed later, during the meeting itself. This feature is typically used for showing documentary evidence.
- *Mouse tracking*: mouse movements by one participant can be shown to all other participants, allowing a participant to point on a map, a plan, a drawing, a bill, etc., i.e., on any part of any uploaded document.
- *Application sharing*: any application that one of the participants has on his computer can be viewed, and even used, by any other participant during an online conference: e.g., one participant can show a video recording even if no other participant has the software to play that recording, or the participants can collectively write a Word document. Virtually any kind of data can be transmitted using this system, as long as the participant transmitting it has the software to read it on his own computer.

- *Recording*: Geneva University's MIRALab computer science center added a feature to ClickToMeet which allows entire sessions to be recorded in either audio or video format.

b. Security

The application used ensures security essentially by password-protecting any access. In order to neutralize the possible consequences of a password being intercepted or stolen (which, it may be recalled, is the most frequent technique used for hacking into computer systems), the videoconferencing platform permanently displays a list of all connected participants, be they active or passive, i.e., be they transmitting video and sound or merely watching and listening in the background. This means that every individual who connects to the platform and follows the proceedings reveals his presence on the platform because of his name appearing on the list. The level of security achieved by these two measures can in principle be considered sufficient.

c. Screenshots

Figure 1. ClickToMeet – eight-participant videoconferencing mode

These screenshots of the ClickToMeet videoconferencing platform reproduce the two main configurations of the application which were used during the experiment. Both images are taken from experimental sessions based on slightly different scenarios than the one described above.

The first image (Figure 1 above) shows the application in videoconferencing-only mode, where the participants may communicate by video and audio transmissions, or by resorting to the message board featured in the lower left corner of the screen. This message board was only used for short notices when, for some reason, the audio and video connection was broken. Although this screenshot only shows eight participants, the application in principle allows up to 16 individuals to appear on the screen. This picture also shows the list of participants mentioned above, on the left-hand side of the image. The second screenshot (Figure 2 below) is a view of the document presentation mode. The document, displayed in the middle of the screen, was in this instance a scanned affidavit.

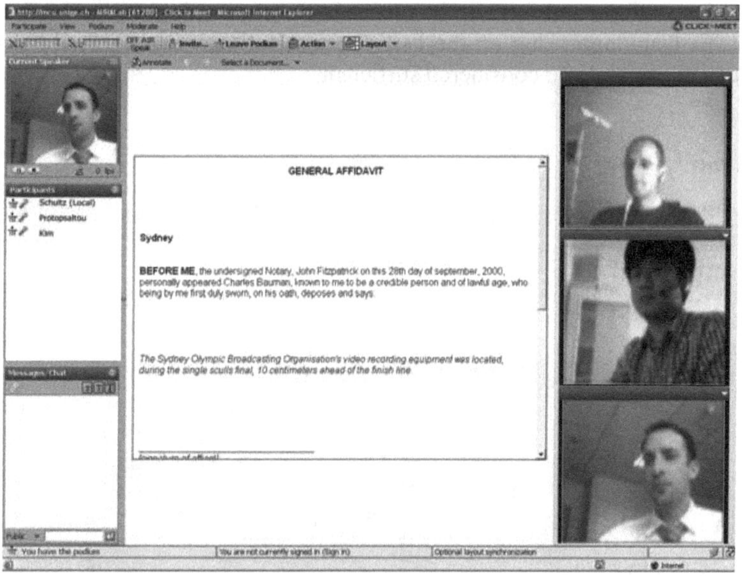

Figure 2. ClickToMeet videoconferencing – document presentation mode

d. Technical requirements

The hardware equipment that each participant must have in order to use this platform is the following:

- Relatively recent Windows PC (roughly not more than 2-3 years old). The optimal configuration is a Pentium 4, 2Ghz, 512Mb)

- Headset, including headphones and microphone, for instance Logitech Internet Chat Headset, costing approximately EUR 30 euros.

- Standard webcam, for instance QuickCam Communicate STX, costing approximately EUR 30.

The software requirements, for each participant, are the following:

- Windows 2000/XP
- Internet Explorer 6.0 or higher

The most important requirement is a high-speed Internet connection. In this regard, the minimum requirement is 600Kbps in reception and transmission speed, which corresponds to a professional Internet connection. For comparison, most common home broadband connections have a download (reception) speed of 600Kbps, but their upload (transmission) speed is often of only 150Kbps.

4. RESULTS OF THE EXPERIMENT

At the end of each videoconferencing test session, a series of questions was submitted to the participants and discussed live and in subsequent e-mail exchanges. Their compiled answers to these questions are summarized below.

The purpose of the present section is neither to set forth a detailed analysis of the issues and questions raised by these questions and answers, nor to provide a reasoned explanation of the pros and cons of videoconferencing, but rather to report the general impressions of the practitioners testing the platform. A more detailed analysis is provided in the next section – which also topically reports the exact answers and comments of the participants in a compiled fashion – when discussing the advantages, disadvantages, and recommendations regarding the use of videoconferencing in relation with arbitral proceedings.

a. Usefulness

The main question posed to the participants which deserves mention here is: 'Would you be willing to use it [this videoconferencing system] in practice?' All participants but one answered 'yes'. The intuitive understanding of the fundamental advantages of videoconferencing, combined with the opportunity to witness that such systems actually work in practice with little effort, generally triggered much interest. Ironically, even some of the most skeptical participants inquired, after much criticism, if it were possible to use the system for one of their cases, as soon as possible. The criticism, in other words, suggested that the fact of holding a meeting online was somewhat unsettling, and that improvements of the platform and its concrete use could always be made. Save in one case, the criticism was never significant enough, however, for the critic to be unwilling to use the system.

The fact that almost all participants in the simulations embraced the idea of using videoconferencing did not mean, of course, that this technology should be used as the new pen and paper (or computer and text-processing software) of arbitration, or that it should or even could be used in any situation. Obviously, this type of videoconferencing is appropriate only for certain cases and situations. Identifying these cases and situations was actually the principal aim of the simulations. They are listed in the next section.[82]

Regarding the overall usefulness of videoconferencing, the recurring statement made by the testers was that this technology was without any doubt far better than a telephone conference, but that it would always remain second-best compared to face-to-face meetings – from the point of view of the quality of the communication. The comments amounted to this: videoconferencing is not the same as a face-to-face hearing, and consequently, if costs and time considerations allow, it is clearly preferable to hold an in-person hearing. On the other hand, it is better to communicate using videoconferencing rather than not at all – hearing a witness using such technology, for instance, is better than simply not hearing him or her. Videoconferencing is also often better than telephone conferences or e-mail exchanges, except when a paper trail is required.

b. Realism

The comparison of videoconferencing and in-person meetings, on the one hand, and videoconferencing and telephone conferences, on the other hand, is to a large extent based on one specific characteristic: the capacity of the technology to create a sense of reality, a feeling of the other participants' presence. The dominant comment of the testers was that they were positively surprised by the system, which provided an impression much closer to a face-to-face meetings than they had expected.

---

[82] See Section C. Uses and advantages, p. 50 below.

Asked about their perception of the other parties' state of mind, the replies were quite variable. Most confirmed that they could easily feel whether the other participants in a session were paying attention or were distracted, were rather nervous or at ease, and were happy with the functioning of the platform and the progress of the simulated case or not.

On several occasions it was noticeable that the absence of physical presence led the participants to be somewhat less inhibited, displaying more facial expressions than they probably would have in a real meeting. This may have compensated to some extent for the fewer clues that image transmission conveys compared to an in-person discussion.

On the other hand, a few testers stated that they were unable to assess the other party's and the arbitrator's states of mind, and that it was even more difficult to do so than during a telephone conference, because they were distracted by the image. This seems to suggest two things. First, one factor of an individual's ability to sense other people's state of mind over a video linkup is the personal ratio of reliance on verbal as opposed to non-verbal aspects of communication. For instance, some testers admitted that not being able to make a real eye-to-eye contact – the camera was not placed behind the screen, but on top or beneath it – was disturbing, while others could barely understand that this was an issue at all. The second suggestion is that this form of communication requires that users get used to it. Indeed, the distraction some felt while using the system is without any doubt due to the novel aspect of the interface.

The reverse situation was strictly unproblematic: all participants stated that they did not have any problem with their own expression. They all declared that they had felt able to express themselves, to make their point, to be heard, to have had 'access' to the tribunal.

More generally, the electronic form of the communications did not raise any issue with regard to the ability to get attention during the sessions or to understand what was occurring. This is especially remarkable considering that, as the screenshots above show, the windows in which the images of the participants appeared were relatively small: about one sixth of the total surface of the screen during most of the conferencing (except during document presentation, at which time they were even smaller) and the screens that were used were only 15 inches in dimension.

c. Technical secretary of the tribunal

One way to reduce many setbacks due to the novelty of the environment in which the parties communicate (such as a certain distraction and consequent lack of concentration), is to have a secretary of the arbitral tribunal handle all technical aspects of the sessions. In the latter stages of the tests, one such person was appointed.

In the experiment, this secretary-technician did generally not appear on the screen but could see and hear the participants. If the testers wanted to change any aspect of the platform (size of windows, switching from conferencing mode with larger images to document-presentation mode with smaller images of the participants, uploading documents, etc.), they would simply say so into their microphone and the secretary would take care of it.

The result was that the testers only had to talk as they would in a traditional meeting. As they knew that they did not have to interact with the platform, they could better focus on the substance of the hearing. Nevertheless, although this measure largely facilitated attention, especially for those less at ease with computers, the testers still stated that such sessions required more effort concentrate than a normal meeting (like telephone conferences).

The implication is that such sessions should be kept relatively short. In addition, it was clear from the behavior of the testers, which evolved during single sessions, that the videoconferencing itself, i.e., the fact of speaking to a screen, requires getting used to, regardless of the simplicity of the system.

d. Document presentation and application sharing

Finally, the usefulness of videoconferencing can be improved beyond the simple possibility of seeing the face of the person addressed. Technology enables the addition of specific features that can make a videoconferencing session more effective.

For instance, with respect to the platform used during the tests, the feature most positively assessed was the document-presentation and application-sharing feature. That is the possibility to present any type of electronic document, in any format, and to point on or highlight specific parts of the document with cursor movements that are reproduced on the other participants' computers.

The shared real-time drafting of documents was also highly valued, as it could be used for collaborative drafting from afar of terms of reference, procedural orders, or arbitral awards (if the videoconferencing is used for arbitrators' deliberations).

C. Uses and Advantages

Among practitioners, the value of videoconferencing gives rise to a controversy. For some, it is a revolutionary development that will profoundly change the practice of arbitration. For others, it is barely more than an interesting but in the end worthless techno-gadget, because the technology is not ready yet, because, as the consideration in this matter is often voiced, 'you try it once, and you know it is not the same as a face-to-face meeting'.

This controversy largely follows from one common Manichean error: the idea that videoconferencing should be a catch-all technology which does away with any need for in-person encounters. In reality, this technology is not and will never be an exact reproduction of real meetings, but many situations of arbitral proceedings either do not require or do not allow face-to-face meetings. On some occasions, the advantages of not having to transport all the participants of an arbitration to a single location may outweigh the disadvantages of the reduced communication abilities of a virtual meeting.

The purpose of this section is to give an account of these advantages and disadvantages, and to discuss the main situations in which videoconferencing could be of interest.

1. ASSESSING VIDEOCONFERENCING

The factors in favor of and against the use of videoconferencing in arbitration may best be considered in comparison to other means of communication or more generally to other ways of communicating. Videoconferencing will thus be compared, first, to telephone conferences, second, to in-person meetings and, third, to e-mail or letter exchanges.

a. Videoconferencing v. *telephone conferencing*

The idea of starting this discussion with a comparison of videoconferencing and telephone conferencing may appear surprising. Indeed, video linkups are usually compared to in-person meetings. Nevertheless, videoconferencing appears in many ways to be a better alternative to telephone calls, in a spirit similar to the many science-fiction movies that feature this technology as replacing the telephone. The clearest advantages of videoconferencing appear when taking this approach.

First of all, the use of videoconferencing bears no disadvantages compared to telephone calls, as the audio transmission may be even better than that of a telephone connection because a higher number of frequencies can be transmitted. Telephones actually only transmit a very limited number of sound frequencies, these frequencies having been identified as those necessary for a person with normal speaking and hearing capabilities to hold a conversation in his or her mother tongue; this explains the additional difficulties we experience when conversing on the telephone in a language different than those we are used to use. Computer microphones and headphones, as well as most videoconferencing systems, do not impose the same restrictions in the frequencies transmitted, with the result that voices can be carried over the network with more clarity in videoconferencing than when using an ordinary telephone.

In addition to this lack of disadvantages, videoconferencing bears a number of advantages compared to traditional telephone conferences. The most obvious advantage is the addition of images. Even in situations where the quality of such images is not outstanding, they provide additional clues as to the state of mind of the person one is speaking to. These clues are more or less significant depending on the quality of the video transmission, but even relatively low-quality images provide at least some indication of the general attitude of the other participants.

Another advantage particularly appreciated by the testers of the videoconferencing platform used at the University of Geneva,[83] was the possibility of adding visual demonstrations and collaborative document management capabilities to the platform. Visual demonstrations are presentations of, for instance, exhibits in the form of text documents, pictures, movies, audio recordings, simulations run on architecture or engineering programs. Collaborative document management provides the possibility of working collectively on a single document, in real time. The research team utilized the videoconferencing platform used for the arbitration simulations to collectively draft, from afar, scientific articles, research proposals, and even some parts of the present book. In the context of arbitral proceedings, collaborative document management capabilities may be used to facilitate the drafting of documents such as the terms of reference or procedural orders. For instance, the chairperson could prepare the bulk of such a document and leave more problematic parts in blank or highlighted. The latter parts could then be discussed and drafted in real time under the eyes of all the participants of the videoconferencing sessions, who could then immediately comment on and approve the final version.

b. Videoconferencing v. *in-person meetings*

Videoconferencing is most often suggested as a replacement for face-to-face meetings. Interestingly, it is precisely the comparison between these two types of communications which drew the most negative criticism of videoconferences. The reason is that, in this respect, videoconferencing shows as many advantages as disadvantages.

The testers in the simulations referred to above generally considered that videoconferencing sessions could only be second best to in-person meetings. The lack of a sense of reality and the consequent difficulty of discerning the other participants' state of mind, though less significant than what most people had expected, led consistently to the view that virtual meetings were not as good as real meetings.

At the same time, testers found that virtual meetings do accomplish a reasonable amount of the communication objectives real meetings usually achieve, such as understanding the facts and issues (be they procedural or related to the merits) and clarifying the parties' positions on specific issues.

Fundamentally, the situation is therefore as follows: videoconferencing will always remain the second-best solution compared to in-person hearings, but it is useful in many respects.

Four considerations, some of which are interrelated, help in assessing in which respects videoconferencing is useful; they are reviewed in the following. In a second step, the paragraphs below review the disadvantages of videoconferencing, and put them in

[83] See Section B. The Geneva experiment, p. 38 above.

context. Finally, undetermined factors are reviewed, i.e., factors that may constitute either advantages or disadvantages depending on the context.

When an in-person meeting is impossible or unreasonable

Virtual hearings are preferable to telephone conferences, as the preceding section has shown; videoconferencing therefore seems adequate in most if not all situations where a face-to-face meeting cannot take place. Such occasions occur, for example, when a witness cannot travel to the hearing site for medical reasons, or when gathering all participants in the same location is unreasonable under the circumstances – this is obviously so when the cost, loss of time, and inconvenience generated by the meeting are disproportionate with regard to (1) the disputed amounts and (2) the expected benefits of the meeting.

If the disputed amounts are low, meeting in person may easily generate costs that are disproportionate in view of the actual monetary value in the dispute. The disputed amount must of course not only be compared to the costs generated by an in-person hearing, but to the total costs of the procedure and assessed against the likelihood of recouping costs in the future.

When an in-person meeting is not required

In other circumstances, an in-person meeting is feasible, but not necessary. The following question should always be asked: what are the expected benefits of an in-person meeting as opposed to a videoconference? Does the first one result in sufficient added value to justify the additional costs involved?

In some situations, one needs something better than a telephone conference, but a face-to-face meeting is not essential. Procedural hearings, for instance, do not necessarily gain much from being held in the actual physical presence of the parties. An exception is often warranted for the first procedural hearing when the arbitrators and the parties or their counsel do not know each other. In this case, holding a face-to-face meeting is useful to build confidence in the process.

Cost advantages

If one of these two conditions is met, i.e., either if the disputed amounts do not allow the expenses of a face-to-face hearing, or if the added value of holding the meeting in person is low, then resorting to videoconferencing may provide significant costs advantages.

The only costs specifically generated by a videoconferencing meeting are the investment in the hardware (which can be very modest);[84] a fee for using the videoconferencing platform; and possibly a fee for the assistance of a technician for the preparation of and during the meeting.

---

[84] See Section II.A.3. IP videoconferencing, p. 37 above.

By contrast, the costs saved by holding a videoconferencing session, rather than a real meeting, appear quite significant. They include the travel expenses of all participants and the rental of conference rooms.[85]

Time constraints

Time may raise a problem in relation to in-person meetings in two respects. First, in urgent situations, it may simply not be feasible to gather all the participants involved on very short notice. This may occur, for example, if a party has requested urgent interim relief. Whatever its benefits, a face-to-face meeting must then be ruled out and a videoconference is certainly the second best solution, preferable to a telephone conference.

Second, time lost before and after an in-person hearing may also play in favor of a videoconference. Because it requires more time overall, it is more difficult to find a time convenient to all participants for an in-person meeting than for a videoconference. Saving time for all participants and allowing for a closer hearing date are additional factors in favor of videoconferences rather than real hearings.

Where videoconferencing fails

The disadvantages of holding a meeting by videoconferencing rather than in person all derive from the lessened sense of reality and the absence of the points of reference people usually use in a discussion. Videoconferencing is not a perfect substitute for in-person interactions because it does not transmit all the elements of non-verbal communication.

For example, videoconferencing does not allow participants to make proper eye contact, making it more difficult to establish trust and to clearly direct attention, approval or disapproval.[86] This also has the effect of reducing the 'vibes' between people during the meetings, thus reducing the ability to 'feel' the other parties' interests, intentions, and positions. If communications during the session can be expected to require many subtleties, the added value of holding a real hearing may become prevalent.

Further, it is more difficult to concentrate in a virtual meeting than in a real hearing, as is the case in a telephone conference. The traditional environment of a real gathering provides many implicit clues that direct our level of attention. These clues being absent when facing a screen, most participants in videoconferencing sessions need more efforts to remain concentrated. This may be an issue in itself if the matters at issue are particularly complex. Furthermore, it implies that a virtual hearing should be scheduled for shorter periods than an in-person meeting.

---

[85] On the general economic efficiency of using electronic communication technologies in arbitration, see Chapter 1, Section II.A.1. Efficiency, p. 12 above. See also B.A. Lenox, 'Personal Jurisdiction in Cyberspace: Teaching the Stream of Commerce Dog New Internet Tricks: Compuserve, Inc. v. Patterson, 89 F.3d 1257 (6th Cir. 1996)' (1997) 22 Dayton L Rev 331, p. 347.

[86] See, for example, J. Lanier, 'Virtually There' (2001) 284-4 Scientific American 66 and L.J. Gibbons, R.M. Kennedy, and J.M. Gibbs, 'Cyber-mediation: Computer-mediated Communications Medium Massaging the Message' (2002) 32 N M L Rev 27, p. 34.

The final disadvantage may seem more trivial, but it is probably not: videoconferencing does away with coffee breaks and other informal discussions. Again, if the case involves subtle balances, unclear positions and interests, this disadvantage may be far from insignificant. This does not mean, however, that such social interactions are needed at every meeting or in every case. It merely suggests that in most cases, there should be a mix of virtual and real meetings.

Undetermined factors

In addition to the factors that constitute clear advantages of videoconferencing vis-à-vis offline sessions, and other factors that amount to clear disadvantages, there are aspects of this form of communication which change the context of the meeting in a way that may be an advantage or a disadvantage depending on the situations or the personalities of the participants.

The first such factor is that a videoconferencing meeting is a less contextual situation, which is thus less impressive and less stressful for the participants. This may make no difference for most lawyers used to speaking before an arbitral tribunal, yet the same may not be true for witnesses or experts. Speaking in front of three senior arbitrators, two teams of lawyers and their clients, a secretary, a court reporter, etc., in rather formal proceedings, compared to sitting alone or with one observer in a room, possibly one's usual office, will certainly bear significant consequences for many witnesses. On the other hand, many rhetorical tricks are unlikely to work from afar. Hence, one may suggest that rather shy witnesses are better served in a virtual hearing, while better speakers would deliver more convincing testimony in a real hearing. Hence, it may also be a question of strategy for a party to accept or to offer to hear a witness over a video linkup.

The second such factor that can be either an advantage or a disadvantage is the fact that videoconferencing allows capturing the data (sound and images) in electronic form. The beneficial aspect of it is that the creation of a record of electronic transmissions can easily be achieved with very limited additional resources and expenses.[87] Such a record may then be used as an augmented form of transcript of the hearing, for instance when preparing post-hearing briefs or the award. Testimonies, for instance, can be watched several times if doubts remain. The downside is that videoconferencing *necessarily* allows the creation of a recording. It is probably impossible to actually prevent the participants from recording the proceedings. Software that records in real time every piece of information that travels through a computer is not difficult to acquire or to create. Such software is already widely used to record live Internet radio broadcasts or to circumvent electronic copyright management systems protecting streaming audio or

---

87 See, for example, W. Krause, 'Do You Want to Step Outside? An Overview of Online Alternative Dispute Resolution' (2001) 19 J Marshall J Computer & Info L 457, p. 489, H.H. Perritt, 'Dispute Resolution in Cyberspace: Demand for New Forms of ADR' (2000) 15 Ohio St J on Disp Resol 675, pp. 680–81, and B. Park Sunoo, 'Hot Disputes Cool Down in Online Mediation' (2001) 48 Personnel J 3.

video files, or to rip music or video contents from any source, provided in can be connected to a computer. Another way to make an unsuspected recording of the proceedings, more analogical in nature, would simply be for any participant to point a camera in its room at the screen used for videoconferencing. Of course, in a traditional arbitration, any participant could also carry a concealed microphone to tape all discussions. But with videoconferencing, all aspects of the proceedings can be recorded, including facial expressions and all documents presented.

c. Videoconferencing v. *e-mail or letter exchanges*

The comparison of videoconferencing and e-mail or letter exchanges calls for much fewer comments. Suffice it to say that, on some occasions, instead of exchanging numerous e-mails or letters, for instance to organize procedural matters, it may be advisable to hold a brief hearing on a videoconferencing platform. The possibility of using shared applications allows, for example, collective work on agendas or on drafting procedural terms in real time and it provides the parties with an opportunity to react instantaneously to organizational matters.

2. SITUATIONS OF USE

On the basis of the discussions above, one may now envisage the situations in which the use of videoconferencing seems particularly advisable. One basic consideration should serve as a starting point: the situations in which videoconferencing should or should not be resorted to may be considered to represent a sliding scale of appropriateness of using this technology. At one end, the scale features contexts in which there is every reason to use this means of communication and, on the other end, contexts in which the use of this technology seems highly unadvisable. These two extreme situations may be described as follows.

Videoconferencing-prone situations

Videoconferencing can in principle always be used if the situation could also have been dealt with in a telephone conference. In such contexts, using videoconferencing per se bears no disadvantages, as the sound transmission is generally of the same quality if not better. Everything that can be done by teleconferencing may also be achieved through videoconferencing.

Admittedly, technical breakdowns are more likely to occur in relation with video linkup sessions than with telephone conferences, be it only because of the fact that computers, rather than telephones, are used on each end. To guard against this eventuality, a back-up solution should always be ready. Such a back-up solution could for instance be a telephone conference, in which case it would be advisable to obtain in advance the information necessary to organize a telephone conference at very short notice (i.e., contact information and availability of telephone conference service providers and the telephone numbers of the participants in the discussions).

Among the advantages of using video linkups, rather than telephone conferences, are the presence of the images of the persons involved, possibly (depending on the videoconferencing system used) the availability of document presentation and shared document editing facilities, and a reduction of costs.

- The presence of images, except if the quality of transmission is poor to the point of becoming a nuisance, always conveys additional information that a pure audio connection does not transmit. The better the image, the more information will be conveyed, but even relatively low-quality images can help assess the other parties' general state of mind or reactions to specific events.
- The possibility of presenting documents and perhaps of collectively editing them may be particularly useful if the objective of the meeting is to discuss the specific contents of a document, for instance a procedural order.
- The reduction of costs depends on the fees charged by the provider of the videoconferencing platform, which are very variable and largely depend on the quality of the service being offered. But at any rate, these fees are much lower than the costs otherwise generated by the need for travel and a conference room.

Videoconferencing-aversive situations

Videoconferencing should never be used if there is no serious reason *not* to meet in person – which would essentially be reasons related to costs and time, as was discussed above. Video linkup, as the testers involved in the Geneva experiment reviewed above have repeatedly asserted, will always remain a second-best solution compared to face-to-face meetings. The following disadvantages of videoconferencing in opposition to in-person meetings may be recalled here:

- the sense of reality and the feeling of the other participants' presence are inevitably weaker;
- the perception of the other participants' states of mind, if better than on a telephone, is not as good as in reality;
- video-based meetings are more demanding in terms of concentration and thus must be held for shorter periods;
- people get fewer 'vibes' from each other over a video linkup as images do not transmit all the elements of non-verbal communications;
- no eye contact can be made; and
- no off-track discussions or informal chats at airports or during coffee breaks may occur.

Other situations: determining the suitability to videoconferencing
In all other situations, the suitability of resorting to videoconferencing should be considered by balancing the interests for and against its use, which first requires an assessment of the concrete needs of the situation in terms, on the one hand, of time and money and, on the other hand, of the richness of the communication in terms of information transmitted.

More precisely, and in between the two extreme types of situations where videoconferencing should either always or never be used, the following occasions can in principle be envisaged as being appropriate for video linkup sessions:

- For *procedural matters*. Videoconferencing can be faster than exchanging written messages to organize procedural matters, and it may conveniently replace procedural meetings between the arbitrators and procedural hearings involving the parties, as these meetings and hearings are frequently held using telephone conferences. An exception must be made when the procedural hearing is also meant as an opportunity to meet for the first time.
- Drafting or reviewing the *terms of reference or mission statement*. This is often done over the telephone or by exchanging faxes. A videoconferencing system featuring document presentation and editing facilities could largely facilitate and accelerate this task, as the parties and the arbitrators would be able to discuss and amend the document in real time, with the text and its revisions right in front of the eyes of all participants in the session.
- *Deliberations* among the arbitrators. When preparing a procedural order or the award, the arbitrators can discuss the contents and amend the text in real time, if the videoconferencing system is equipped with document presentation and editing features. This can typically be done by one arbitrator (in principle the chairperson) preparing most of the text and highlighting the critical passages or those that may have to be debated.
- *Meetings with co-counsel*. When several teams of counsel work for one party, they may often be located in different countries if not on different continents. A videoconferencing meeting can provide a good opportunity to assess each other's position and style, and to get each other's ducks in a row.
- *Assessing and preparing witnesses*. Counsel may want to simulate a hearing with the witnesses they intend to hear during the proceedings, both to assess their credibility and their actual knowledge of the facts they will be called to testify on, and to prepare them for cross-examination. Instead of traveling to meet these witnesses, or having them travel to the counsel's location, it would save time and costs to assess and prepare them over a video linkup. The lack of a sense of reality and of the possibility to feel their state of mind is unlikely to constitute any real disadvantage in this context.
- When *a witness cannot be present in person*, especially but not exclusively if this problem occurs on very short notice, the possibility of hearing this person from afar, although less satisfactory than hearing him or her in person, may constitute a good compromise.

- Serious problems of *availability*. It may happen that an arbitrator or a counsel is unexpectedly prevented from attending at the last minute. Rather than postponing the hearing altogether, a videoconference would ensure the presence, even though only virtual, of the missing person.
- *Hearings on interim measures*. By their very nature, hearings on interim measures must often take place on short notice. As a result, it may be difficult to identify an available date for an in-person hearing. Finding the time for a two-hour videoconference hearing would be much easier in most circumstances and may largely contribute to clarifying the parties' positions and grant them an opportunity to be heard. It is at any rate more profitable to hold a brief hearing over video linkup rather than not to hold a hearing at all and rely solely on the parties' briefs.
- *Expedited arbitration*. Videoconferencing can meet the needs of expedited arbitration in several ways. First of all, there are situations in which decisions must be reached so quickly that they do not permit gathering all the required participants – as is for instance typically the case during the Olympic Games, where the awards must in principle be rendered within 24 hours even though the case may require hearing witnesses literally residing on other side of the planet.[88] In such situations, the only choice is to forego the in-person participation of these individuals. To allow these individuals to participate over videoconferencing is obviously the best solution, and it is preferable over hearing them by telephone. Second, there are less dramatic situations in which the travel time of the various participants could in principle be tolerable, but the difficulty of finding common availabilities may substantially delay the actual date for a possible meeting. Here again, the best solution is obviously to meet via a video linkup system.
- For *cases involving large distances* between the various participants in the arbitration and a rather *low amount in dispute*. Typical of the online dispute resolution movement, these situations call for every available means of communication that can reduce the costs (especially those related to travel), which must always remain proportionate to the amount in dispute.

D. Caveats

Some concerns about the use of videoconferencing arise continuously. They are voiced, in principle, by those individuals who have little or no experience with this technology. These concerns call for clarification; some of them correspond to real issues or to actual limitations of this means of communication, while others merely constitute exaggerated apprehensions caused by a lack of knowledge in this field. The concerns voiced most

---

[88] On arbitration at the Olympic Games: G. Kaufmann-Kohler, *Arbitration at the Olympics*, n. 81 above.

often are technological insufficiencies and limitations; security, privacy, and confidentiality; as well as legal issues in general.

1. Technological Insufficiencies and Limitations

The most frequent fears expressed by arbitration practitioners in relation to videoconferencing are the three following: the technology will not work properly when they need it most; the quality of the image will not be sufficient; and an image transmitted by a camera can never be trusted entirely, as it shows only what is in the picture, and not everything that occurs in the room in which a participant is located.

a. Technical breakdowns

The issue of technical breakdowns is a real issue. Imagine being in the meeting room of a hotel somewhere with all the other parties, arbitrators, witnesses, experts, and running the risk of becoming suddenly blind, deaf, and dumb. Understandably, such a risk puts a damper on the enthusiasm of many people. But it should be remembered that the handicaps just mentioned are reversible and that the risk that they actually occur can be significantly reduced by implementing some common basic safety measures, outlined below and discussed in further detail elsewhere.[89]

The most important safety measure is to run a test of the system some time in advance, with exactly the same configuration that will be used for the real meeting. A videoconferencing system should never be tried for the first time on the occasion of the actual event which matters; too many aspects of the setup could fail. Most dysfunctions of a videoconferencing system may be dealt with within a few hours, but it is extremely difficult to avoid or handle them 'in abstracto', without actually running the application in realistic conditions with the computer systems of the other projected participants connected,[90] i.e., without undertaking a trial run beforehand.

Moreover, according to the principle of dedication,[91] one should be very careful when using a given computer for anything else than its attributed arbitration-related task – in the present situation video linkup meetings. It is even recommended to reserve a specific computer for the exclusive use of videoconferencing. As a recent (two years old or less) laptop of medium capacity, costing approximately EUR 1,000–1,500, is in principle suf-

[89] These measures, which apply generally to all technologies, are discussed in more detail in Chapter 5, Section I.B. Breakdowns, p. 145 below and Chapter 1, Section IV. How to use IT?, p. 21 above.

[90] On such trial runs, see further Chapter 1, Section IV.B. Lack of experience: IT as a trump card?, p. 22 above and, more specifically on videoconferencing, Chapter 5, Section III.B. Setting up a videoconferencing session, p. 170 below.

[91] This principle is presented in Chapter 5, Section I.B. Breakdowns, p. 145 below.

ficient for most IP-based videoconferencing applications,[92] meeting this requirement of dedication should be feasible for the vast majority of participants. If dedicated videoconferencing[93] is used instead of an IP-based system, this requirement is automatically met, as dedicated systems rely on equipment that can in principle not be used for a lawyer's other tasks.

To reinforce the preceding measure, one may even suggest, in line with the principle of redundancy,[94] that each participant be equipped with not one, but two such dedicated computers. Both of these computers should in addition be available at all times, so as to be perfectly interchangeable. If possible, but this is admittedly much more difficult to achieve, these two computers should connect over two different broadband networks.

Furthermore, provisions should always be made for fallback solutions, such as telephone conferences or alternative dates.

Finally, a videoconference should not be planned for situations of major importance if an in-person meeting can reasonably be arranged instead.

b. Image quality

The broadcast quality of videoconferencing depends essentially on the bandwidth used; the quality of the hardware and software used is much less important in this regard. This issue is indeed a true limitation of the technology: without a good high-speed connection, an online video meeting will not allow the establishment of an interpersonal rapport and will merely cause frustration. However, this problem is decreasing as compression rates for images are being improved and connections gradually become faster. Nevertheless, bandwidth considerations remain a knockout factor; below approximately 500 Kbps downloading *and* uploading speed, the quality of the image transmission (more precisely the image refresh rate or 'frames per minute' factor) becomes poor enough to make the whole exercise useless.

Most home broadband connections can reach a download speed of 600Kbps, but their upload speed is often of only 150Kbps. Most professional connections, however, provide the required bandwidth. It may further be noted that the connection speed also depends on the Internet 'pipe' into a city or a region. Working with people from the America's Cup, we once tried a videoconferencing session with a party located in Trapani, a remote city of 70,000 inhabitants in Sicily, and realized that although the party had a very fast connection into the local network, the pipe in was shared by too many users to allow any satisfactory image refreshment rate. Setting up a videoconferencing session with participants located in remote areas should thus involve extensive tests carried out at the same time of day as the scheduled real meeting, in order to reproduce the same conditions of network demand.

---

[92] See Section 3. IP videoconferencing, p. 37 above.

[93] See Section 2. Dedicated videoconferencing, p. 36 above.

[94] This principle is discussed in Chapter 5, Section I.B. Breakdowns, p. 145 below.

c. Camera view

The fact that the participants cannot see what lies out of view of the camera is certainly a genuine issue, but it seems highly overrated. The reason why it is a concern in the first place is the fear that a participant – especially a witness or an expert – is being prompted answers or a general line of conduct during his or her examination or cross-examination, or that he or she is being threatened by a person positioned just out of shot of the camera.

A series of measures can be taken to reduce this risk. For instance, one may utilize cameras that can be controlled from afar to pan, tilt, and zoom; hence, one may at irregular intervals scan the entire room in which the person in question sits. Such cameras may be standard webcams mounted on a rotating and inclining platform that can be controlled by a distant computer; both together should not cost more than a few hundred euros.

Another measure may be to use two webcams, one in its traditional function, that is with a close-up on the participant's face and upper body, and the other one sitting in the corner of the room, capturing a wide-angle image that shows everything that goes on in the room.

Finally, if there are indications of a possible risk under the specific circumstances, the tribunal may order the other party to send an observer to sit in the room with the witness, or delegate an observer itself. That observer can then be given special instructions about how to contact the tribunal during the conference if anything suspicious occurs.

Eventually, to place this concern in context, one should not forget that silent pressure and latent threats are certainly not impossible in face-to-face hearings either.

2. Security, Privacy, and Confidentiality

The issue of security is the subject of the most diverse reactions of practitioners. Some believe security, as the means to ensure privacy and confidentiality, is of the utmost importance and that every connection to the Internet amounts to a serious security risk; they believe that one can never be sure that the data transmitted for the videoconferencing session is not being intercepted. Conversely, others state that bugging a conference room in a hotel is probably far easier than breaking into a reasonably secured videoconferencing platform. Suffice it to say that the latter are, by and large, right. The anxieties of the former are, most of the time, not grounded in reality, and are indeed usually the consequence of a lack of understanding of technological realities.

With regard to a video linkup system, the task of overcoming the security protections is made even more difficult by the fact that, in most circumstances, the hacker will only have the time of the videoconferencing session itself to perform the feat. The reason is that the data of the session does usually not remain available on the platform or the server. Even if the session is recorded, it will in principle be edited to be sent on a DVD, rather than remaining available online from the platform or the server, because the recorded data may easily amount to several gigabytes, which takes an inconsiderate amount of time to download, even with high-speed Internet connections. The editing of the DVD is in principle done on a local machine, which is in principle much better protected against intrusions than servers – it may even be disconnected from the Internet.

Nevertheless, it is recommended to always enquire about the security measures (password protection, secure sockets layer or SSL, firewalls, permanent list of participants logged in, etc.) of the videoconferencing software one plans to use.[95]

3. LEGAL ISSUES

The legal issues raised by the use of videoconferencing in relation to arbitral proceedings are relatively unproblematic.[96] As they fundamentally correspond to the issues that apply to IT usage generally, which are reviewed in detail in the next chapter, the following only sketches the main points in this respect.

- A technical failure in a videoconference could result in ex parte communications, which is a violation of a party's due process right to rebut its opponent's case. This right guarantees each party an opportunity to comment on the submissions of the other party and to produce evidence in rebuttal, and also requires that the arbitral tribunal has no private communications with one party only (so called ex parte communications). However, this risk can be significantly reduced by using certain tools, such as software that automatically signals when a participant is disconnected, or a direct telephone line parties can use to report a breakdown to the arbitral tribunal.
- The use of videoconferencing may also raise equal treatment issues. Under this due process right, no technology may be used that is inaccessible or too complicated to be used by one of the parties. A tool's compatibility, costs of acquisition and the parties' familiarity with it must be discussed before its use. In addition, the use of a similar size broadband connection by both parties will help avoid significant differences in transmission quality that would put one party at a disadvantage.

---

[95] For further technical information on security in IP-based videoconferencing, including encryption protocols and firewalls, see e.g., M. Brandl and others, 'IP Telephony Cookbook', University of Bremen, <www.informatik.uni-bremen.de/~prelle/terena/Cookbook.pdf>, 9 March 2004 and Tandberg Corp., 'Tandberg and Security', D50172, Rev 3.1, <www.-tandbergusa.com/collateral/white_papers/whitepaper_TANDBERG_Security.pdf>, last visited 17 January 2006.

[96] This book specifically excludes issues of liability for security breaches and for damages caused by inoperative technology (which are in principle exclusively governed by the respective applicable national law). Such issues are beyond the scope of this book, because they do not relate directly to the relationship between the conduct of arbitral proceedings and IT-usage.

III. OTHER USES OF TECHNOLOGY

Myriad technologies, much too numerous to all be reviewed here, can assist practitioners in their everyday work. For this book, a choice had to be made as to which technologies should be discussed and which should be left out. The decision was to exclude all secondary technological tools which have no specific use in arbitration. Accordingly, technical instruments such as the following, although interesting, had to be left out: legal thesauri; glossaries used to homogenize the terminology of a law firm; databases cataloguing standard contracts, statutes and case-law; commentaries hyperlinked to documents, to be used by co-counsel or staff; information retrieval technologies based on lists of url addresses; integrated time sheet organizers; automated deadline reminders; and voice recognition software. Such technologies, which globally fall into the category of so-called 'legal practice management software', have been omitted because, first, they bring about less fundamental changes to arbitral proceedings and, second, they are of the same nature as the decision to use, for instance, a BlackBerry or a laptop equipped with a WiFi/UMTS/GPRS connection card, Windows computers or Macintoshes, or even hanging folders or binders; in other words, such choices in tailored work organization are eminently personal, or at best depend on each law firm's internal policy. Advice for such choices may only be seriously obtained from specialized software or hardware producers,[97] and possibly from some law firms which have dedicated a considerable amount of effort to such issues.[98]

However, in addition to the main technologies discussed in the bulk of this book, some further IT systems and uses deserve to be mentioned here, because they may constitute significant aspects of an arbitration procedure and are much less frequently discussed in legal technology forums. The following will thus consider live notes systems; the eventuality of resorting to ODR platforms; and the use of claim forms.

A. Live notes

Live notes software, also called 'live minutes', 'live transcripts, or 'realtime transcripts', is a technology that allows transcripts taken by court reporters to be immediately accessible on screens to all participants at a hearing, and possibly to other individuals as well.[99]

Such software usually operates in the following way: an ordinary court reporter – a highly trained individual who takes down in shorthand, on a stenotype, a verbatim account of all which is said during a hearing – transmits his or her transcript of the

97 See n. 53 above. In addition, see, for instance, the application developed by Amicus Attorney, which is very comprehensive, at <www.amicusattorney.com/index.html>.

98 See, for example, the various applications developed by Förster & Bülow, in Nuremberg, <www.fr-lawfirm.de/en/tools.htm> and <www.fr-lawfirm.de/en/winjur.htm>.

99 See, for example, <www.livenote.com>.

discussions to a specifically equipped computer. This transmission occurs instantaneously, during the hearing itself. The specific equipment of the computer plays the role of an electronic scopist, i.e., normally a person who converts the account from shorthand into longhand, from phonetic stenographic writing into plain language. The computer thus translates the court reporters' stenographic notes into English (or into any other language actually being spoken), recognizing which combination of the syllables is most likely to make sense in the situation. This is achieved in real time by the technology. The text produced in plain language is then line-numbered and formatted into a relatively well-presented document, which forms the transcript of the hearing. This transcript is instantly transmitted to the selected participants in the arbitral proceedings, typically onto their laptops.

Although the use of such systems in arbitration is relatively recent, the technology has in fact been tested as early as 1985 in certain courts in Michigan to allow deaf people to sit on juries, and it is commonly used in the broadcasting environment to close-caption TV news.

The transcript may then be used to cross-examine witnesses or experts. It may also be annotated in real time, or other reference tools may be used to pinpoint any important information, for subsequent reference. The more sophisticated systems also allow linking, using a hyperlink, specific passages of the transcript to exhibits produced during the hearing or to any other document in electronic format, stored in a database or not. If the hearing has been recorded in video format, some systems further allow the synchronization of the written transcript with the images and sound of the video recording, enabling users to scroll through the text and, when the relevant passage is found, click on a hyperlink that opens the video recording at the corresponding moment. This is particularly useful to subsequently assess the credibility of a witness or an expert.

The transcript, as it consists merely of text, may also be transmitted over the Internet outside of the room in which the hearing takes place, for instance to associate practitioners already preparing the next phase of the proceedings. If desirable, the entire audio or video recording may be transmitted instantly to external participants as well.

Such software typically costs less than USD 1,000 – to which, of course, the costs of the court reporter must be added, which form the bulk of the expenses. To use such systems, it is preferable to employ so-called 'real time court reporters', who are usually real data management specialists and are used to troubleshooting technological issues related to such systems.[100]

[100] For further information, see, for instance, the presentations on the matter by the National Court Reporters Association, <www.ncraonline.org/about/history/CAT.shtml>.

B. Online dispute resolution platforms as a standalone solution

Online dispute resolution (ODR) platforms could be put to use in the context of offline, traditional arbitration as a standalone IT solution which has had all initial IT difficulties already ironed out and has hit its stride. It would simply be resorted to as an already smoothly running system, by an arbitration institution or an ad hoc arbitral tribunal.

More precisely, such platforms could be used either as a permanent tool, in which case the arbitration institution or the arbitral tribunal would liaise with the ODR provider on a lasting basis and typically offer the use of the platform as an additional service for the parties to its proceedings. Or such platforms could be used as an ad hoc, detached collection of communication tools for arbitration institutions or arbitral tribunals which are unexpectedly confronted with parties or situations calling for IT solutions; just as there are videoconferencing service providers which typically handle every aspect related to the use of this technology, there are also ODR service providers, which can take care of every IT aspect of the procedure. Utilizing ODR platforms in such situations may have advantages related to prior experience, user-friendliness, and costs, as discussed in the following paragraphs.

First of all, ODR platforms are in principle particularly user-friendly. In understanding why, it is useful to remember first that ODR may be defined as those dispute resolution processes which take place essentially, if not exclusively, using electronic communication means.[101] Accordingly, the ODR sector has a strong focus on small disputes, because parties to larger disputes usually wish to meet in-person with the arbitral tribunal and their opponent.

One of the consequences thereof is that the technical services ODR providers offer must be easily accessible to consumers and other one-shot players. Investing time to master the technicalities of a specific ODR platform would be particularly inefficient in situations where only low amounts are at stake; ODR procedures must never be time-consuming epics and hence the technology must be particularly user-friendly. Such user-friendliness is assuredly very welcome in the context of traditional arbitration, whose main actors are usually senior practitioners with little background in IT and no time to waste mastering complex technologies

Second, another consequence of the focus of the ODR sector on small disputes is that ODR providers make their business by the number, and not the size, of cases handled. Consequently, they frequently have much experience with regards to IT usage in dispute resolution procedures, in terms of the amount of disputes that they solve. To take an extreme example, the most successful ODR provider, SquareTrade, has solved over two million disputes in the last five years (of which more than half were dealt with in 2005 alone) and has recently been working on a new system which it believes could be used

[101] Further on the definition of ODR, see, for example, G. Kaufmann-Kohler and T. Schultz, *Online Dispute Resolution: Challenges for Contemporary Justice* (The Hague, Kluwer Law International, 2004), p. 5 *et seq.*

for handling up to 25 million disputes a year.[102] Other ODR providers report much lower figures, but they are still much higher than what any traditional arbitration institution may achieve with respect to cases involving IT usage.[103] Even if the vast majority of disputes submitted to ODR is not resolved by ordinary arbitration, but rather by mediation, automated or computer-assisted negotiation, or non-binding arbitration, the sheer wealth of experience of such organizations in the matter of IT and dispute resolution appears extremely valuable.

In other words, ODR is no doubt the field in which the use of technology in dispute resolution is the most advanced, where one finds the most experience with the issues that technology poses for dispute resolution, such as technical problems or how communications should be adapted to compensate for the lack of non-verbal clues. To put it simply, ODR providers have specialized in ready-to-go dispute resolution platforms which are at the forefront of IT solutions, thanks to their longstanding experience with a large quantity of disputes.

Finally, as a consequence of the amount of cases handled, ODR platforms may provide significant advantages in terms of costs, primarily because of economies of scale (i.e., decrease of the price per unit as the quantity of output increases). As the number of disputes being solved is high, the costs of referring to an ODR platform as a permanent or ad hoc tool for an arbitration institution or an arbitral tribunal should in principle be lower than what may be achieved if the arbitration institution or arbitral tribunal in question creates its own IT platform. In other words, the idea is to externalize IT aspects to an organization for which handling a few more cases, or even adapting its services to a specific procedure, should be achievable at reduced marginal costs.

Looking back on the evolution of these last years in the field of IT and arbitration, one is left with the impression that some dispute resolution institutions have been investing considerable efforts and resources to create, almost from scratch, IT systems that existed in very similar forms elsewhere, where they were already fully operational. In the current era of open source, constant technological remix, and global interconnections, the most economically efficient solution is often to integrate IT developments achieved elsewhere, or even to simply refer to them as a standalone IT solution. Reinventing the wheel is not to be favored. Moreover, it should be recalled that dispute resolution represents only a very small portion of the market of electronic communications. The global market of electronic communications has experience and means to develop IT solutions that the dispute resolution sector will never have.

In addition, the ODR sector is a market with an extremely high concentration ratio, a few ODR providers servicing 99 per cent of market shares. But there are between 100 and 150 providers in activity throughout the world and, hence, it is notorious in the ODR

---

[102] E. Katsh, 'Online Dispute Resolution: Some Implications for the Emergence of Law in Cyberspace' (2006) 10 *Lex Electronica* <www.lex-electronica.org/articles/v10-3/katsh.pdf>, p. 5.

[103] For an overview of ODR providers and their case loads, see, for example, G. Kaufmann-Kohler and T. Schultz, *Online Dispute Resolution*, n. 101 above, p. 249 *et seq.*

field that ODR providers have a strong interest in connecting to any source of referral, among which traditional arbitration institutions could occupy a particularly interesting position. Indeed, traditional arbitration institutions could confer on the ODR provider whose services they use a strong symbolic capital, i.e., they would show to the market that they trust the services of the ODR provider in question, which may in turn attract referrals from other sources. ODR platforms used by arbitration institutions would thus become well-recognized providers of such services, meaning that they would have an economic incentive to accommodate the procedural requirements of arbitration institutions at relatively low costs.

IV. TECHNOLOGIES OF THE FUTURE? 3D SHARED VIRTUAL WORKSPACES

The main current technologies having thus been reviewed, it may now be useful to take a look ahead, to see where IT usage in arbitration may have arrived in a decade or more. Technology is indeed constantly evolving, and it is increasingly pervasive. Those who had embraced computers 25 years ago now have a significant advantage in terms of efficiency and effectiveness over those who have only recently developed an interest in technology. The individuals, industry sectors, companies, and even countries that have been monitoring technological development are now largely on the forefront of their respective activities. It is a matter of preparation for the future to remain interested not only in what everyone already uses, but also in the most recent trends of development.

For this purpose, this section introduces a new technology currently under study in computer science in relation to dispute resolution: 3D shared virtual workspaces. This is fundamentally an interactive platform, accessible from afar over the Internet, which helps reconstruct complex fact patterns by representing them in three dimensions.

Such virtual workspaces are not currently used in arbitration at all, but their study has at least two rationales, in addition to the general importance of monitoring technological development. First, it helps understand certain psychological and organizational aspects of IT usage in dispute resolution generally, as it sheds a new light on the possibilities of collaboration and interaction from afar. Second, such a study provides an indication on some of the most radically new possibilities that IT is being equipped with as regards the re-creation, from afar, of reality, which may offer significant advantages for specific aspects of an arbitration procedure.

This section first presents this new technology, describing how it operates and what its purpose is. Thereafter, it reviews its actual uses and advantages, providing a concrete example in the form of a scenario, with a screenshot of such a system.[104]

---

[104] For a more detailed presentation of this technology, see D. Protopsaltou, T. Schultz, and N. Magnenat-Thalmann, 'Taking the Fourth Party Further? Considering a shared virtual workspace

A. What is a 3D shared virtual workplace?

Today's cutting edge technology in computer graphics and virtual reality offers a number of tools, where, rather than trying to describe an inaccessible environment or an event using words, sketches, or pictures, the entire object or scene can be reconstructed realistically in virtual reality, viewed from various angles and modified according to the users' needs. This is the purpose of 3D shared virtual workspaces.

In essence, a virtual workspace is a computer program allowing the presentation of virtual objects. To say that a virtual workspace is shared means that the same object can be viewed in exactly the same status (i.e., position, rotation, aspect, etc.) at the same time, on several computers. Its three-dimensional aspects refer either to the fact that the virtual object appears as if it were indeed three-dimensional (which usually requires wearing special glasses) or that the object is simply computed in three dimensions, i.e., that it can be rotated in pan and tilt but appears like any ordinary object on television – flat on the screen.

In the context of arbitration, virtual objects represent in principle real objects that are part of the factual situation in a given case, and the sharing of and interaction with the workspace is meant to be operated from afar, over the Internet. The idea is thus that any party can easily create and upload any type of object, in three dimensions, onto a common platform accessible to the arbitrators, the other party, the witness or expert, and any other participant. All participants may then interact with the object, i.e., rotate it, zoom, modify specific aspects of it, in order to give emphasis to their statement of fact or their testimony, or to clarify a specific question related to this object. Complex fact patterns, involving an object that can be reconstructed in virtual reality, may thereby be grasped more easily by their visualization in three dimensions. The use of a shared virtual workspace can provide the parties and the arbitrators with a better sense of reality.

On the front of technology, two brief remarks should be made. First, the platform supporting the shared virtual workspace may also provide for other means of communication, such as videoconferencing to accompany the 3D presentation with an oral explanation. A typical configuration would be a videoconferencing system featuring a document presentation tool, which would itself allow the presentation of three-dimensional 'documents'.

Second, the technology used to create shared virtual workspaces is called 'replicated application sharing'. In replicated application sharing, separate instances of the same application are run on each participant's computer. Events occurring on the computer of one participant (e.g., mouse events, keystrokes) are broadcast to the other copies where they are processed as if they had been generated locally, allowing the distributed applications to stay synchronized. The flexibility and efficiency of this technology, in terms of computer resources, is noteworthy.

---

for arbitration' [2006] *Information and Communication Technology Law*, special issue on the virtualization of justice, in press.

B. Uses and Advantages

The general idea having thus been sketched of what shared virtual workspaces are and what properties they provide, the question arises as to the concrete applications they enable: which situations pertaining to arbitral proceedings could they be useful for and how? To answer these questions, the following first describes the main situations which could lend themselves to their use, then provides a concrete example of such an application, including a screenshot of the system used for the simulation of the example given. Finally, the value of sharing visual information – which is the main property of a 3D shared virtual workspace – is explained.

1. Situations

In the context of arbitral procedures, shared virtual workspaces could be used during the hearings with the parties and during the deliberations of the arbitrators.

- With regard to *hearings*, shared virtual workspaces may constitute an additional tool that increases the possibilities of the parties to make their case. In complex factual situations, the ability to share visual information about an object that forms part of the facts of the case may allow the party to make a clearer, more convincing allegation of the facts and to better explain the evidence it puts forth. Typical uses may thus be the 3D reconstruction of events, such as virtual visits of factories or simulations of industrial accidents based on engineering models.
- After the hearings and before the award is rendered, the arbitrators usually meet – face-to-face or virtually – to discuss the case and to *deliberate* on the facts alleged by the parties, the evidence submitted, and the rights invoked. With respect to facts and evidence, the discussion among the arbitrators may be improved if they have the possibility of sharing the visual representation of what they are discussing. One arbitrator can for instance manipulate an object – for the other arbitrators to see – to express his or her view on the case.

In addition, shared workspaces improve collaboration, as will be shown below. While it is obvious that deliberations are a form of collaboration, there is no doubt that the same is true for hearings, which imply a cooperation between the arbitrators and the parties.

2. Example – scenario

The following scenario may assist in understanding how shared virtual workspaces can be used during hearings.

Let us assume that the parties and the arbitrators examine a 3D object that constitutes evidence related to the case being arbitrated. The parties, the arbitrators, the witnesses and the experts share a visual space consisting of a view of a given object, rendered on each of their computer screens, as shown in Figure 3 below. On this image, the object at issue (technical computer parts) is represented in three dimensions in the upper part of the screen, viewed from two different angles. This object can be manipulated (rotated, zoomed, modified as to its structure, etc.) by any user.

The facts of the dispute on which this sample scenario is based, and for which this virtual workspace was used, are the following. Party A orders a load of custom-made computer chips, graphic cards and other interfaces from party B. A specifies that the chips must be adapted to the motherboard type ZZ55. B builds and delivers the chips, graphic cards and other interfaces. A installs them, but the computer system they are meant for does not work.

Figure 3. The 3D shared virtual workspace developed by MIRALab, at the University of Geneva[105]

[105] For those with a special interest in technology, this system used the Macromedia Communication Server MX 1.5 platform to build the shared objects. The system is made up of two parts: the

A claims that the chips do not fit correctly onto ZZ55 motherboards, because the chips do not have the correct number and position of pins. B claims that A is not using the chips correctly, that the fact that the computer system does not work is due to a bad interconnection of the chips, the graphic cards and the other interfaces. The interconnection, B claims, is unusual and B could not have known that A wanted parts built for that specific use.

The dispute is over the question whether the number and position of the pins constitutes a defect or not. The purpose of the 3D visualization of the motherboard and the chips, which simulate the fitting, is to help the arbitrators determine whether the number and position of the pins is correct or not.

Once constituted, the arbitral tribunal orders a double exchange of written briefs. The parties file these briefs, which contain their description of the facts and legal arguments, and the reactions to the statements of their opponent. After the second round of briefs, both parties, the arbitrators, the witnesses and the experts (some of which have been appointed by the arbitrators, others by the parties) gather in a shared virtual workspace for a hearing. There, the parties argue their case in turn, question the witnesses and experts, and answer the arbitrators' questions. During the hearing, all parties utilize, among other technologies, a 3D modelling feature, which helps them explain their views or questions about the interconnection of chips, graphic cards, other interfaces, and motherboards. The 3D feature allows a visual demonstration, instead of a verbal explanation, of the problem from the participants' different points of view. Finally, the arbitrators meet among themselves, using the shared virtual workspace, to deliberate upon the case.

3. ENHANCED VIRTUALIZATION: SHARING VISUAL INFORMATION

The goal of a virtual reality system, in this case a shared virtual space, is to simulate sensory information in such a way that the participant feels that the generated experience resembles the real world – i.e., to enhance virtualization. This simulation helps participants understand the current state of action and enables them to communicate and ground their conversations more efficiently. Incidentally, increasing realism by sharing visual information on one another's work space may also promote group dynamics, in the sense that the parties, the arbitrators, and all other participants may more easily get the feeling that they form a group working towards the resolution of a concrete problem, namely the dispute to be resolved. As was indeed briefly suggested above, it is evident that hearings

server, which provides the means of communication, and Macromedia Flash Player. The application consists of a client Macromedia Flash movie (SWF) and a server component that communicates with the client. The server component consists of an application folder created on the server running Communication Server. The server and the client communicate over a persistent connection using Real-Time Message Protocol (RTMP). The Flash client is delivered to the Flash Player by a Web server over http. The Flash client then establishes a persistent connection to Communication Server using RTMP, allowing an uninterrupted data stream to flow between client and server.

are a form of collaboration, implying a real cooperation between the arbitrators and the parties, whether the general climate between the parties is antagonistic or not.

As research in computer science has shown, enhanced virtualization is especially associated with faster and better performance when the task carried out involves a concrete object; this benefit becomes gradually more significant as tasks are visually more complex, because such complexity implies a reduced simple vocabulary for each actor describing his or her world.[106]

Several studies in computer science have sought to identify the precise conditions under which visual information is valuable, and how a shared visual environment improves communication.[107] The main conclusion of these studies, for present purposes, is that the benefit of visual information comes from allowing participants to share the 'work area', rather than from seeing one another.

This conclusion was derived first from comparing pairs performing a given communication task using only an audio channel, with pairs working face-to-face or using an audio/video connection. The pairs could see each other, but not the objects they were working on. The results was that seeing each other barely improved the efficiency of their work.[108] Further research then shifted the focus from a view of the participants' faces to a shared view of the work area, and the result suggested a clear gain in efficiency in the realization of the task, which included mechanical operations on a concrete object.[109] For example, one experiment involved dyads repairing a bicycle while

---

[106] R.E. Kraut, S.R. Fussell, S.E. Brennan, and J. Siegel, 'Understanding effects of proximity on collaboration: Implications for technologies to support remote collaborative work' in *Distributed work*, P. Hinds and S.B. Kiesler (eds) (Cambridge MA, MIT Press, 2002).

[107] S.E. Brennan, 'How conversation is shaped by visual and spoken evidence' in *World Situated Language Use: Psycholinguistic, Linguistic and Computational Perspectives on Bridging the Product and Action Traditions*, J. Trueswell and M. Tanenhaus (eds) (Cambridge MA, MIT Press, 2005). Older studies along the same lines include: S.R. Fussell, R.E. Kraut, and J. Siegel, *Coordination of communication: Effects of shared visual context on collaborative work* (New York, ACM Press, 2000); L. Karsenty, 'Cooperative work and shared visual context: An empirical study of comprehension problems and in side-by-side and remote help dialogues' (1999) 14-3 *Human-Computer Interaction* 283; E. Veinott, J. Olson, G. Olson, X. Fu, 'Video helps remote work: Speakers who need to negotiate common ground benefit from seeing each other' in *Proceedings of CHI'99* (1999); S. Whittaker and B. O'Conaill, 'The role of vision in face-to-face and mediated communication' in *Video-mediated communication*, K. Finn, A. Sellen, and S. Wilbur (eds) (Mahwah NJ, LEA Press, 1997); H.H. Clark and S.E. Brennan, 'Grounding in communication' in *Perspectives on socially shared cognition*, L.B. Resnick, R.M. Levine, and S.D. Teasley (eds) (Washington DC, APA Books, 1991); P.-G. Maillot, 'Using quaternions for coding 3D transformations' in *Graphic Gems*, A.S. Glassner (ed) (Boston, Academic Press, 1990).

[108] J. Short, E. Williams, and B. Christie, *The Social Psychology of Telecommunications* (London, Wiley, 1976); A. Chapanis, R.B. Ochsman, R.N. Parrish, and G.D. Weeks, 'The effects of four communication modes on the behavior of teams during cooperative problem-solving' (1972) 14 *Human Factors* 487.

[109] H.H. Clark and S.E. Brennan, 'Grounding in communication', n. 107 above.

conversing virtually side-by-side, using a head-mounted camera, opposed to the same task being carried out via audio collaboration only. Pairs were substantially faster when they worked virtually side-by-side.[110] This was confirmed by other studies indicating that seeing the staging or work area improved performance by enabling more rapid entrainment on pair-specific referring expressions (i.e., the pairs could more efficiently refer to specific parts of the object they or one of them was manipulating), but that seeing the partner's face had little benefit – this time the task was to place a series of picture cards in a specific order.[111]

This suggests that ordinary videoconferencing in arbitration may not be the best choice for tasks that involve a concrete object to be described or more generally discussed; a simple solution would be to point a camera at the object in discussion, a more sophisticated one would be to use the technology discussed here.

---

110 S.R. Fussell, R.E. Kraut, and J. Siegel, *Coordination of communication*, n. 107 above.

111 S.E. Brennan and C.B. Lockridge, 'How visual co-presence and joint attention shape speech planning', in preparation, as cited in R.K. Kraut, D. Gergle, and S.R. Fussel, 'The Use of Visual Information in Shared Visual Spaces: Informing the Development of Virtual Co-Presence' in Proceedings of CSCW 2002 <www-2.cs.cmu.edu/~kraut/RKraut.site.files/articles/kraut02-VisualInfoInSharedVisualSpaces.pdf>.

CHAPTER 3

CURRENT PRACTICE AT ARBITRATION INSTITUTIONS

Available IT services and guidelines provided by arbitration institutions

Bill Gates, as we remember, started Microsoft in his garage. Linus Torvalds basically did the same many years later with Linux. Whether or not such inventions are indeed typical examples of the unobtrusive beginnings of IT-induced revolutions, online dispute resolution (ODR) seems to have followed, during the last decade, a similar path. When the ODR movement started out as a peripheral phenomenon in the nineties, it essentially took the form of start-up companies experimenting with more or less successful concepts, oftentimes much to the amusement of the legal community. But gradually the benefits of the dematerialization of communications and the assistance that computers could provide by 'massaging the medium' became clear.[112] Moreover, some ventures have developed into particularly successful enterprises, such as SquareTrade for instance, a Californian provider of ODR services that now has solved over two millions disputes. Interest then started to grow on many different fronts. It is in this context that the juggernauts of arbitration have recently embraced IT usage and are now offering sophisticated electronic communication platforms. This chapter is about where this development stands, about what the arbitration practitioner may currently find available at arbitration institutions.

Chapter 1 provided a general introduction on information technology; it portrayed in general terms its potential benefits and presented ways to take advantage of them, suggesting what could be done. Chapter 2 then took these general considerations further towards concrete situations and applied them to the two main technologies of interest to arbitration: case management websites and videoconferencing.

Chapter 3, as was suggested above, now discusses what is actually being done: how the world of arbitration has taken advantage of IT tools to date, in terms of technical services and recommendations offered by arbitration institutions.

I. STATE OF PRACTICE

Three of the world's most significant arbitration institutions have embraced the necessity of providing parties and arbitrators wishing to use IT with reliable systems. All three institutions have thus developed – or are in the last stages of the development of – insti-

[112] L.J. Gibbons, R.M. Kennedy, J.M. Gibbs, 'Cyber-Mediation: Computer-Mediated Communications Medium Massaging the Message' (2002) 32 N M L Rev 27.

tutionalized IT services specifically adapted to the procedures they administer. The following describes, in chronological order of launching, the systems of the AAA (WebFile), WIPO (ECAF), and ICC (NetCase).

A. AAA – WEBFILE

The American Arbitration Association (AAA) provides an online service, AAA WebFile, which allows users to file claims online and to 'make payments, perform online case management, access rules and procedures, electronically transfer documents, select neutrals, use a case-customized message board', and check a case's status.[113]

WebFile is accessible using an ordinary Web browser; no specific technology is required. The image (Figure 4) below shows the secure, SSL-protected start page of the system, accessible after having logged in.[114]

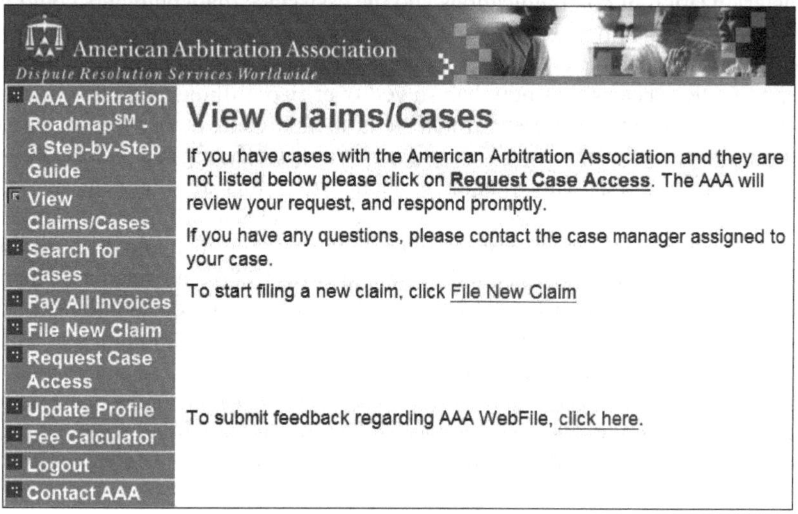

Figure 4. WebFile: user's start page

To use the service, parties must complete a registration form and select a password in the 'Online Filing' section of the AAA's website.[115] The username and password enable the

---

[113] American Arbitration Association, 'AAA WebFile: all online', <https://apps.adr.org/webcase2/-demo/pages/Slide02.htm>, last visited 12 December 2005. A brochure for WebFile may be downloaded at <www.adr.org/si.asp?id=1839>.

[114] See <https://apps.adr.org/webcase2/index.jsp>.

[115] See <www.adr.org>File a Case>File a Claim with AAAWebFile>.

parties to file an online claim and later return to view and manage the case or cases (several cases may be filed with WebFile at the same time) they have filed with the AAA.[116]

Filing a claim online involves the following steps:

1. Selecting the appropriate procedure.[117]
a. This selection first implies determining the applicable rules, as shown by Figure 5 below:

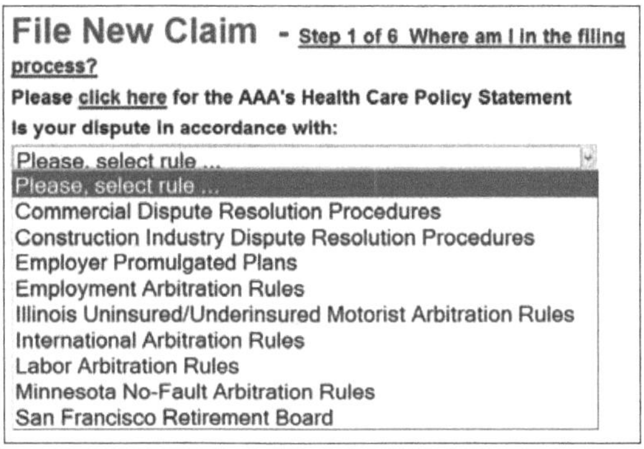

Figure 5. WebFile: filing a claim – selecting the applicable rules

b. The second step of the selection of the appropriate procedure is to select the dispute resolution method. In Figure 6 below, the selected rules provide for arbitration and mediation:

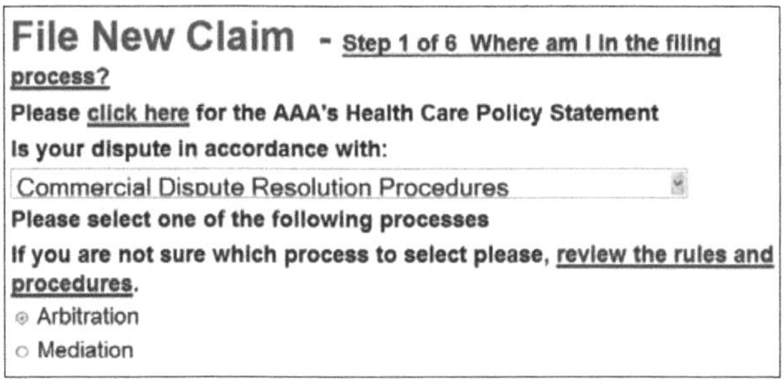

Figure 6. WebFile: Filing a claim – selecting the dispute resolution method

[116] American Arbitration Association, 'Frequently Asked Questions', <https://apps.adr.org/webcase2/index.jsp>, last visited 12 December 2005.
[117] Ibid.

2. Once the applicable rules and the appropriate dispute resolution method have been selected, the user is invited to indicate whether it is the claimant or her representative who is filing the claim.[118]

3. The claimant is then, on the same Web page, also invited to review the agreement upon which the dispute is based, and to confirm either that the AAA is named in the arbitration or mediation clause or that all parties consent to submit to the AAA.[119] Figure 7 below reproduces the wording of this statement on the AAA's jurisdictional basis.

> **Check "Yes" if your agreement contains a clause providing for the administration of arbitration or mediation by the American Arbitration Association, or if all parties consent to using the services of the AAA. If there is an arbitration provision in your contract but it does not specifically name the American Arbitration Association, please contact the AAA office nearest you for more information.**
>
> ☑ **Yes**
>
> ***Please note that by completing this form and submitting the claim, you have authorized the American Arbitration Association to begin proceedings.**

Figure 7. WebFile: Filing a claim – confirming the jurisdictional basis of the AAA

4. The next step of the filing process consists of providing information about the claimant. The user can search for a party from a previously filed case, and has the option of adding more claimants if necessary.[120]

5. At this stage of the filing process, the user is required to provide information about the claimant's representative, as well as the respondent and her representative. In case of multiple parties or representatives, their details may be added at a later stage, from the claim overview or summary page, described in Paragraph 8 below.[121]

   Figure 8, on the following page, reproduces the standard forms being used for entering the information required in steps 4 and 5.

6. Thereafter, the user is requested to submit information about the claim, including its amount and other details. At this stage, the filing party is also invited to select the number of arbitrators and the place of the hearing. As a means of confirming the correctness of this information, the user is required to reproduce the arbitration

---

118 American Arbitration Association, 'AAA WebFile: all online', <https://apps.adr.org/webcase2/-demo/pages/Slide05.htm>, last visited 12 December 2005.

119 Ibid.

120 American Arbitration Association, 'AAA WebFile: all online', <https://apps.adr.org/webcase2/-demo/pages/Slide06.htm>, last visited 12 December 2005.

121 American Arbitration Association, 'AAA WebFile: all online', <https://apps.adr.org/webcase2/-demo/pages/Slide07.htm>, last visited 12 December 2005.

clause.[122] Figure 9 below shows the different types of information that need to be entered in order to complete the filing process.

Figure 8. WebFile: Filing a claim – entering claimant and representative information[123]

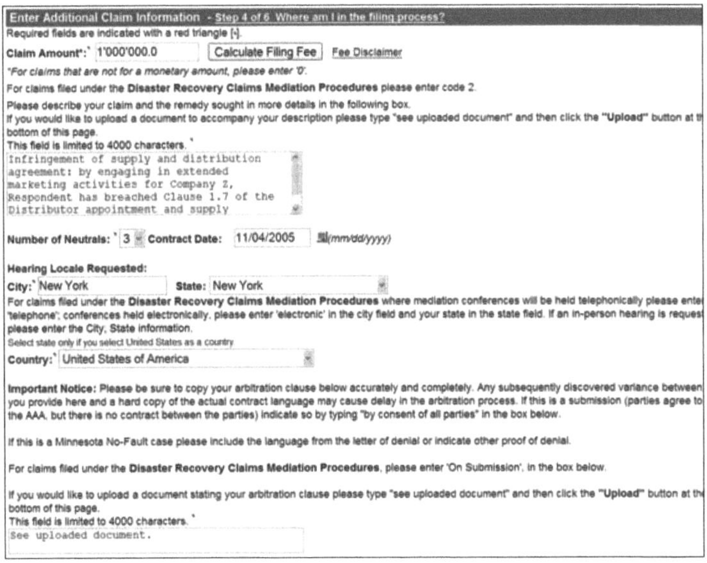

Figure 9. WebFile: Filing a claim – additional claim information page

[122] American Arbitration Association, 'AAA WebFile: all online', <https://apps.adr.org/webcase2/-demo/pages/Slide08.htm>, last visited 12 December 2005.

[123] All data appearing in this and the following screenshots are fictitious and have been created exclusively for the purpose of tests and demonstrations.

7. The system then offers to estimate the initial administrative fee that the claimant must pay when submitting a new claim – this can be done even before the claim is completed.[124] The amount of the fee varies depending upon the type of dispute, the amount of the claim, and the chosen dispute resolution method (arbitration or mediation). In some circumstances, additional fees may also be charged, which are not automatically determined by the system. Information on possible additional fees is provided at a later stage by the case manager.[125] Figure 10 below shows these different elements selected on the website of WebFile.

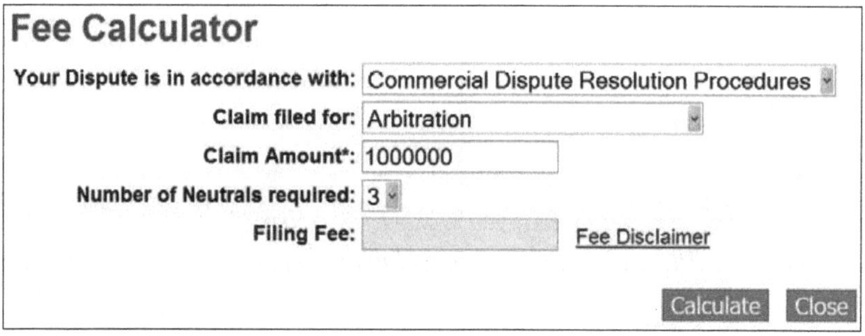

Figure 10. WebFile: Filing a claim – calculating the initial filing fee

8. At this stage, it is highly recommended to print, for the record, an overview or summary page showing the main details of the claim.[126] Such an overview page takes the form reproduced in Figure 11 on the following page. This page must also be used to institute the proceedings – it may be sent either in electronic format or in paper form to the opposing party.

9. The user is then taken to a payment form.[127] It may be noted that payments through the website may only be made by credit card. Payments made by check will soon also be possible; in this case, the user will need to print the overview page referred to in the preceding paragraph and send it, along with the check, to the nearest AAA office.[128]

---

[124] American Arbitration Association, 'AAA WebFile: all online', <https://apps.adr.org/webcase2/-demo/pages/Slide09.htm>, last visited 12 December 2005.

[125] American Arbitration Association, 'Frequently Asked Questions', n. 116 above.

[126] American Arbitration Association, 'AAA WebFile: all online', <https://apps.adr.org/webcase2/-demo/pages/Slide10.htm>, last visited 12 December 2005.

[127] American Arbitration Association, 'AAA WebFile: all online', <https://apps.adr.org/webcase2/-demo/pages/Slide11.htm> and continue to slides 12, 13, and 14, last visited 12 December 2005.

[128] American Arbitration Association, 'Frequently Asked Questions', n. 116 above.

Claim Summary - Step 5 of 6 Where am I in the filing process?

Your dispute has been filed in accordance with: Commercial Dispute Resolution Procedures
This Claim has Been Filed For: Arbitration
Filing Fee:

Additional Claim Information Edit

Claim Amount: $1,000,000.00
Claim Description: Infringement of supply and distribution agreement: by engaging in extended marketing activities for Company Z, Respondent has breached Clause 1.7 of the Distributor appointment and supply agreement between Claimant and Respondent.
Arbitration Clause: "In the event of any dispute arising out of or in connection with the present contract, the parties agree to refer such dispute to arbitration by the American Arbitration Association (AAA). In relation to such arbitral proceedings, the parties agree to discuss and consider resorting to any electronic communication system provided by the AAA."
Hearing Locale Requested: New York, NY
Contract Date: 11/04/2005
Number of Neutrals: 3

Attached Files Edit

You have uploaded one file.
Add Claimant Add Respondent

Claimant # 1 Edit

Name: Arjun Metha
Company Name: The Boarding Pass Corp.
Address: 17, Russell Square
WC1B 5JP London, UK
Tel#: +44-20-7862 5199
Fax#: +44-20-7862 5190
Email: ametha@boarding.com
Include in Caption: Company

Representatives Add Representative

Edit Delete
Name: Dr Thomas Schultz
Company Name: Lauterpacht Center
Cambridge University
Address: 5, Cranmer Road
Cambridge CB3 9BL
United Kindgom
Tel#: +44-1223-335-358
Fax#: +44-1223-300-406
Email: ts395@cam.ac.uk

Respondent # 1 Edit

Name: Hew Probono
Company Name: The Electric Co.
Address: Slane Castle,
Temple Bar Lane South,
Dublin 2, Ireland
Tel#: +353-960-5555
Fax#: *353-980-556
Email: hp@electric.co.ie
Include in Caption: Company

Representatives Add Representative

Edit Delete
Name: Prof. Gabrielle Kaufmann-Kohler
Company Name: Schellenberg Wittmer
Address: 15bis, rue des Alpes
P.O. Box 2088
1211 Geneva 1
Switzerland
Tel#: +41-22-707-8000
Fax#: +41-22-707-8001
Email: gabrielle.kaufmann@swlegal.ch

WebFile accepts credit card payments only. If you wish to pay by check, please print this page and mail it along with your che payment directly to the AAA office nearest you.

Figure 11. WebFile: Filing a claim – claim overview page

The payment of the filing fee completes the claimant's tasks with regard to the online filing procedure with WebFile. The claim is now listed under 'Pending Claims', as Figure

12 below shows, in the 'View Claims/Cases' page of the WebFile site[129]. At this point, a case manager reviews the claim and, if the case is approved, he notifies the user by e-mail, usually within 2-3 days,[130] and transfers the case to the appropriate section of the 'View Claims/Cases' page. This page is organized in three categories, listing incomplete claims (when the user has not provided all the information required for filing), pending claims, and filed cases (claims filed by the user that have been approved by a case manager). Incomplete claims may be modified, pending claims are under review by a case manager, and filed cases are ready to proceed to the next step, which is the selection of the arbitral tribunal (or the mediator).[131]

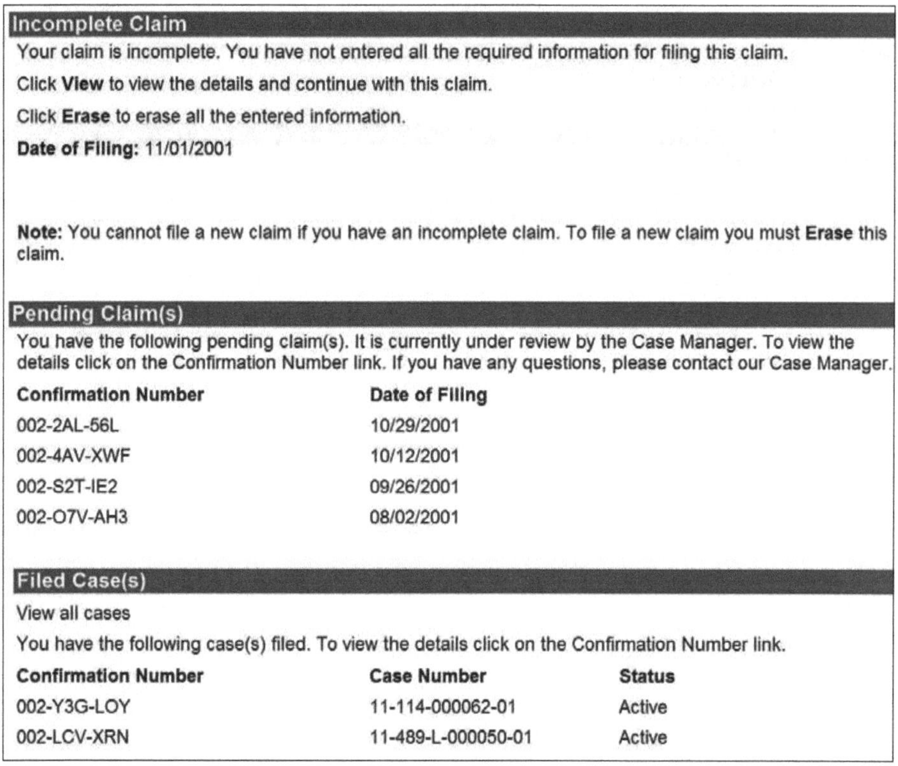

Incomplete Claim

Your claim is incomplete. You have not entered all the required information for filing this claim.

Click **View** to view the details and continue with this claim.

Click **Erase** to erase all the entered information.

Date of Filing: 11/01/2001

Note: You cannot file a new claim if you have an incomplete claim. To file a new claim you must **Erase** this claim.

Pending Claim(s)

You have the following pending claim(s). It is currently under review by the Case Manager. To view the details click on the Confirmation Number link. If you have any questions, please contact our Case Manager.

Confirmation Number	Date of Filing
002-2AL-56L	10/29/2001
002-4AV-XWF	10/12/2001
002-S2T-IE2	09/26/2001
002-O7V-AH3	08/02/2001

Filed Case(s)

View all cases

You have the following case(s) filed. To view the details click on the Confirmation Number link.

Confirmation Number	Case Number	Status
002-Y3G-LOY	11-114-000062-01	Active
002-LCV-XRN	11-489-L-000050-01	Active

Figure 12. WebFile: 'View Claims/Cases' page

129 For the 'View Claims/Cases' page, see Figure 4 above.

130 Ibid.

131 American Arbitration Association, 'Frequently Asked Questions', n. 116 above. See also American Arbitration Association, 'AAA WebFile: all online', <https://apps.adr.org/webcase2/-demo/pages/Slide16.htm>, last visited 12 December 2005.

Once a claim has been filed and approved by a case manager, a list of neutrals (arbitrators or mediators) will be prepared and can be accessed by a link from the 'Filed Case Information' page,[132] Figure 13 below (the image of Figure 13 does not show a link to the selection of the arbitrators or mediator, as the list of neutrals had not yet been constituted by the case manager). This Web page also provides a description of the claim, contact information for the parties, a list of scheduled hearings, and the documents that the parties have uploaded, the latter being shown in Figure 14 below.

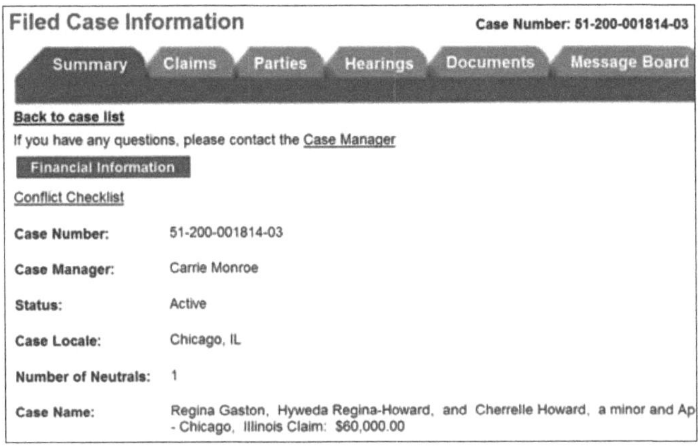

Figure 13. WebFile: Filed case information

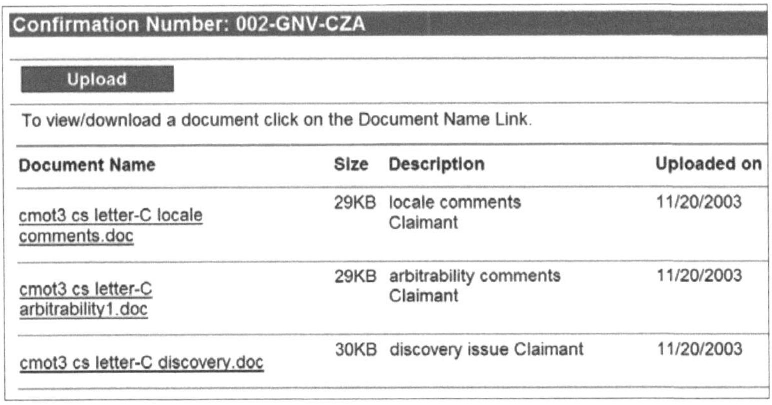

Figure 14. WebFile: Filed case information

[132] American Arbitration Association, 'AAA WebFile: all online', <https://apps.adr.org/webcase2/-demo/pages/Slide17.htm>, last visited 12 December 2005.

This Web page is interactive, in the sense that a user can, for example, submit an online request to postpone a hearing, or upload, review, and download documents (exhibits, briefs, comments, etc.).[133] It also features a message board, on which the parties and the arbitrators (or the mediator) may leave short text messages. Typically, this would be used by a case manager for posting non-urgent messages about a case. Only the case manager, the parties and the neutral(s) involved in a case can access the message board for that case.[134] Figure 15 below shows an example of a message posted on the board and Figure 16 reproduces the interface used for posting messages.

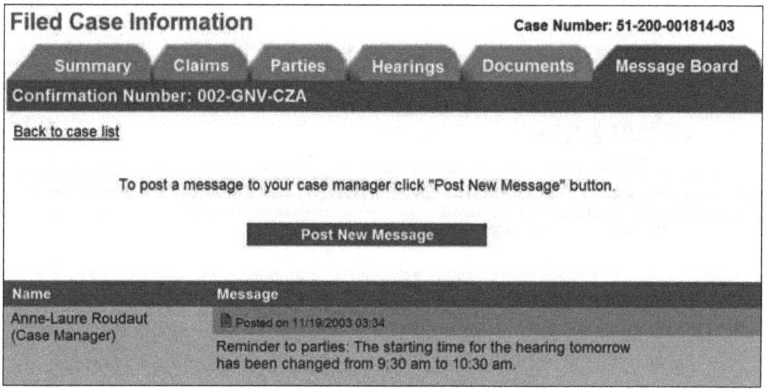

Figure 15. WebFile: Message board – example of posted message

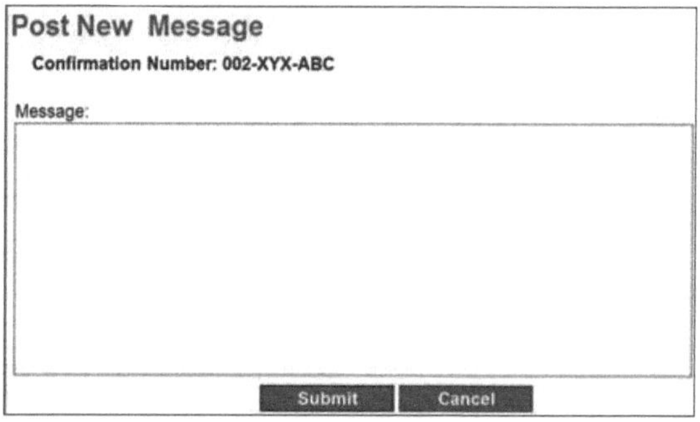

Figure 16. WebFile: Message board – messaging posting

[133] American Arbitration Association, 'AAA WebFile: all online', <https://apps.adr.org/webcase2/-demo/pages/Slide20.htm>, last visited 12 December 2005.

[134] American Arbitration Association, 'Frequently Asked Questions', n. 116 above. See also American Arbitration Association, 'AAA WebFile: all online', <https://apps.adr.org/webcase2/-demo/pages/Slide16.htm>, last visited 12 December 2005.

B. WIPO – ECAF

The Arbitration and Mediation Center of the World Intellectual Property Organization (WIPO) was created in 1994.[135] Its role is to assist in resolving private international commercial disputes by providing Alternative Dispute Resolution (ADR) services including mediation, arbitration, expedited arbitration, and mediation followed by arbitration (med-arb). The cases administered by the Center generally deal with disputes related to intellectual property, in the areas of technology and entertainment in particular.[136]

WIPO provides several online facilities, which seek to facilitate communication and organization in the resolution of international private commercial disputes. These facilities are flexible and provide a choice of IT options. Ease of use and interoperability are key aspects. In general terms, one may note that the facilities are based upon widespread existing tools, and are scalable so that new functions can be added over time.

The following reviews, first, the general IT facilities at WIPO, i.e., the Electronic Case Facility, which may be used by all parties to an arbitration or mediation procedure conducted under the aegis of WIPO, except for cases under the Uniform Domain Name Dispute Resolution Policy (UDRP). The second part of this section then shortly considers IT facilities provided by WIPO for specific types of cases, i.e., disputes related to the 32nd America's Cup and domain name cases submitted to the UDRP.

1. General IT facilities at WIPO

The Center recently created a secure Web facility for use in its proceedings, which seeks to facilitate the conduct of cases under the WIPO Mediation, Arbitration, and Expedited Rules. This facility, the WIPO Electronic Case Facility (ECAF), enables parties, the arbitral tribunal and the Center to file, store, and retrieve case-related submissions electronically. It is secure and allows for access from anywhere in the world, using an ordinary Web browser to log into the system through the Center's website.

This IT facility is a case management system, providing for facilitated communications, documents exchange, and case administration or organization. It takes the form of a central database accessible via the Internet, which allows participants in a case to upload and submit documents online and to communicate by exchanging text messages posted on a message board. The system also features Web pages providing information about the case, such as contact information, time tracking, docket listing, a finance overview, and a general case overview.[137]

---

135 See <arbiter.wipo.int/center/index.html>.

136 See World Intellectual Property Organization, 'The WIPO Arbitration and Mediation Center', <arbiter.wipo.int/center/background.html>, last visited 16 December 2005.

137 See World Intellectual Property Organization, 'WIPO Electronic Case Facility (ECAF)', <arbiter.wipo.int/ecaf/introduction.jsp>, last visited 16 December 2005.

The following presents the Web pages of ECAF used to provide:

- case overview information;
- contact information;
- time tracking;
- a docket listing;
- a financial overview; and
- a text-based communication facility.

ECAF's case overview page, reproduced in Figure 17 below, provides basic information about a case, such as its status, the type of dispute resolution clause or submission agreement, the governing law and the place of arbitration, and upcoming action in the case.[138]

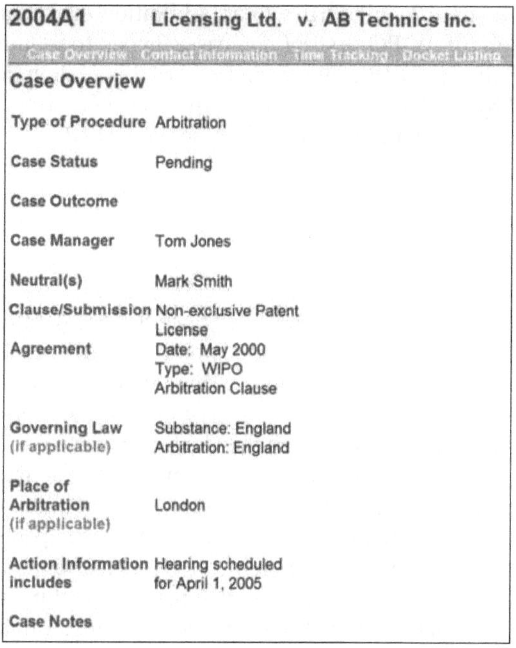

Figure 17. ECAF: Case overview[139]

---

[138] Ibid.

[139] All data appearing in this and the following screenshots are fictitious and have been created exclusively for the purpose of tests and demonstrations.

The contact information page of ECAF (Figure 18 below) provides contact details for all participants in a given case[140].

Figure 18. ECAF: Contact information page. It includes information about the case manager, the claimant, the respondent, and the arbitrator(s).

[140] Ibid.

The time tracking page, presented in Figure 19 below, serves as an informal agenda of the important dates in the case.[141]

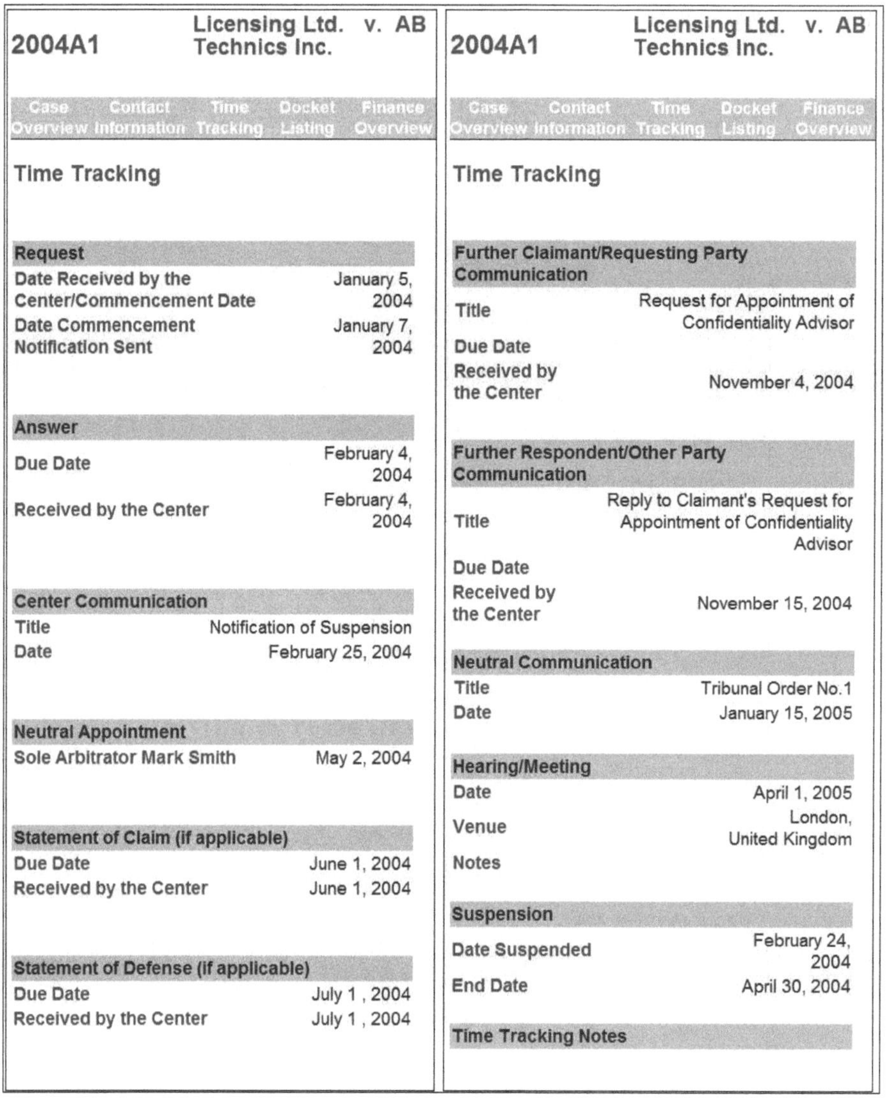

2004A1 Licensing Ltd. v. AB Technics Inc.

Case Overview | Contact Information | Time Tracking | Docket Listing | Finance Overview

Time Tracking

Request

Date Received by the Center/Commencement Date	January 5, 2004
Date Commencement Notification Sent	January 7, 2004

Answer

Due Date	February 4, 2004
Received by the Center	February 4, 2004

Center Communication

Title	Notification of Suspension
Date	February 25, 2004

Neutral Appointment

Sole Arbitrator Mark Smith	May 2, 2004

Statement of Claim (if applicable)

Due Date	June 1, 2004
Received by the Center	June 1, 2004

Statement of Defense (if applicable)

Due Date	July 1 , 2004
Received by the Center	July 1 , 2004

2004A1 Licensing Ltd. v. AB Technics Inc.

Case Overview | Contact Information | Time Tracking | Docket Listing | Finance Overview

Time Tracking

Further Claimant/Requesting Party Communication

Title	Request for Appointment of Confidentiality Advisor
Due Date	
Received by the Center	November 4, 2004

Further Respondent/Other Party Communication

Title	Reply to Claimant's Request for Appointment of Confidentiality Advisor
Due Date	
Received by the Center	November 15, 2004

Neutral Communication

Title	Tribunal Order No.1
Date	January 15, 2005

Hearing/Meeting

Date	April 1, 2005
Venue	London, United Kingdom
Notes	

Suspension

Date Suspended	February 24, 2004
End Date	April 30, 2004

Time Tracking Notes

Figure 19. ECAF: Time tracking page

[141] Ibid.

The docket listing page provides, as shown in Figure 20 below, an overview, organized in a searchable format, of the various communications and documents filed in relation to a given case. As a participant submits a communication electronically into the online docket, the system automatically notifies, via e-mail, the other participants of the submission. The users may also view and search the docket at any time. In order not to be technology restrictive, the online docket can also be used to record submissions made in hardcopy outside ECAF.[142]

2004A1 **Licensing Ltd. v. AB Technics Inc.**

Case Overview Contact Information Time Tracking Docket Listing Finance Overview

Docket Listing

Only documents to be recorded as part of the casefile should be submitted in the Docket

Search Docket **Sub**

To sort, you may click on the column headers

Item No	Submitted By	Date	Subject
7	John Doe Claimant Representative	23/02/05 14:52:51	Claimant's Reply to Response
6	Sophie Cloakville Respondent Representative	23/11/04 17:10:02	Comments re: Confidentiality Advisor
5	John Doe Claimant Representative	22/11/04 14:52:24	Proposals re: Confidentiality Advisor
4	John Doe Claimant Representative	14/05/04 17:16:46	Mark Smith
3	Sophie Cloakville Respondent Representative	14/05/04 17:13:50	Answer to Request for Arbitration
2	Tom Jones Case Manager	14/05/04 17:09:56	Acknowledgment of Receipt of Request
1	John Doe Claimant Representative	14/05/04 16:59:10	Request for Arbitration

Figure 20. ECAF: Docket listing page

[142] Ibid.

All case fees due and received may be reviewed, at any time, using an informal tool accessible on ECAF's finance overview page (Figure 21).[143]

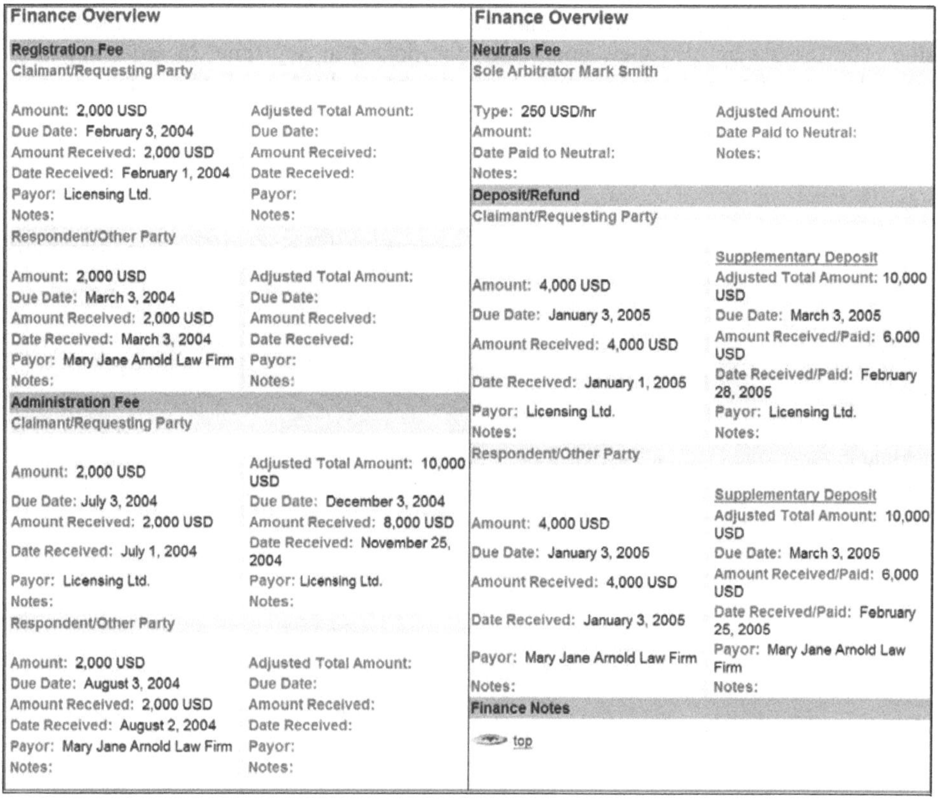

Finance Overview

Registration Fee

Claimant/Requesting Party

Amount: 2,000 USD	Adjusted Total Amount:
Due Date: February 3, 2004	Due Date:
Amount Received: 2,000 USD	Amount Received:
Date Received: February 1, 2004	Date Received:
Payor: Licensing Ltd.	Payor:
Notes:	Notes:

Respondent/Other Party

Amount: 2,000 USD	Adjusted Total Amount:
Due Date: March 3, 2004	Due Date:
Amount Received: 2,000 USD	Amount Received:
Date Received: March 3, 2004	Date Received:
Payor: Mary Jane Arnold Law Firm	Payor:
Notes:	Notes:

Administration Fee

Claimant/Requesting Party

Amount: 2,000 USD	Adjusted Total Amount: 10,000 USD
Due Date: July 3, 2004	Due Date: December 3, 2004
Amount Received: 2,000 USD	Amount Received: 8,000 USD
Date Received: July 1, 2004	Date Received: November 25, 2004
Payor: Licensing Ltd.	Payor: Licensing Ltd.
Notes:	Notes:

Respondent/Other Party

Amount: 2,000 USD	Adjusted Total Amount:
Due Date: August 3, 2004	Due Date:
Amount Received: 2,000 USD	Amount Received:
Date Received: August 2, 2004	Date Received:
Payor: Mary Jane Arnold Law Firm	Payor:
Notes:	Notes:

Finance Overview

Neutrals Fee

Sole Arbitrator Mark Smith

Type: 250 USD/hr	Adjusted Amount:
Amount:	Date Paid to Neutral:
Date Paid to Neutral:	Notes:
Notes:	

Deposit/Refund

Claimant/Requesting Party

	Supplementary Deposit
Amount: 4,000 USD	Adjusted Total Amount: 10,000 USD
Due Date: January 3, 2005	Due Date: March 3, 2005
Amount Received: 4,000 USD	Amount Received/Paid: 6,000 USD
Date Received: January 1, 2005	Date Received/Paid: February 28, 2005
Payor: Licensing Ltd.	Payor: Licensing Ltd.
Notes:	Notes:

Respondent/Other Party

	Supplementary Deposit
Amount: 4,000 USD	Adjusted Total Amount: 10,000 USD
Due Date: January 3, 2005	Due Date: March 3, 2005
Amount Received: 4,000 USD	Amount Received/Paid: 6,000 USD
Date Received: January 3, 2005	Date Received/Paid: February 25, 2005
Payor: Mary Jane Arnold Law Firm	Payor: Mary Jane Arnold Law Firm
Notes:	Notes:

Finance Notes

top

Figure 21. ECAF: Financial overview of the case

Finally, informal communications, which are not part of the record and hence are not listed on the docket listing presented above, may be posted (Figure 22) on a specific message board (Figure 23). These messages are accessible to all participants using the system.[144]

---

[143] Ibid.

[144] Ibid.

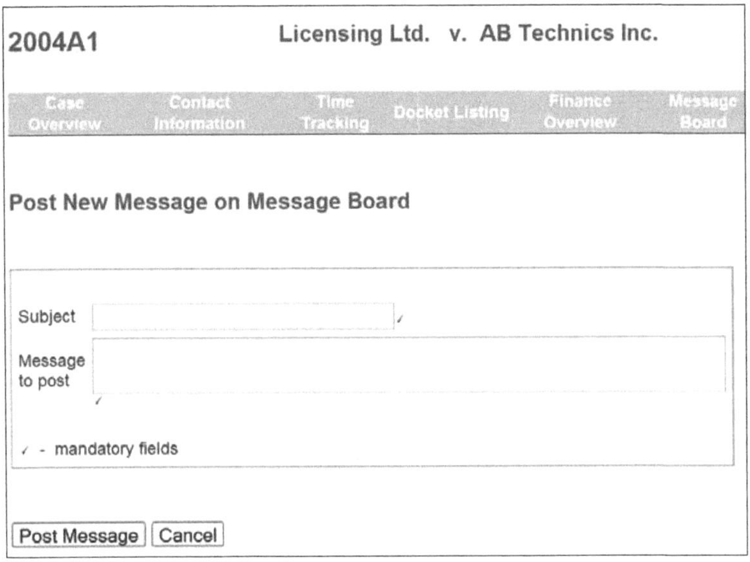

Figure 22. ECAF: Message posting

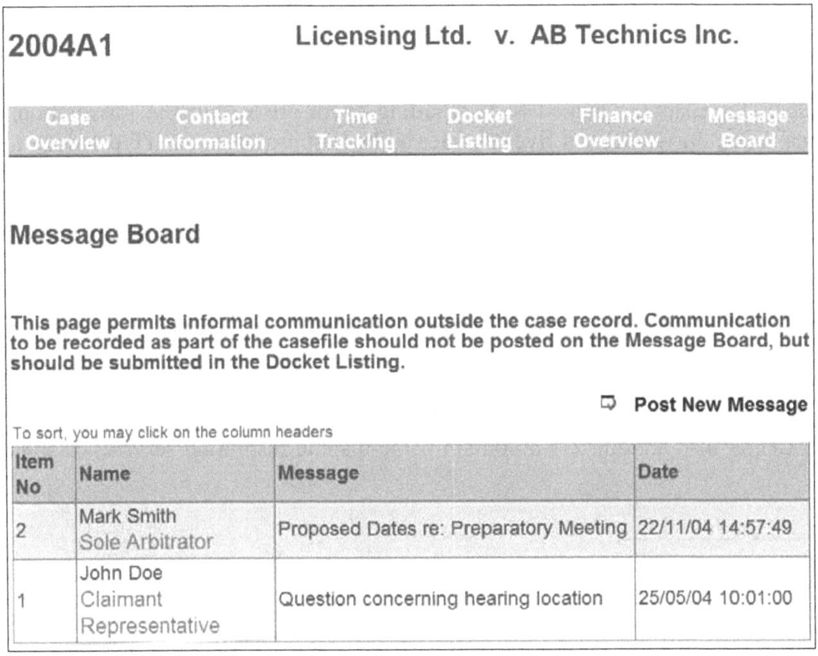

Figure 23. ECAF: Message board

With the exception of the docket listing and message board, which are used exclusively by the participants in a case and update themselves automatically, all the pages in the ECAF system are maintained and updated by the staff of the WIPO's Arbitration and Mediation Center.[145]

Security of the information transmitted to and from the server on which the ECAF system runs as well as the data stored in ECAF's electronic repository is ensured by three measures. First, a username, a password, and a passcode are required to access the system. The passcode changes constantly, in the sense that a new code is delivered for each time a participant wishes to access the system. The code is delivered by RSA SecurID card, a hand-held device, similar to those used by some banks for e-banking, that converts data provided by the access website into a code, using a long and secret algorithm specific to each user. Second, ECAF's servers, and all information stored on them, are firewall protected. Third, all communications to and from ECAF are encrypted by using state-of-the-art Secure Sockets Layer (SSL) technology.[146]

2. America's Cup Arbitration and Domain Names Dispute Resolution

In addition to the ECAF system available for all types of disputes submitted to WIPO arbitration or mediation (barring UDRP cases), the Center has recently developed a specific case management website for use in the 32nd America's Cup, in 2006 and 2007. This website is an adaptation of ECAF to the specific needs of dispute resolution at the America's Cup.

Most of the disputes related to this sailing event are within the jurisdiction of the America's Cup Jury (ACJ), a five-member ad hoc arbitral tribunal. IT provides obvious benefits for the ACJ, whose work is constrained by two main factors. First, the five members of the ACJ reside on four different continents. Second, the time constraints of the issues to be solved are sometimes harsh. This is similar in many sports contexts, but the issue is particularly acute in the context of the Cup, because ACJ proceedings involve all 12 teams and the official bodies of the Cup, with the consequence that numerous submissions are addressed to numerous participants. The multiplicity of actors makes such an electronic filing facility particularly useful.[147] In addition to using ECAF, the ACJ is also experimenting with the use of specific videoconferencing technologies.

Finally, in a different context, it may be recalled that the WIPO Arbitration and Mediation Center also administers a domain name dispute resolution service, established in

145 Ibid.

146 Ibid.

147 Further on the ACJ and the 32nd America's Cup, see e.g., T. Schultz, 'Sailing away from judicial interference: Arbitrating the America's Cup' [2006] 1-2 *International Sports Law Journal*, in press.

December 1999.[148] This service, which operates mainly using electronic communication and repository facilities, resolves mainly domain name disputes under the Uniform Domain Name Dispute Resolution Policy (UDRP), for the .com, .net, .org, .biz, .info and .name domains, and other procedures, adapted from the UDRP for over 45 national domains (for instance .fr, .ie, .nl, .ch). The IT features of these domain name dispute administration services include model forms in Word format and Web-based forms, various online resources, and the general acceptance of online communications. The services also provide IT case management support.

C. ICC – NetCase

NetCase is a case management website for participants in ICC arbitration proceedings,[149] launched in late 2005. It is accessible by the parties, their counsel, the arbitrators and the Secretariat. Its goal is to allow participants, if they consent to its use, to communicate and share information rapidly and securely using the Internet,[150] yet it does not exclude the use of traditional, offline means of communication. This platform is restricted to proceedings conducted under the auspices of the ICC. NetCase constitutes neither an arbitral procedure in itself nor a stand-alone service for dispute resolution, but merely a way to facilitate communication and organization between the parties and the arbitrators by offering instantaneous information 24 hours a day.[151]

The NetCase environment provides security and confidentiality, speed, organization, accessibility, private forums and cost savings.

- Security and confidentiality: all communications and documents traveling between the user's browser and NetCase are encrypted. Before accepting documents for posting, NetCase first automatically checks them for viruses and refuses any infected document. In addition, access to NetCase is password-protected.
- Speed: documents are available to all participants as soon as they are posted on NetCase. In addition, documents are transferred as quickly as by e-mail, with the advantage of a secured environment.
- Organization: all information and documents are organized in a uniform manner (as correspondence, memoranda, procedural orders, terms of reference or award[152]) in order to lessen the risks of confusion and conflict that can arise from multiple filing

[148] World Intellectual Property Organization, 'Frequently Asked Questions: Internet Domain Names', <arbiter.wipo.int/center/faq/domains.html#7>, last visited 15 December 2005.

[149] For the moment, NetCase is only intended for use in proceedings subject to the ICC Rules of Arbitration: M. Philippe, 'NetCase: A New ICC Arbitration Facility' in *Using Technology to Resolve Business Disputes*, Special Supplement ICC Bull (Paris, ICC Publishing, 2004), p. 53.

[150] Ibid.

[151] Ibid, p. 56.

[152] Ibid, p. 56.

systems. The origin of the documents is indicated so as to make them easily identifiable,[153] and all submissions and exchanges are tracked to help participants follow the chronology of a case.[154] The system accepts pdf and tiff formats. Figure 24 below reproduces the correspondence overview page of NetCase.

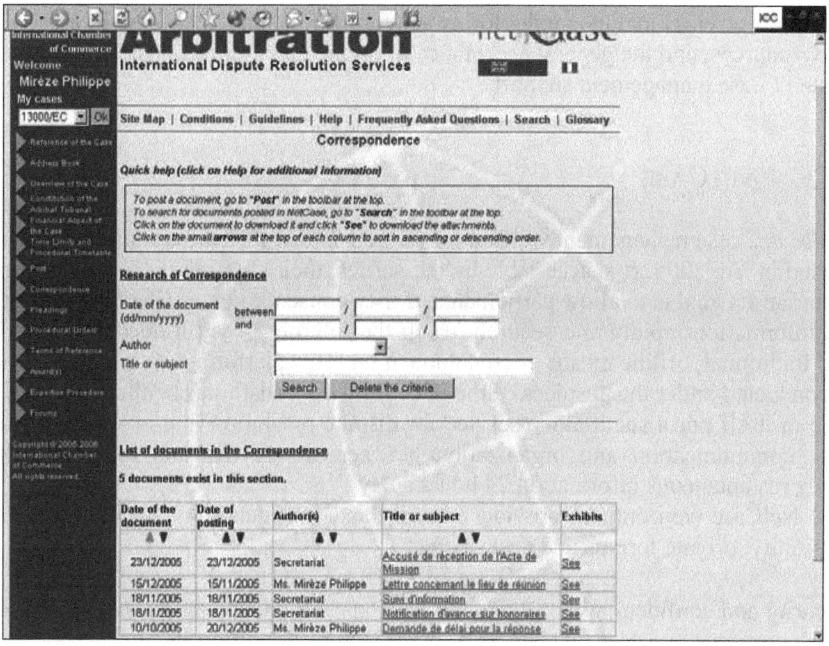

Figure 24. NetCase: Overview of correspondence[155]

- Uniformity: NetCase allows all participants to view the same content at the same time in the same display form and environment.
- Accessibility: NetCase is accessible anywhere, anytime, using the Internet, regardless of the browser and operating system used. Users are thus able to consult the documents posted on NetCase or information on the status of proceedings 24 hours a day using any computer simply by logging in with their ID and password. In addition, message alerts inform participants when a new message or document has been posted on NetCase.

---

[153] Ibid, p. 54.

[154] Ibid.

[155] All data appearing in this and the following screenshots are fictitious and have been created exclusively for the purpose of tests and demonstrations.

– Private forums: these allow participants to communicate in an access-restricted environment that is more secure than the exchange of unprotected e-mails. Furthermore, within the forum, more restricted rooms may be created that can be accessed only by specified participants in the proceedings, e.g., the arbitrators, or one party and its counsel, or the arbitrators and the arbitral institution. Figure 25 below shows the interface used for such forums.

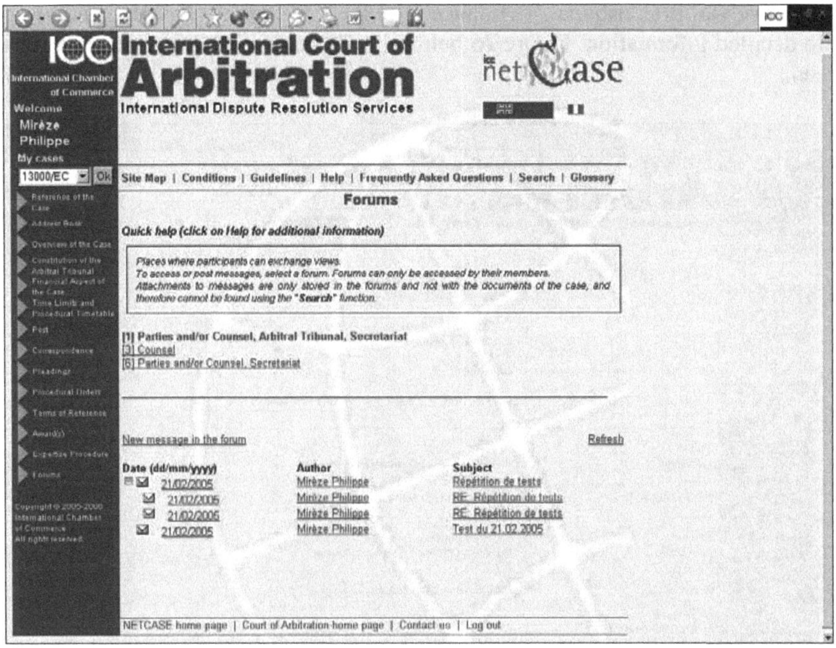

Figure 25. NetCase: Example of discussion forum

– Cost savings: by allowing the electronic exchange of documents, NetCase reduces the costs of preparing, handling and sending hard copies, although it does not completely eliminate the need for them, as national legal requirements may require some communications, such as the notification of an award, to be sent by traditional mail.[156]

[156] Ibid, p. 55. On the requirement of a written award, see e.g., J. Arsic, 'International Commercial Arbitration on the Internet – Has the Future Come Too Early?' (1997) 14 J Int Arb 209, p. 217; M.E. Schneider and C. Kuner, 'Dispute Resolution in International Electronic Commerce' (1997) 14 J Int Arb 5, p. 24; and G. Kaufmann-Kohler and T. Schultz, *Online Dispute Resolution. Challenges for Contemporary Justice* (The Hague, Kluwer Law International, 2004), pp. 216–223.

The NetCase platform offers a number of functions, including:

- An address book containing the details of all participants, including those of the Secretariat team in charge of the case.
- General information giving an overall picture of the case, with party, counsel and arbitrator names, the chronology of the proceedings (including dates of different stages of the case)[157] and a financial overview. Specific sections relating to the various aspects of the case (arbitral tribunal,[158] finance,[159] expert witnesses,[160] and forums) contain more detailed information. Figure 26 below shows the upper part of the case overview screen.

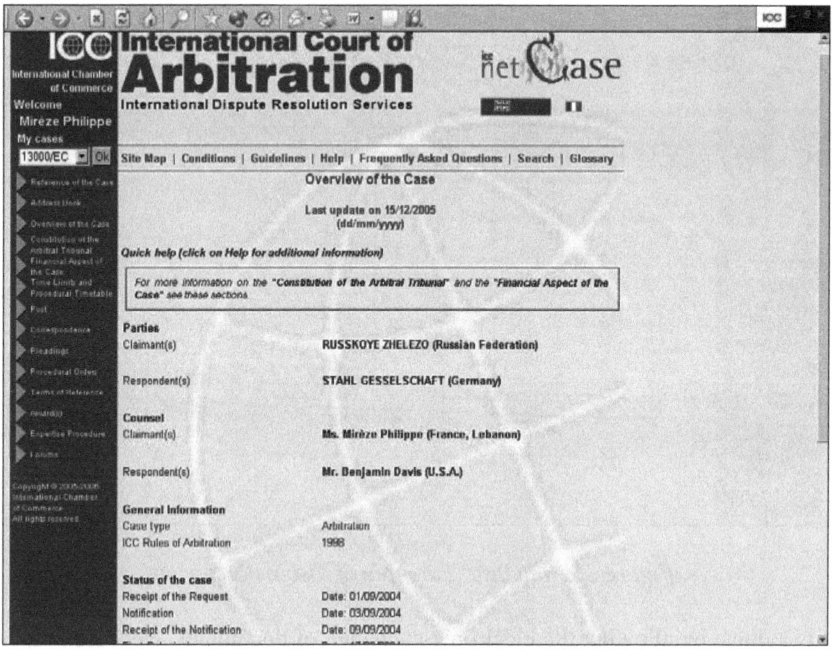

Figure 26. NetCase: Case overview screen

[157] M. Philippe, 'NetCase: A New ICC Arbitration Facility', n. 149 above, p. 55.

[158] Including information about the constitution of the arbitral tribunal, the curriculum vitae of arbitrators and their declarations that they will act independently.

[159] Including information about securities, payments made by the parties, fees paid to arbitrators, and arbitration fees.

[160] Used for expert procedures and containing experts' contact data and financial information regarding these specific proceedings.

– A calendar of the proceedings with the deadlines fixed by the Secretariat or the arbitral tribunal.[161]
– Assistance in the form of an e-mail address at which participants can contact the Secretariat for help, and guidelines explaining the different sections and the system as a whole.[162]

In its first version, the NetCase platform still has some limitations, which are intended to be improved in future versions:

– Language: the use of an extensible mark-up language format (xml)[163] has been set aside for the time being due to compatibility issues. The first version uses html format in English and French, and future versions could be proposed in German and Spanish and even in other languages.
– Search function: the initial version does not incorporate a search function since it requires a complex work of compilation, updating and listing of keywords. This function may be included in a future version when the optical recognition of characters improves.
– Digital signatures: there is no uniformity regarding this issue because of varying national legislations. However, the ICC recommends that parties discuss this issue if they wish to use means providing additional certainty with respect to authentication.
– Digital certificates: similarly, there is no uniformity concerning the entities authorized to provide digital certificates and the kind of information they must contain.[164]

II. GUIDELINES OF THE INTERNATIONAL CHAMBER OF COMMERCE

The International Chamber of Commerce (ICC) is one of the most important global players in the field of arbitration. In addition to administering the largest number of important international arbitration procedures in the world, the ICC is also a significant think-tank and leading force for new developments in the field of dispute resolution. Its

---

161 M. Philippe, 'NetCase: A New ICC Arbitration Facility', n. 149 above, p. 56.
162 Ibid.
163 The specificity of xml formats is that they inform about content, and not merely display: html files tell the browser information about the style and display of text on a Web page, but xml informs the browser about what the text on a Web page actually represents. An xml tag may for instance indicate that some piece of text is in fact the price of an object, or a deadline, or the name of an individual, etc. For further information on xml, see for instance <www.w3.org/-XML> and N. Walsh, 'XML.com: A Technical Introduction to XML' <www.xml.com/pub/a/-98/10/guide0.html>, 3 October 1998.
164 M. Philippe, 'NetCase: A New ICC Arbitration Facility', n. 149 above, p. 60.

activity could not have overlooked IT usage in arbitral procedures. In this context, the ICC has, further to developing the NetCase system presented above, issued a series of green papers, including practice guidelines on the use of electronic communication technologies. Due to the pioneering character of its endeavor in this regard and the usual benchmarking effect of much of its activities, its work deserves to be mentioned here.

This section starts with a short summary of the ICC's main report on IT, and then reviews in more detail its practical recommendations.

A. Report on Special IT Requirements in International Arbitration

The ICC has a special section on information technology, whose overall objective is 'to address the relevant possibilities and risks resulting for international commercial arbitration from (a) the deepening penetration of access and use of IT by arbitration users and (b) the increase of information transmission and processing capabilities of IT.'[165]

In March 2002, this ICC Section on IT issued a preparatory paper considering the role of the ICC in encouraging the use of IT in international arbitration.[166] This paper addressed a series of underlying considerations which led to the actual guidelines issued by the ICC. Such considerations are presented in the next section.

The paper reviews the uses of IT in international arbitration, the most obvious of which is the 'formal exchange and manipulation of data within any single arbitration process'[167] through physical storage media, e-mail and shared access to a website (e.g., a virtual case room).[168] It surmises that the use of IT has the potential to greatly increase the efficiency of international arbitral proceedings in terms of speed, cost, and ease of use of the information exchanged,[169] especially in the case of large submissions.[170]

The report also notes that information technology can be used effectively during hearings: to present technical evidence[171] or to allow real-time collaboration through telephone conferencing, videoconferencing, and through the production of electronic transcripts of the hearings.[172] It further mentions that IT also facilitates access to legal

165 International Chamber of Commerce, Section on IT Mission Statement of 24 January 2001, cited in International Chamber of Commerce, Commission on Arbitration, 'Report by the Section on Information Technology on Special IT Requirements in International Arbitration', Doc. 420/21-005, 18 March 2002, para. 2.

166 ICC, 'Report by the Section on Information Technology on Special IT Requirements in International Arbitration', n. 165 above, para. 5.

167 Ibid, para. 7.1.

168 Ibid, para. 7.2.

169 Ibid, para. 7.3.

170 Ibid, para. 7.4.

171 Ibid, para. 8.1.

172 Ibid, para. 8.2.

resources such as all types of legal texts as well as information on comparative law and practice.[173]

The report goes on to observe that information technology is not used widely yet in international arbitration. It suggests the following possible general reasons:

- the adversarial nature of arbitration;
- the difficulty of adopting a uniform approach when parties already have their own IT 'habits';
- the expense involved in maintaining and using the necessary IT infrastructure;
- lack of skills or willingness to use IT solutions;
- inadequacy of the legal environment related to the use of IT in international arbitration; and
- conservatism.[174]

The report further identifies four types of more specific issues related to the actual use of IT in international arbitration, which explain why IT usage is not yet more widespread than it is:[175]

- *Technical issues*: they include technical compatibility (capability related to hardware, software, word-processed documents, spreadsheets, images, databases, specialist programs, compression, encryption, electronic signatures, and information and document integrity),[176] the 'lowest common technical denominator',[177] and system failure.[178]
- *Inherent practical issues*: they include unique 'project' characteristics,[179] confidentiality and security,[180] and other specific issues relating to the use of computerized data storage.[181]
- *Legal issues*: the principal legal issues relate to ensuring that the use of IT does not compromise the integrity of the arbitral proceedings.[182]
- *Financial issues*: they may arise in particular in relation to the allocation of additional expenses incurred by the use of IT.

---

[173] Ibid, para. 9.1.
[174] Ibid, para. 10.
[175] Ibid, para. 11.
[176] Ibid, para. 12.
[177] Ibid, para. 13. The 'lowest common denominator' refers to the fact that participants may have different levels of technical capability (related to hardware, software and technical skills). A more IT-capable participant may have to align himself to the level of less capable counterparts.
[178] Ibid, para. 14.
[179] Ibid, para. 15.
[180] Ibid, para. 16.
[181] Ibid, para. 17.
[182] Ibid, para. 18.

On the basis of these factors and issues, the ICC has developed guidelines on the use of IT to resolve business disputes; these guidelines are the topic of the next section.

B. Guidelines on 'Using Technology to Resolve Business Disputes'

In a special supplement to the Bulletin of the ICC Court of International Arbitration, the ICC Task Force on IT in Arbitration issued guidelines on 'Using Technology to Resolve Business Disputes'. This supplement provides a series of Operational Standards,[183] whose purpose is to provide standard, optional[184] solutions to facilitate the use of IT in international arbitration. The Standards are intended to be adapted to each arbitration proceedings and modified as necessary.[185] They are only mandatory if they are expressly incorporated as procedural rules.[186] All, some or none of the Standards can be used.[187] It is suggested that they be referred to in the arbitration agreement, or adopted at the outset of the arbitration.[188]

As a general assessment of the Standards, one may suggest that they are remarkably complete, but sometimes give the impression that the ICC over-egged the pudding, in the sense that their over-specification may lead many practitioners to view IT usage as requiring overly complex and pedantic procedures, which does not need to be the case. Nevertheless, if not considered to be crucial requirements to be carried out to the letter, the Standards offer a very useful instrument for parties or arbitrators considering recourse to IT. The following paragraphs summarize these standards.

1. General procedures

The use of the Standards can be initiated by any party or the arbitral tribunal; this is done by transmitting a completed initiation form (a model of which is included in the annex to the supplement) to the other parties and to the members of the tribunal.[189] Each recipient should then complete the form and send a copy to the other parties and to the members of the tribunal.[190] The Standards suggest that they be not applied unless and until every party has acquired the necessary IT capacity, or if the parties agree on measures to overcome any obstacle related to IT capacity. The arbitral tribunal may also give instructions for the

---

183 'Operating Standards for Using IT in Arbitration', [2004] ICC Bull, special supplement on 'Using Technology to Resolve Business Disputes'.
184 Ibid, Part A.
185 Ibid, Part B.
186 Ibid, Standards G1 and G3.
187 Ibid, Part C.
188 Ibid, Part D.
189 Ibid, Standard G4.
190 Ibid, Standard G5.

harmonization of the parties' IT capacity.[191] In any case, the Standards state that the parties' final agreement as to the use of IT during the arbitration proceeding should be consolidated in writing.[192]

The Standards further provide that any problem or incident with the application of the IT agreement, whether permanent or temporary, should be notified to the other parties and to the arbitral tribunal as soon as possible, using the so-called incident report form.[193] Once a problem is reported, the Standards suggest that each party take all reasonable measures to remedy the problem or prevent it from occurring again, and inform the other participants of the measures taken.[194] It is recalled that, in general, the parties should cooperate in good faith and use all reasonable efforts to remedy or overcome any obstacle or incident.[195]

Finally, the Standards recommend consigning any modifications to the Standards in writing.[196] If the parties cannot agree, the arbitrators can make the modifications.[197]

2. Paperless files

A second section of the Standards covers documents that are submitted to the arbitral tribunal or institution and copies of these documents provided to the other participants (i.e., the documents in an arbitrator's file of the case).[198]

This section applies if each participant agrees to convert all the documents it would normally submit in paper form into the agreed electronic format.[199] In this regard, wherever possible, each physical document should be converted into a single electronic document, as identical to the original as possible, including pagination.[200]

On the organization of files, it is recommended that the participants use a logical naming system for the files to identify the participant who submitted them, their category, and their place in that category. The name and date of the original document should appear on the first page of the electronic document.[201] The ICC suggests one such naming system,[202] but the parties are free to agree on their own system.[203] The parties can also

[191] Ibid, Standard G6.
[192] Ibid, Standard G7.
[193] Ibid, Standard G8.
[194] Ibid, Standard G9.
[195] Ibid, Standards G10–11.
[196] Ibid, Standard G12.
[197] Ibid, Standard G13.
[198] Ibid, Standard P1.
[199] Ibid, Standard P3.
[200] Ibid, Standard P4.
[201] Ibid, Standard P5.
[202] Ibid, Standard P6.3.
[203] Ibid, Standards P6.1–2.

agree on a system for sharing structured information about the documents (e.g., a searchable document database).[204]

All parties who submit electronic documents should retain the paper original at least until the end of the arbitration proceeding, and longer if required by other rules or applicable law.[205] They should also use reasonable efforts to protect their own files from corruption, damage or destruction, and archive backup copies in a safe place.[206]

One point on which the Standards are particularly cautious is that they recommend that 'paper' documents should not be exchanged in electronic format only, be it on CD or DVD, but rather in their original paper format, with a copy of all documents in electronic copy. The Standards further provide that if the first option is chosen nonetheless, the participants should verify that this is admissible under the applicable law, and then clearly state their choice in writing.[207] This might be over-cautious. Of course, some documents, such as awards, should definitely be notified in paper form, but the vast majority of national arbitration laws do not set formal requirements on the exchange of briefs. The parties must be heard in adversary proceedings and be treated equally, but this does not in itself imply that the communications be made in paper form.[208] It must be admitted, though, that exchanging documents in electronic format seems more practicable if they are not exceedingly long: sometimes a submission composed of a brief and documentary evidence may amount to several thousand pages, which may be particularly annoying to print out in their entirety – even though this is in principle feasible.

Lastly, the Standards recommend that, upon receiving any submission in electronic format, each participant should always verify that they can open and read the file. If not, they should immediately issue an incident report form. The participant who provided the file should investigate the problem promptly and provide a replacement file within seven working days.[209]

3. Electronic communications

A third section of the Standards, which considers the technologies to be used for electronic communications, suggests that the exchange of written communications (briefs, documentary evidence, other written correspondence) may take place either by e-mail or through a case management website (i.e., a virtual case room). The Standards then also address audio and video communications. The following reviews, in turn, the provisions of the Standards on these four types of communications.

[204] Ibid, Standards P9–11.
[205] Ibid, Standard P8.
[206] Ibid, Standard P15.
[207] Ibid, Standards P12–13.
[208] See further Chapter 4, Section I. Due process issues, p. 108 below.
[209] 'Operating Standards for Using IT in Arbitration', n. 183 above, Standard P 14.

a. Written communications

If the parties decide to communicate via e-mail (instead of either exchanging paper documents or making submissions to a case management website), each participant is required to save, both electronically and in paper form, the e-mails he sends and receives in the context of the arbitration proceedings. These must be stored for a 'reasonable' time period after the end of the proceedings,[210] i.e., at least until the end of the time limit for actions to challenge the award.

Most likely in order to minimize the risk of virus transmission and to maximize compatibility, the Standards suggest that e-mails should be sent in ascii format rather than html. For organizational and filing purposes, the e-mails should include a clear reference to the case as well as the date, the name and the postal address of the sender. Any attachments should be listed in the body of the e-mail.[211]

The Standards address one interesting point, which is often left out of negotiations on the use of IT: the frequency with which e-mails are retrieved. Under the Standards, the participants must check their e-mail inbox at least once every two working days.[212] In order to ensure non-repudiation, the Standards further judiciously require the participants to generate manually an acknowledgement of receipt of the e-mails which includes the entire text received.[213] Moreover, if an acknowledgement of receipt has not been received within two days, the participant expecting the receipt is advised to issue an incident report form.[214] The sender will then retransmit the message via e-mail or by another reliable method.[215]

The parties may wish to use encryption or electronic signatures to provide for extra protection of the confidentiality and authenticity of their e-mail communications.[216] After discussion, they should draw up an agreement that can be implemented after approval by their counsel.[217]

b. Case management websites

The Standards also suggest that participants in the arbitration proceedings may wish to communicate using a virtual case room accessible via the Web,[218] which has the advantage, compared to e-mails, of centralizing all communications. If the parties decide

[210] Ibid, Standard E5.
[211] Ibid, Standard E10.
[212] Ibid, Standard E8.
[213] Ibid, Standard E6.
[214] Ibid, Standards E7–8.
[215] Ibid, Standard E9.
[216] Ibid, Standard E13.
[217] Ibid, Standards E13–15.
[218] Ibid, Standard E17.

to use such a technology, they may do so using the NetCase system accessible via the Web, now that it is operational, if the procedure is an ICC arbitration. The Standards recognize that other ad hoc virtual case rooms may also be used, including for ICC arbitrations.[219]

The Standards recommend that such a case room should be hosted by a neutral entity not controlled by any of the parties, or preferably controlled by the arbitral tribunal or institution; in the case of an ICC arbitration, the Standards suggest the NetCase system.

The selected case room should be set up so as to track the participants' access, and records of access should be available to all participants during the arbitration proceedings and for a period thereafter.[220] Furthermore, the case room should permit each participant to post messages, with or without attachments.[221] As for e-mails, the Standards advise to provide for a specific frequency with which messages are retrieved: all participants should visit the case room at least once every two working days or, if the case room generates automatic e-mail notifications whenever a document is uploaded or a message is posted (which is generally the case), they should check their e-mail inbox with the specified frequency.[222]

c. Audioconferences

If the parties have agreed to resort to audioconferencing (be it an ordinary teleconference or an IT-based audioconference of the type Skype provides for), the Standards suggest that, after consultation with the parties, the arbitral tribunal issue instructions on the organization of the conference, including timing, identity and connection of participants, and any special needs. It is important that these instructions are issued sufficiently in advance of the audioconference.[223]

The audioconference should be led by the single arbitrator or the president of the arbitral tribunal, who verifies that all participants are properly connected. Each participant will then introduce himself before speaking and should not disconnect before the audioconference is declared finished.[224]

Any technical problems should be notified to the single neutral or president as soon as possible.[225]

[219] Ibid, Standard E1.
[220] Ibid, Standard E18.
[221] Ibid, Standard E23.
[222] Ibid, Standard E24.
[223] Ibid, Standard A2.
[224] Ibid, Standard A4.
[225] Ibid, Standard A5.

d. Videoconferences

If the participants agree to use videoconferences, the Standards suggest that, just as for audioconferencing, the arbitral tribunal issue instructions after consultation with the parties on the logistics of the videoconference, including the timing of the conference, the sites used, the participants, and any special needs. Here too, it is essential that the instructions be issued sufficiently in advance of the conference.[226]

The participants' designated technicians should then confer to determine whether the participants have the necessary equipment or whether external resources are needed, what the anticipated costs would be and how these costs should be allocated.[227] All this information should be memorialized in a protocol which must be approved before implementation.[228]

Any technical problems should be notified to the sole arbitrator or president of the arbitral tribunal as quickly as possible.[229]

---

[226] Ibid, Standard V2.
[227] Ibid, Standard V3.
[228] Ibid, Standard V4–5.
[229] Ibid, Standard V6.

CHAPTER 4

LEGAL FRAMEWORK

In the context of arbitral proceedings, resorting to IT tools raises surprisingly few real legal issues. Despite the many differences that we may strongly perceive between the familiar analogical world and electronic environments, the real substance and consequences of the vast majority of actions achieved through technology do not really differ from what we may do with pen, paper, and documents sent by courier. The many new ways of handling certain situations, made possible by the technologies reviewed in the preceding chapters, rarely involve a fundamentally different legal framework from that of arbitral proceedings conducted in the absence of technology.

In principle, arbitration law intervenes to prohibit certain courses of action only in extreme situations. In the absence of extreme cases, it leaves a regime of flexibility. This flexibility is generally sufficient to accommodate the transition from traditional means of communication to electronic ones. But there is one proviso: the law requires that proper common sense actions be taken.

Think, for instance, of the validity of a digitally signed and electronically notified award in an enforcement procedure: while it is true that the validity of such awards may in some contexts be doubtful, there is no reason not to print out the award (which is, of course, almost always written in an electronic format in the first place), to sign it manually, and to notify it to the parties by the usual channels.[230] This example is a reminder of the basic principle suggested in Chapter 1 that one should not overuse IT.[231] Using electronic means of communication is not a goal in and of itself; IT should only be used if it provides a real advantage. Sending an award in paper form avoids uncertainty without creating a significant disadvantage.

Another imperative of common sense is that the opportunities technology provides should never be used to gain or give advantages to one party only, to the detriment of the other party; a recourse to technology should not modify the balance of powers between the parties. Similarly, an arbitral tribunal may only use technology to simplify the procedure to a certain extent; simplification beyond a certain baseline may jeopardize the parties' fundamental rights.

---

[230] See, for example, G. Kaufmann-Kohler and T. Schultz, *Online Dispute Resolution: Challenges for Contemporary Justice* (The Hague, Kluwer Law International, 2004), pp. 217–223; J. Arsic, 'International Commercial Arbitration on the Internet – Has the Future Come Too Early?' (1997) 14 J Int'l Arb 209, p. 217; and M.E. Schneider and C. Kuner, 'Dispute Resolution in International Electronic Commerce' (1997) 14 J Int'l Arb 5, p. 24.

[231] See Chapter 1, Section IV.A. Creeping featurism: the more IT, the better?, p. 21 above.

This chapter translates these common sense recommendations into a legal analysis of the main issues that IT usage raises with respect to arbitration law, namely due process issues and questions of confidentiality.

I. DUE PROCESS ISSUES

Due process issues raised by the use of IT in arbitration essentially relate to the right to be heard; the right to adversary proceedings; and the right to be treated equally. After addressing these three questions, this section reviews the possibilities of judicial review of awards rendered after proceedings during which difficulties involving due process arose. Finally, this section addresses the questions posed by the recognition and enforcement of such awards.

A. THE RIGHT TO BE HEARD

The legal rules on arbitration were not drafted with technologies like case management websites and videoconferencing in mind. Consequently, the legal framework must be tested against such new technologies, essentially to see how they could be used and if they should be adapted. The following thus examines the legal requirements posed by the various forms of due process.

1. A REASONABLE OPPORTUNITY TO PRESENT THE CASE

In arbitral proceedings, the parties have the right to be heard, which means that they must be granted a reasonable opportunity to present their case, i.e., to allege facts, present legal arguments, and produce evidence on relevant facts.[232] In relation to arbitral proceedings using electronic communication technologies, this right of the parties sets two types of limitations to the organization of the procedure: first, the technology being used must be simple, yet, second, the procedure itself should not be oversimplified.

a. Real opportunities to present the case

Can the use of a specific technology breach the parties' right to be heard? The question may arise in connection with sophisticated communication technologies that cannot be

[232] On the right to be heard in arbitration generally, see, for example, C. Liebscher, *The Healthy Award – Challenge in International Commercial Arbitration* (The Hague, Kluwer Law International, 2003), pp. 243–273, 344 and J.-F. Poudret and S. Besson, *Droit comparé de l'arbitrage international* (Zurich, Schulthess, 2002), p. 499.

easily accessed and mastered by the parties, for instance if very complex Web interfaces are necessary for the parties to present their case. This question calls for the following indirect answers.

First, the arbitral tribunal should always seek the parties' consent to the use of such technology.[233] This will in principle resolve the issue: although the parties cannot validly waive all opportunities to present their case, they can jointly choose the method to allege facts, present legal arguments, and produce evidence.[234] If the parties consent to the use of even a very complex technology, there is no reason to object to it.

If the consent of the parties cannot be obtained, the question whether the possibility of presenting the case using a complex technology constitutes a real opportunity or merely an illusory right will depend on the technical skills of the parties and the user-friendly character of the technology. The more complex a given technology, the higher the parties' technical skills and the user-friendliness must be in order to be able to validly obligate them to use it.

Second, imposing on the parties the use of a particularly complex communication system should also be acceptable if there are additional, not too technically complicated opportunities to allege facts, present legal arguments, and produce evidence. One may imagine, for instance, that the rules of procedure for an arbitration require the parties to make their case using a specific highly complex IT system, for example a particular engineering application for the simulation of specific aspects of a construction dispute or a 3D shared virtual workspace. Such a mandatory recourse to complex IT should be considered acceptable in regard to the right to be heard if the parties are also allowed, in addition to the submissions made through the mandatory IT tool, to present their allegations and evidence in writing, be it in paper form or electronic format. Of course, the communication to the tribunal of these written documents must then be achievable by means that every reasonably IT-literate person can master: e-mails, a simple case management website, etc. The written submissions would satisfy the requirements of the right to be heard – at least as long as the right to be heard does not include a right to be heard orally. This is discussed in another section.[235]

---

[233] See for instance J. Hörnle, 'Online Dispute Resolution' in *Bernstein's Handbook of Arbitration and Dispute Resolution Practice*, J. Tackaberry and A. Marriott (eds) (4th edn, London, Sweet and Maxwell, 2003), para. 12.043.

[234] For a discussion of such waivers, see for instance G. Kaufmann-Kohler and T. Schultz, *Online Dispute Resolution*, n. 230 above, p. 204 and T. Schultz, 'Human Rights: A Speed Bump for Arbitral Procedures? An exploration of safeguards in the acceleration of justice' (2006) 9-1 Int A L R 8, pp. 17–19.

[235] See Section I.A.2. Oral hearings, p. 111 below.

b. Sufficient opportunities to present the case

The second issue is more theoretical and in a sense less directly related to technology. It is about the fact that the acceleration opportunities offered by IT may tempt the arbitration institution or the arbitral tribunal to set up an oversimplified procedure.

On the one hand, technology may be configured (or the rules of procedure may be drafted) so as to limit the size, and thus the length, of the documents admissible for uploading to a communication platform. A case management website may for instance restrict the length of briefs to a certain number of pages, so as to keep the arbitral tribunal's workload low enough to allow it to conduct speedy proceedings. A general tendency in this direction can be observed in connection with a number of IT-intensive procedures.

The minimum in this respect seems to be that this fixed length or size should be sufficient for the parties to realistically allege facts, submit legal arguments, and include evidence produced. Beyond this general statement, the concrete minimal limit, i.e., what will be a sufficient length or size, depends, first, on the complexity of the type of case involved – standard consumer cases, for example, require smaller submissions than large international commercial cases. Second, it depends on the type of dispute resolution method (expedited or not, inexpensive or not), because the parties can be considered to have accepted to limit their right to be heard in exchange for faster proceedings.

On the other hand, a fast-track arbitral tribunal, in order to provide speedy and inexpensive procedures, may wish to limit the taking of evidence to the parties' written submissions, excluding recourse to witnesses and experts. This may seem particularly advantageous in the context of procedures resorting strongly to IT, because hearing witnesses or experts over a video linkup is one of the most problematic aspects of videoconferencing. It raises the classical issues of being less able to 'feel' persons who are not physically present and of not knowing who else is in the room.[236] Such an exclusion of witnesses and experts should preferably be subjected to the parties' informed consent, meaning that the parties should be informed by the arbitral tribunal, at the beginning of the procedure, that their right to be heard will be limited, and their express approval should be requested.

In any event, the strict minimum is that the parties be offered at least *one* opportunity to allege facts and submit evidence on relevant facts, likely to prove or disprove possibly decisive aspects of the case. Less than that would not only violate the parties' right to be heard, but it may also void the process of arbitration of its very essence, which is to

236 For general responses to these concerns, which involve, respectively, scheduling a videoconferencing session only if all participants have already met at least once before, and providing for an addition camera showing the entire room, see Chapter 2, Section II.D.1.c. Camera view, p. 62 above. See also Chapter 5, Section III.B. Setting up a videoconferencing session, p. 170 below.

adjudicate a dispute with full legal authority conferred to the arbitrators.[237] In order to adjudicate the dispute, the arbitral tribunal must be provided with at least one presentation of the elements necessary to apply law to facts.

2. ORAL HEARINGS

If there is no face-to-face hearing during the procedure, but only, for instance, a videoconference during which the parties present their case and make their allegations of facts, can this amount to a violation of the right to be heard because no oral hearing was granted?

The answer is that, in most situations, it does not amount to such a violation, at least if the parties have consented to the absence of oral hearings. First, as such, the right to a reasonable opportunity to be heard does not include, in and of itself, a right to an oral hearing; it does not necessarily guarantee an opportunity to be heard orally in all circumstances.[238] Moreover, the right to be heard, in the specific sense of the respective applicable law, does in most cases not extend to a mandatory right to be heard orally. The following provides an overview of the general situation in this regard.

- The law governing the arbitration procedure,[239] which may provide for a possible right to an oral hearing, varies from one arbitration law to another, but one can make out two main situations. Either there exists no right to an oral hearing (as is the case under English[240] and Swiss law,[241] for instance), or there is a right to an oral hearing

---

[237] C. Jarrosson, 'Les frontières de l'arbitrage' [2001] 1 Rev Arb 5, p. 19 (providing that, regarding arbitration, the requirements are, inter alia, full legal authority to adjudicate the dispute ('*mission juridictionnelle*') conferred to the third neutral by the parties); J.-F. Poudret and S. Besson, *Droit comparé de l'arbitrage international*, n. 232 above, p. 3 ('authority to adjudicate in lieu of national courts'); T.E. Carbonneau, *Cases and Materials on The Law and Practice of Arbitration* (2nd edn, Yonkers NY, Juris Publishing, 2000), p. 2 ('The parties confer upon the arbitrators full legal authority to adjudicate disputes').

[238] J.-F. Poudret and S. Besson, *Droit comparé de l'arbitrage international*, n. 232 above, pp. 499–500, 779.

[239] This is generally the law of the seat of the arbitration: A. Redfern and M. Hunter, *The Law and Practice of Commercial Arbitration* (4th edn, London, Sweet and Maxwell, 2004), paras 2.14–2.18 and 6.12–6.13 and A.J. van den Berg, *The New York Convention of 1958: Towards a Uniform Judicial Interpretation* (Deventer, Kluwer Law International, 1981), p. 307.

[240] See English Arbitration Act 1996, s. 34(2)(h), which provides that it shall be for the tribunal to decide all procedural and evidential matters, subject to the right of the parties to agree any matter. (2) Procedural and evidential matters include . . . (h) whether and to what extent there should be oral or written evidence or submissions'.

[241] See, e.g., the decision of the Swiss Federal Supreme Court in *U. v. Epoux G.*, 1 July 1991, RO 117 II 346, (1991) 9 ASA Bull 415. See J.-F. Poudret and S. Besson, *Droit comparé de l'arbitrage international*, n. 232 above, pp. 500, 780–781. See also *Fouchard Gaillard Goldman*

but it can be waived (this is the case under German,[242] French,[243] Italian,[244] Dutch,[245] Belgian,[246] and Swedish law,[247] as well as under the UNCITRAL Model Law[248]).
- The European Convention on Human Rights, which might be referred to at least *per analogiam* in order to explore the minimal requirement of due process of our legal systems,[249] requires an oral hearing only if it is indispensable to the protection of the 'interest of the person concerned' and if the person concerned has not waived that right.[250]

Consequently, the need for an oral hearing is in principle not a legal obstacle, either because the applicable law does not provide such a right, or because this right can be waived.[251]

Nevertheless, the situation may arise where the parties have not validly waived their right to be heard orally. Hence, the question again: does a videoconference, or any other technology-based 'meeting', constitute a valid opportunity to be heard orally, i.e., a valid equivalent to a face-to-face meeting? Two responses to such a situation may be suggested

on International Commercial Arbitration, E. Gaillard and J. Savage (eds) (The Hague, Kluwer Law International, 1999), para. 1296.

242 Para. 1047 German ZPO.

243 See the decisions of the Paris Court of Appeal in *Compagnie Honeywell Bull SA v. Computacion Bull de Venezuela CA*, 21 June 1990, [1991] Rev Arb 96, p. 100 and in *Boccard v. SARL Stapem*, 26 January 1990, [1991] Rev Arb 125. See J.-F. Poudret and S. Besson, *Droit comparé de l'arbitrage international*, n. 232 above, p. 500; C. Kessedjian, 'Principe de la contradiction et arbitrage' [1995] Rev Arb 381. Contrast *Fouchard Gaillard Goldman on International Commercial Arbitration*, n. 241 above, para. 1296.

244 See P. Bernardini, National report: Italy, in *International Handbook on Commercial Arbitration*, Suppl. 31 of September 2000, J. Paulsson (ed.) (The Hague, Kluwer Law International).

245 See Dutch WBR, art. 1039(2).

246 Belgian *Code judiciaire*, Art. 1694(3), and see J. Linsmeau, *L'arbitrage volontaire en droit privé belge* (Brussels, Bruylant, 1991), para. 245; P. de Bournonville, *Droit judiciaire: l'arbitrage* (Brussels, Larcier, 2000), p. 175.

247 Swedish Arbitration Act 1999, s. 24(1).

248 UNCITRAL Model Law on International Commercial Arbitration, art. 24(1).

249 On the influence of the ECHR on the concept of due process in arbitration, see e.g., G. Kaufmann-Kohler and T. Schultz, *Online Dispute Resolution*, n. 230 above, pp. 198 *et seq.*, 204 *et seq.* and T. Schultz, 'Human Rights: A Speed Bump for Arbitral Procedures?', n. 234 above.

250 See the report of the European Commission on Human Rights in *Schuler-Zgraggen v. Switzerland* (App 14518/89), 7 April 1992, (1993) 16 EHRR 393, para. 96. See also the decision of the European Court of Human Rights in *Zumtobel v. Austria*, Series A No 268-A, (1993) 17 EHRR 116, para. 34. See also C. Liebscher, *The Healthy Award*, n. 232 above, pp. 96–97 and 109.

251 See generally D. Girsberger and D. Schramm, 'Cyber Arbitration und prozessuale Fairness' in *Geschäftsplattform Internet IV. Open Source – Multimedia – Online Arbitration*, R.H. Weber, M. Berger, and R. auf der Maur (eds) (Zurich, Schulthess, 2003), p. 198 and J. Hörnle, 'Online Dispute Resolution', n. 233 above, para. 12.024.

– it being understood that if the applicable law does not provide for a right to be heard orally, there is a fortiori no right to be heard face-to-face.

First, one may submit that there is no such thing as a right to be heard *in person* rather than over a video linkup, that the right to be heard orally only guarantees an opportunity to react instantaneously to arguments and submissions of the other party and to statements or questions from the arbitral tribunal. A videoconferencing session certainly offers such an opportunity – provided of course that the technology used is easily accessible to the parties; otherwise, as suggested above, the opportunity to be heard may not be deemed to be real.[252] The increasingly pervasive concept of 'functional equivalence' (i.e., that legal requirements should be media-neutral as long as the same functions are fulfilled) certainly argues in favor of this contention.[253] Similarly, telephone conferences should be deemed to provide equivalent opportunities to be heard. Taking the argument further, one may even maintain that the gist of the right to be heard orally is not a right to speak rather than to write, but a right to immediate reactions and to a more flexible and dialogical form of rhetoric than sending a request for arbitration, a response, a reply, and a rejoinder. Consequently, real-time communication mechanisms other than videoconferencing and teleconferences could also validly replace an in person meeting with respect to satisfying the right to be heard orally, even if these communication systems were text-based, such as online chat rooms.

Alternatively, if a right to be heard in person, in a face-to-face meeting, were deemed to exist, it must be admitted that it can be waived implicitly for the benefit of an IT-based meeting. For example, the parties may have agreed that specific parts of the proceedings, or the procedure in its entirety, would be held exclusively online. This is certainly the most common and the most advisable situation for an arbitral tribunal wishing to resort to IT usage, i.e., to obtain the parties' agreement on the use of electronic communication technologies before implementing them. In this case, with regard either to specific parts of the proceedings or to the procedure in its entirety (depending on the extent of the parties' consent to online proceedings), the parties must be deemed to have validly waived in-person hearings, even if they have not expressly waived them. Indeed, online proceedings, by definition, involve no face-to-face hearings.

---

[252] See Section A.1.a. Real opportunities to present the case, p. 108 above.

[253] On the concept of 'functional equivalence', which in principle applies to electronic versus paper documents, see UNCITRAL Model Law on Electronic Commerce, art. 5; UCITA, s. 107(a); UETA, s. 7; European Directive on Electronic Commerce (Directive 2000/31/EC of 8 June 2000), art. 9(1); US E-Signature Act, s. 101(a)(1); H.D. Gabriel, 'The New United States Uniform Electronic Transactions Act: Substantive Provisions, Drafting History and Comparison to the UNCITRAL Model Law on Electronic Commerce' [2000] *Revue de droit uniforme* 651, p. 654; and D.L. Kidd and W. Daughtrey, 'Adapting Contract Law to Accommodate Electronic Contracts' (2000) 26 Rutgers Computer & Tech L J 215, p. 269.

B. ADVERSARY PROCEEDINGS

In application of the right to be heard in adversary proceedings – in French terminology the *principe de la contradiction* – the parties must be provided with an opportunity to respond to the allegations, arguments and evidence submitted by their opponent, by making allegations and submitting arguments and evidence in rebuttal.[254]

Most arbitral proceedings take the form of a request for arbitration, a response, a reply, and a rejoinder. These rounds of briefs are usually followed by one or several hearings and end with post-hearing briefs. The right to be heard in adversary proceedings imposes two requirements with respect to these communications:

- The arbitral tribunal or members thereof must have no contact with a party that excludes any other party ('ex parte communications'), because all parties must be able to take a position on one another's arguments and evidence.[255]
- Both parties must have equal access to the record, again to allow them to take a position on the submissions filed by their opponent.

In the context of arbitral proceedings making use of electronic communication technologies, issues may primarily arise in connection with a technical failure in the transmission of documents using a case management website, or of images and sound or other information in a videoconferencing session (online hearing). In such events, one of the parties may indeed be prevented from receiving the submissions of its opponent and thus responding to them. This amounts to a restriction (but not yet a violation) of the right to be heard in adversary proceedings.

Such a restriction could constitute a violation of the right to be heard in an adversary proceeding on two conditions – and an award may then be challenged on this ground.[256]

---

[254] See for instance J.-F. Poudret and S. Besson, *Droit comparé de l'arbitrage international*, n. 232 above, p. 792; K.P. Berger, *Internationale Wirtschaftsschiedsgerichtsbarkeit* (Berlin, de Gruyter, 1992), p. 374; *Fouchard Gaillard Goldman on International Commercial Arbitration*, n. 241 above, para. 1638; C. Kessedjian, 'Principe de la contradiction et arbitrage', n. 243 above, pp. 389–390. See also Swiss PIL Act, art. 190(2)(d) (providing that the award can be challenged if 'the equality of the parties or their right to be heard in an adversarial proceeding was not respected'); French New Code of Civil Procedure, art. 1502(4) (providing for a ground to set aside the award if the principle of contradiction has not been respected); and English Arbitration Act 1996, s. 33(1) (stating that the parties must be granted a 'reasonable opportunity of putting his case and dealing with that of his opponent').

[255] See for instance A. Redfern and M. Hunter, *The Law and Practice of Commercial Arbitration*, n. 239 above, para. 4.66 ('In principle all communications with only one of the parties should be reduced to writing and furnished to the other party, and in no event should there ever be discussions regarding the merits of the case').

[256] See D. Girsberger and D. Schramm, 'Cyber Arbitration und prozessuale Fairness', n. 251 above, p. 198

(a) First, the restriction must be significant enough, i.e., the information exchanged while only one of the parties and the arbitrators had access to it must be sufficiently substantial.
(b) Second, the arbitral tribunal must not have ordered a replay of the submissions or provided the opposing party with the submitted information in another way and allowed a specific opportunity to react to it.

This problem can be avoided by using software that automatically interrupts the hearing of one party if the computer of the other party is disconnected, or by using a reliable means of instant communication to alert the arbitral tribunal of the disruption – a direct telephone connection for instance.

As a matter of fact, some IT tools might even carry a lower risk of ex parte communications between one party and the arbitrators than exists in the offline context, not accounting for technical breakdowns. Indeed, technology can be configured so as to prevent ex parte communications. Further, some means of communication, such as chat rooms and bulletin boards, do not allow ex parte communications. E-mails, obviously, are a different matter. On a more theoretical ground, academic experiments have even suggested resorting to messaging software with an embedded electronic agent that monitors all communications between the parties and the arbitral tribunal. The agent then either permits or blocks these transmissions.[257] The contention that technology can be configured so as to prevent ex parte communications should not be misunderstood as meaning that all such communications then become impossible; technology cannot prevent the parties or the arbitrators from placing phone calls or sending e-mails to one recipient only. But technology can bring the participants in an arbitration to use a preferred system of communication that does not itself allow such private contacts, requiring them to switch to another system of communication to accomplish such contacts. In other words, ex parte communications, especially those that arise from simple mistakes, are more likely to be avoided while using chat rooms or bulletin boards than by sending letters, which may be sent to the wrong person or may never arrive.[258]

---

257 The use of such an agent is considered in the E-Arbitration-T online arbitration platform, see E-Arbitration-T, 'Online Arbitration: What Technology can do for Arbitral Institutions', IST-2000-25464/11.5/UBRUN/2048/R/2 <www.e-arbitration-t.com/papersadr/ubrun_seminar_content.pdf>, 20 January 2003, p. 12.

258 O. Cachard, 'Electronic Arbitration', module of the UNCTAD Course on Dispute Settlement in International Trade, Investment and Intellectual Property, UNCTAD/EDM/Misc.232/Add.20 <www.unctad.org/en/docs/edmmisc232add20_en.pdf> (Geneva, United Nations Publications, 2003), p. 36.

C. EQUAL TREATMENT

In arbitral proceedings, the parties have a right to be treated equally by the tribunal.[259] This does not mean that they must be treated identically, but rather that none of the parties may be put at a disadvantage as a result of the conduct of the proceedings.[260]

With regard to IT usage, issues may arise if the technology used cannot be equally accessed and mastered by both parties and that, as a consequence, one party is at a substantial disadvantage. If the use of such technology has been imposed by the arbitral tribunal and if the technology in question requires more than a reasonable training in IT matters, then such a disadvantage may constitute a violation of equal treatment.

This general statement calls for further specification. The discrepancies between the technological capabilities of the parties, which could jeopardize the right to equal treatment, may be due to factors related to the parties, the technology itself, or to the dispute.

With regard to the parties, typical factors influencing their technological capabilities are geographical location, some countries offering better IT support than others and some areas being less well served by broadband access, sometimes to the point of not permitting the use of certain technologies;[261] firm size; resources; and personal experience with IT.

Regarding the technology itself, disparities between the parties will in general largely depend on the complexity of the technology being used; on what computer scientists call its 'deployment', i.e., how widespread its use is; and on its overall acquisition costs. These three elements are often intertwined, as particularly complex software is typically less widely 'deployed' and often entails higher acquisition costs. Deployment is an issue because widely used software is less likely to raise difficulties with regard to compatibility (which may involve acquisition costs if one party's computer system must be adapted to the new technology) and general familiarity or prior personal experience. Some

---

259 See e.g., UNCITRAL Model Law on International Commercial Arbitration, art. 18; Swiss PIL Act, art. 182(3); A. Redfern and M. Hunter, *The Law and Practice of Commercial Arbitration*, n. 239 above, para. 9.21; J.-F. Poudret and S. Besson, *Droit comparé de l'arbitrage international*, n. 232 above, pp. 507–508; *Fouchard Gaillard Goldman on International Commercial Arbitration*, n. 241 above, paras 1638–1639. In *Dombo Beheer BV v. Netherlands*, the European Court of Human Rights held that equal treatment 'implies that each party must be afforded a reasonable opportunity to present its case – including evidence – under conditions that do not place it at a substantial disadvantage vis-à-vis his opponent': Series A No 274-A, (1994) 18 EHRR 213.

260 J.-F. Poudret and S. Besson, *Droit comparé de l'arbitrage international*, n. 232 above, p. 507.

261 Some areas of even usually well-equipped countries may be poorly served by broadband, to the point of not allowing to participate in a videoconferencing session: see Chapter 2, Section II.D.1.b Image quality, p.. 61 (reporting on an instance where videoconferencing failed with a small city in Italy because of the limited capacity of the pipe into the city).

authors consider that even the imposition of videoconferencing by the arbitral tribunal could constitute unequal treatment of the parties.[262]

In relation to the dispute, the factor that may cause a disparity between the parties is its value, in the sense that one party may already be equipped with a specific technology that is too expensive for the party to acquire based on the value of the case. Conversely, large cases make certain discrepancies between the parties less relevant. For instance, the larger the case, the lesser the role acquisition and training costs will play, because they will be proportionately less significant compared to the total expenses incurred.[263]

There is, however, a minimal threshold to technical qualifications: in some cases, the technological capabilities of the parties must be a legal fiction. If the tools in question are very widely deployed, the parties must be deemed to be fully and equally able to use them. This for instance applies to Adobe Acrobat; Microsoft Word, PowerPoint, and Excel; but also to e-mailing. It may be noted that courts have gradually increased the level of what should be considered normal with regard to IT usage, for instance holding that an e-mail message is an admissible means of service for arbitration.[264] Indeed, the ability to use such software is nowadays almost as self-evident in business activities as sending a letter by courier or fax.

Moreover, once it has been established that the parties are supposed to have equivalent IT capabilities, inept use of technology should not give grounds to objections based on unequal treatment. Typically, an arbitral tribunal will seek to organize the procedure and the use of IT tools in such manner as to ensure that the proceedings are not disrupted by the voluntary or involuntary inept use of the technology. This organization should in principle not amount to a violation of the right to equal treatment. For example, the parties have to cope with their own lack of IT competence in order to meet the time limits set by the tribunal. If a party misses a time limit due to its own inept use of a technology it is supposed to master, then the arbitral tribunal does not violate the right to equal treatment if it does not grant an extension of the time limit.

As a final general recommendation, one may suggest that, as in connection with the right to be heard, the arbitral tribunal would be well advised to obtain the prior consent of

---

262 See for instance O. Cachard, 'Electronic Arbitration', n. 258 above, p. 36 (providing that oral statements of claim and statements of defense must be made from identical electronic hearing rooms in order not to put due process at risk). See also J. Hörnle, 'Online Dispute Resolution', n. 233 above, paras 12.042 and 12.054–12.056.

263 With respect to smaller disputes, see for instance G. Kaufmann-Kohler and T. Schultz, *Online Dispute Resolution*, n. 230 above, pp. 203–204.

264 See, e.g., *Bernuth Lines Ltd v. High Seas Shipping Ltd* [2005] EWHC 3020 (Com Ct) ('There is no reason why, in this context, delivery of a document by e-mail – a method habitually used by businessmen, lawyers and civil servants – should be regarded as essentially different from communication by post, fax or telex.')

the parties regarding the technology to be used. It is further advisable, whenever possible, to use software as user-friendly as possible and only well known formats.[265]

D. JUDICIAL REVIEW OF ARBITRAL AWARDS RENDERED AFTER PROCEEDINGS MAKING USE OF IT

Violations of due process rights may, in certain circumstances, constitute grounds for an application to challenge the validity or effect of an arbitral award, in order to have it modified or, more frequently, set aside. The following provides a brief overview of these circumstances.

First of all, an arbitral award may only be challenged in the country in which it was made, i.e., in the country of the seat of the arbitral tribunal, which is not necessarily the actual place where the proceedings were held. The applicable law, which defines the admissible grounds for a challenge, is in principle that of the seat of the arbitral tribunal as well, although it may also be the procedural law chosen by the parties to govern the procedure.[266]

The admissible grounds for an application to challenge an award vary from one country to another. As Alan Redfern and Martin Hunter put it, 'each national court approaches the question from its own particular national standpoint'.[267] Exactly what constitutes a 'fair hearing' depends on national conceptions. Nevertheless, as a general rule, all legal systems provide for an action to set aside the award if the arbitrators have committed one of the following procedural violations:

- They have not given the parties a sufficient opportunity to present their case.[268]
- They have not granted the parties an opportunity to be heard orally in a country where such a right exists and this right has not been waived.[269]

---

[265] By analogy, one may mention that, eight years ago, in *Yukiyo Ltd v. Watanabe*, 111 Fed 3d 883 (Fed Cir 1997), the US Court of Appeal for the Federal Circuit held that a brief submitted on a CD-Rom while the other party was not equipped to read it was a violation of due process. Nowadays, in 2005, it has become exceptional indeed that a law office is not equipped to read CD-Roms. Examples of usual standards include rtf for text documents (rather than doc documents, which more easily carry viruses and might require the use of proprietary software or a compatible version of the same software program) or pdf. For images, typical formats are gif, jpeg, and bmp (although bmp encodes every pixel and thus produces very large files).

[266] A. Redfern and M. Hunter, *The Law and Practice of Commercial Arbitration*, n. 239 above, para. 9.11.

[267] Ibid, para. 9.22.

[268] J.-F. Poudret and S. Besson, *Droit comparé de l'arbitrage international*, n. 232 above, pp. 779–780.

[269] H. Raeschke-Kessler and K.P. Berger, *Recht und Praxis des Schiedsverfahren* (3rd edn, Cologne, RWS, 1999), p. 229; M. Huys and G. Keutgen, *L'arbitrage en droit belge et*

- They have not granted the parties sufficient opportunity to respond to the other party's submissions.[270]
- They have not treated the parties equally.[271]

One may recall, however, that an objection based on the violation of procedural rights must be raised immediately, before the arbitral tribunal, or else the procedural right is considered waived.[272]

E. Enforcement of Awards

An arbitral award may also be refused enforcement or recognition based on a violation of one of the due process rights discussed in this chapter. As the enforcement and recognition of arbitral awards is essentially governed by the New York Convention of 1958, the following considerations will review the three provisions of the Convention that may allow a refusal of enforcement on grounds of due process.

1. Article V(1)(b) of the New York Convention

For present purposes, the most important provision of the Convention with respect to resisting enforcement is Article V(1)(b). It states that enforcement may be refused if the party against whom the award is invoked was 'unable to present his case'. This refers to the violation, by the arbitral tribunal, of a fundamental due process right of one of the parties, and more precisely of the right to be heard in one of its different forms reviewed above.[273] Only very serious irregularities, however, are sanctioned by the provision.[274] With respect to case management websites, videoconferencing, and the use of other

---

international (Brussels, Bruylant, 1981), p. 358; Swiss law is an exception to this general rule: see *U. v. Epoux G.*, n. 241 above.

270 J.-F. Poudret and S. Besson, *Droit comparé de l'arbitrage international*, n. 232 above, pp. 780, 782.

271 D. Hascher, 'Principes et pratique de procédure dans l'arbitrage commercial international' (1999) 279 *Collected Courses of the Hague Academy of International Law* 50, pp. 126–133.

272 On the challenge of an award on the ground of a violation of fundamental procedural rights, see J.-F. Poudret and S. Besson, *Droit comparé de l'arbitrage international*, n. 232 above, p. 779 and K.P. Berger, *Internationale Wirtschaftsschiedsgerichtsbarkeit*, n. 254 above, p. 664.

273 See in general *Fouchard Gaillard Goldman on International Commercial Arbitration*, n. 241 above, paras 1696–1699; A.J. van den Berg, *The New York Convention of 1958*, n. 239 above, pp. 306–311; J.-F. Poudret and S. Besson, *Droit comparé de l'arbitrage international*, n. 232 above, pp. 886–888; A. Redfern and M. Hunter, *The Law and Practice of Commercial Arbitration*, n. 239 above, paras 10.39–10.40.

274 A.J. van den Berg, *The New York Convention of 1958*, n. 239 above, pp. 297, 306; J.-F. Poudret and S. Besson, *Droit comparé de l'arbitrage international*, n. 232 above, p. 887; *Fouchard Gaillard Goldman on International Commercial Arbitration*, n. 241 above, para. 1698.

electronic means of communication, one may assume that examples of very serious irregularities could derive from one of the following situations:

- A true inability for one or both parties to allege facts, submit arguments, or produce evidence due to the technology chosen by the arbitral tribunal, for instance because such technology was particularly difficult to use and prevented a party from filing its submissions on time (violation of the right to be heard *stricto sensu*, i.e., to be granted a reasonable opportunity to present the case).
- In the absence of a videoconferencing session and an in-person meeting, the parties may oppose enforcement on this basis if the law governing the arbitration provides for a right to be heard orally and the parties have not waived it. If the right to an oral hearing exists and a videoconferencing session but no in-person meeting was held, it may be recalled that this should not amount to a violation of this right, as the goal of an in-person meeting is to be able to react instantaneously to the allegations of one's opponent, and this goal is met in a videoconferencing session. Videoconferencing should be regarded as a valid form of oral hearing[275] (violation of the right to be heard orally).
- Lengthy technical failures, e.g., disruption of sound and image transmission, in a videoconference allowing one party to make its case without the other being online (violation of the right to be heard in adversary proceedings).
- Gross inequalities in the use of the technology selected by the arbitral tribunal (violation of the right to equal treatment).

2. Article V(1)(d) of the New York Convention

Another important provision of the Convention with regard to opposing enforcement on the basis of an inadequate use of technology is Article V(1)(d). It provides that recognition or enforcement may be refused if (1) the arbitral procedure was not in accordance with the agreement of the parties, or (2), in the absence of such an agreement, was not in accordance with the law of the country where the arbitration took place.

The considerations involved in connection with the conformity of the procedure with the law of the place of arbitration are not essentially different from the ones just discussed in the context of Article V(1)(b).

The issue of the conformity of the procedure with the agreement of the parties (for instance an agreement that there should be no videoconferencing, or that a specific technology should be used) calls for the following three comments:

- First, although the majority of commentators state that the agreement of the parties prevails in any case over the law of the place of arbitration, more convincing recent

275 See Section A.2. Oral hearings, p. 111 above.

views hold that Article V(1)(d) applies only to agreements that meet the mandatory requirements of the law of the place of arbitration.[276]

- Second, although the Convention provides 'no criteria enabling the determination of which procedural rules are sufficiently important to justify the refusal . . . in the event that the arbitrators fail to comply with them',[277] US and English courts have held that only those violations of agreed rules that work 'substantial prejudice to the complaining party' are covered by Article V(1)(d).[278]
- Third, it is in practice quite rare that courts refuse to enforce or to recognize an award based on this provision.[279] In other words, successfully contesting enforcement on Article V(1)(d) is rather unlikely, and in some countries it requires proof of substantial prejudice and that the rules agreed upon, which were violated, complied with the mandatory provisions of the place of arbitration.

3. Article V(2)(b) of the New York Convention

According to Article V(2)(b), enforcement and recognition may also be refused if the award is contrary to the public policy of the enforcement state. The public policy addressed here is international; but its source is national: it is specific to each state. The provision does not refer to ordinary (internal) public policy, which is broader and varies more significantly from one state to another. Neither does it refer to transnational public policy, which is narrower; transnational public policy, which overrides local laws, is supranational and fundamentally composed of principles of universal justice.

The substance of international public policy, with regard to Article V(b)(2), is to be construed narrowly,[280] with the consequence that, although this provision is often relied upon, courts very rarely accept this ground for denying enforcement or recognition.[281]

---

[276] See J.-F. Poudret and S. Besson, *Droit comparé de l'arbitrage international*, n. 232 above, pp. 890–891.

[277] *Fouchard Gaillard Goldman on International Commercial Arbitration*, n. 241 above, para. 1701.

[278] See for instance *Compagnie des Bauxites de Guinée v. Hammermills Inc.*, 1992 WL 122712 (DDC 1992) and *China Agribusiness Development Corp v. Balli Trading* [1998] 2 Lloyd's Rep 76 (QB).

[279] A.J. van den Berg, *The New York Convention of 1958*, n. 239 above, p. 323 and J.-F. Poudret and S. Besson, *Droit comparé de l'arbitrage international*, n. 232 above, p. 892.

[280] H. Raeschke-Kessler and K.P Berger, *Recht und Praxis des Schiedsverfahren*, n. 269 above, p. 249; A.J. van den Berg, *The New York Convention of 1958*, n. 239 above, p. 366; J.D.M. Lew, L.A. Mistelis, and S.M. Kröll, *Comparative International Commercial Arbitration* (The Hague, Kluwer Law International, 2003), pp. 721, 729; *Fouchard Gaillard Goldman on International Commercial Arbitration*, n. 241 above, paras 1710–1711.

[281] *Fouchard Gaillard Goldman on International Commercial Arbitration*, n. 241 above, para. 1713; J.D.M. Lew, L.A. Mistelis, and S.M. Kröll, *Comparative International Commercial Arbitration*, n. 280 above, pp. 723–729.

Nevertheless, in one landmark case, the *Oberlandsgericht* of Hamburg refused enforcement because the arbitrator relied on documents submitted by one party but not communicated to the other party.[282] Such a violation of the right to be heard in adversary proceedings may be considered part of the international public policy of most countries. Hence, similarly, an error (voluntary or not) in the transmission of an electronic document, which is not received by one of the parties, may amount to a violation of international public policy. The arbitral tribunal would be well advised to make sure, in this regard, that every document that it receives and that is relevant to the case (i.e., not mere billing matters, for example) is also properly transmitted to the other party before taking the document into consideration. The same holds true for documents that are uploaded to a case management website but are not accessible or readable by one party, for instance because of the use of a format that was unusual and had not been agreed upon. In other words, serious violations of the right to be heard are likely to amount to a violation of public policy under Article V(2)(b) in the conception most countries have of international public policy.

The absence of oral hearings, however, is very unlikely to constitute such a violation, as such hearings are not even mandatory in the vast majority of countries, and the concept of public policy embedded in Article V(2)(b) is much stricter than the concept of mandatory provisions, whose substance may globally be compared to that of ordinary or internal public policy.[283]

II. CONFIDENTIALITY ISSUES

Although confidentiality does not raise specifically novel legal issues with respect to IT usage in arbitration, its practical relevance is increased in this context by the ease with which confidentiality breaches may occur. Such breaches are made easier than in the offline world by several common, if not inherent, properties of electronic data.

First, every electronic document, once transmitted from one person to another, necessarily exists in several copies, at least one on the sender's computer and one on the recipient's. As David Post, one of the most prominent early experts of cyberspace law, puts it:

> File copying is not merely inexpensive in cyberspace, it is ubiquitous. And it is not merely ubiquitous, it is indispensable, a necessary precondition to the existence of the medium, because all basic computer functions, and therefore all computer-mediated communication, rely on reproducing information in some manner or another.[284]

---

[282] *Firm P v. Firm F*, 3 April 1975, [1977] 2 Yearbook Comm. Arb'n 241.

[283] J.-F. Poudret and S. Besson, *Droit comparé de l'arbitrage international*, n. 232 above, p. 907.

[284] D. Post, 'Controlling Cybercopies' [1996] *Legal Times* 44.

Moreover, backup copies of documents are also frequently made in several electronic locations. And most people do not use the available means to limit the consequences of copying – such as protecting Word files with a password. In addition, electronic data is much easier to transmit, including to the wrong addressee; who has never sent or received an e-mail to or from the wrong person, or a wrong attachment, or forwarded or been forwarded an e-mail containing information that the addressee was not meant to see? Admittedly, the results of such errors also wind up in our postal mailboxes, but that happens less often. Furthermore, other electronic information, such as audio and video data transmitted during a videoconferencing session, may easily be recorded without anyone noticing.[285] In fact, every piece of information exchanged through electronic communication means leaves a trace, can be uncovered, copied, and transmitted to anyone. In this regard, one may simply remember the archetypical issue that dragging a document to the trash or 'recycle bin' on one's computer does not actually delete the information constituting the file from the hard disk. It merely marks the file in such manner that the disk file system of the computer simply ignores it, does not show it to the user, and allows it to be overwritten if space comes to lack on the disk. Every deleted document on a hard disk can be uncovered for a long period if no specific software has been used to actually overwrite it with blank or random data. Hence, keeping track of information and controlling access to it is generally much more uncertain than in the offline world.

Because of the increased confidentiality concerns in arbitration when electronic means of communication are used, it seems necessary to provide a brief reminder of the legal status of confidentiality in arbitration and what should be done, legally, to ensure it. This is not only, as Ethan Katsh suggests, to address 'the concerns and interests served by confidentiality',[286] i.e., to ensure that the proceedings are indeed private and confidential; it is also a matter of trust in IT usage. In offline settings, the parties can assume from the very context whether transmitted information is treated as confidential or not, because of the organization of the physical premises. But with electronic means of communication, the clues that signal that an environment is secure are more difficult to interpret. Hence, increased attention should be paid to the rules protecting confidentiality, which should be clear and predictable. Generally speaking, it is advisable for an arbitral tribunal to address the issue at the outset of the proceedings, because this will allow it to record the existence and scope of confidentiality and to choose methods of electronic transmission that preserve confidentiality.

---

[285] See Chapter 2, Section II.C.1 Assessing videoconferencing, p. 51 above.

[286] E. Katsh, 'The Online Ombuds Office: Adapting Dispute Resolution to Cyberspace' NCAIR Dispute Resolution Conference <mantle.sbs.umass.edu/vmag/katsh.htm>, Washington, 22 May 1996 ('In a digital world, where copying and communication are intertwined and where anything that appears on screen can be copied and preserved by one party, it may be that it is the concerns and interests served by confidentiality that need to be addressed, and not simply to try to make sure that information is controlled as tightly as it might be in the physical world.')

In order to provide such an overview on confidentiality, this section first reviews its possible sources, i.e., the law and the parties' consent. Then it details the contents of the confidentiality requirement, including the persons bound by the duty and the type of information covered.

A. CONFIDENTIALITY BY VIRTUE OF LAW

Currently, the most internationally relevant national legislations do not provide expressly for a general duty of confidentiality in arbitration.[287] When provisions exist in national legislations, they are in principle limited to some specific aspects of confidentiality.

Some national courts, however, have found that there is an *implied* duty of confidentiality in arbitration. For the Paris Court of Appeal, ruling in *Aita v. Ojjeh*, such a duty is 'in the very nature of arbitral proceedings'.[288] For the English Court of Appeal, in *Dolling-Baker v. Merrett*, the 'nature of arbitration' creates an implied duty of confidentiality, subject to some exceptions.[289]

On the other hand, a US District Court found in *United States v. Panhandle Eastern Corp* that the private nature of commercial arbitration did not create a general obligation of confidentiality.[290] The High Court of Australia followed a similar reasoning in *Esso Australia Resources Ltd v. Plowman*,[291] where it concluded that confidentiality is not an essential attribute of the arbitral procedure, and an arbitration clause does not imply a confidentiality duty. That court then went on to hold that some technical and commercial information should be maintained confidential, but that public interest must sometimes prevail over the parties' interest in maintaining confidentiality.[292]

At any rate, even when it is recognized, there are generally accepted exceptions to the general duty of confidentiality. For instance, courts, arbitrators and even the parties

---

287 A general duty of confidentiality essentially exists under the New Zealand Arbitration Act 1996, art. 14, and the Spanish Arbitration Act 2003, art. 24.

288 Decision of 18 February 1986, [1986] Rev Arb 583, n. Flecheux. The same court was less categorical in *Nafimco v. Foster Wheeler Trading Co AG*, of 22 January 2004.

289 [1990] 1 WLR 1213 (CA). The Court later reaffirmed the *Dolling-Baker* finding in *Ali Shipping v. Shipyard Trogir*, holding that 'confidentiality attaches to arbitration agreements as a matter of law', yet admitting that some exceptions could arise: [1999] 1 WLR 314 (CA).

290 118 FRD 346 (D Del 1988). See also F. Fracassi, 'Confidentiality and NAFTA Chapter 11 Arbitrations' (2001) 2 Chi J Int'l L 213.

291 (1995) 128 ALR 391. See also F. Fracassi, 'Confidentiality and NAFTA Chapter 11 Arbitrations', n. 290 above.

292 *Esso*, n. 291 above, paras 34–35.

themselves may impose disclosure and publicity[293] or national courts may have to intervene to enforce provisional measures or compliance with an arbitral award.[294]

B. Confidentiality by Virtue of the Parties' Agreement

In the absence of legal provisions in this regard, confidentiality in arbitration may also be a creature of contract. If the arbitration agreement or the institutional arbitration rules agreed upon contain an express provision on confidentiality, then there clearly is a requirement of confidentiality. But what if neither the arbitration agreement nor the procedural rules expressly provide for such a requirement?

A number of commentators maintain that some general duty of confidentiality is implied in every arbitration agreement. The precise scope of this duty, however, is usually left undefined.[295] By contrast, others consider that there is no such duty in the absence of any provision in this regard, and that such a duty does not even exist if the parties' arbitration agreement contains a clause requiring the proceedings to be conducted 'in private'.[296] Still others hold an intermediary position, arguing that since the parties have the option of agreeing that their arbitration process be confidential, a legal requirement of confidentiality does only exists if they have expressly so chosen.[297] Hence, generally speaking, parties seeking confidentiality would be well advised to include a clear confidentiality clause in the arbitration agreement or choose an institution whose procedural rules contain a clear provision to this effect.

The procedural rules of all major arbitration institutions do contain a provision on confidentiality, but the degree of confidentiality required varies depending on the institution.[298] Most institutions regulate the issue of confidentiality only partly. Mainly, they require the 'confidentiality of the arbitration'; provide for the private nature of the hearings, meaning that persons not involved in the proceedings may not attend; and impose a duty of confidentiality on the institution and the arbitral tribunal.[299] This suggests that the

---

293 A.C. Brown, 'Presumption Meets Reality: An Exploration of the Confidentiality Obligation in International Commercial Arbitration' (2001) 16 Am U Int'l L Rev 969, pp. 970–71.

294 J. Rosell, 'Global Development: Confidentiality and Arbitration' (2002) 9 Croat Arbit Yearb 19, p. 20.

295 See further J. Paulsson and N. Rawding, 'The Trouble with Confidentiality' (1995) 11 *Arbitration International* 303 and Y. Fortier, 'The Occasionally Unwarranted Assumption of Confidentiality' (1999) 15 *Arbitration International* 131, p. 132 and 138.

296 F. Fracassi, 'Confidentiality and NAFTA Chapter 11 Arbitrations', n. 290 above.

297 E.C. Chiasson, 'Confidentiality and Arbitration' (2000) 58 *Advocate* 417.

298 For an overview of this variance, see, for example, M. Collins, 'Privacy and Confidentiality in Arbitration Proceedings' (1995) 30 Tex Int'l L J 121. See also H. Smit, 'Breach of Confidentiality as a Ground for Avoidance of the Arbitration Agreement' (2000) 11 Am Rev Int'l Arb 567.

299 See, e.g., the International Arbitration Rules of the AAA, art. 20(4); the ICC Rules of Arbitration, art. 21(3), and the Rules Appendix II, art. 1(3)–(6); the Arbitration Rules of the

parties should consider completing the procedural rules, either through a more specific arbitration agreement, or by requesting a procedural order to this effect from the arbitral tribunal.

Further determining how complete the duty of confidentiality is, or defining how such completion may be achieved, should consider two aspects: on the one hand, who is bound by the duty of confidentiality and, on the other hand, what information is covered by such a duty. These two aspects of the duty of confidentiality form the substance of the following sections.

B. Who is Bound by the Duty of Confidentiality?

The duty of confidentiality in arbitration may concern four types of participants in arbitral proceedings. The most obvious holders of a duty of confidentiality are the arbitrators. Nevertheless, only a few national legislations expressly provide for a duty of confidentiality on their part,[300] but other countries clearly provide for such a duty on an indirect basis, deriving from the contractual relationship of the arbitrators with the parties.[301] The matter is better regulated by the arbitration institutions, the majority of whose procedural rules impose a duty of confidentiality upon arbitrators.[302]

Second, the parties to arbitration proceedings may also have such a duty. As a matter of fact, very few national legislations prohibit them expressly from making public information regarding an arbitral proceeding or an award rendered in the context of an arbitration proceeding.[303] But, again, in some countries it is generally recognized that the

LCIA, art. 19(4); the Rules of the Arbitration Institute of the Stockholm Chamber of Commerce, art. 20(3); the CIETAC Arbitration Rules, art. 33; the WIPO Arbitration Rules, art. 53(c); the Rules of the Russian ICAC, art. 27; the Règlement pour montants inférieur à € 12.500, art. 18(5), and the Règlement pour montants supérieur à € 12.500, art. 17(5), both of CEPANI. See also the UNCITRAL Arbitration Rules, art. 25(4).

300 So, for instance, the Spanish Arbitration Act, art. 24.

301 So, for example, Switzerland: see A. Jolles and M. Canals de Cediel, 'Confidentiality' in *International Arbitration in Switzerland*, G. Kaufmann-Kohler and B. Stucki (eds) (The Hague, Kluwer Law International, 2004), pp. 93–94.

302 See, e.g., the International Arbitration Rules of the AAA, art. 34; the CIETAC Arbitration Rules, art. 33; the JCAA Commercial Arbitration Rules, r. 40(2); the SCC Arbitration Rules, art. 20(3); the Arbitration Rules of the LCIA, art. 30(2); the Swiss International Arbitration Rules, art. 43; and the WIPO Arbitration Rules, art. 76(a).

303 See the New Zealand Arbitration Act, art. 14, commented by J. Rosell, 'Global Development: Confidentiality and Arbitration', n. 294 above, p. 21. See also the Spanish Arbitration Act, art. 24.

same prohibition is implied under the agreement to arbitrate.[304] The rules of many arbitration institutions require the parties to keep the proceedings confidential.[305]

The third type of participants concerned are the witnesses. The duty of confidentiality of witnesses is only infrequently regulated. Courts in England have interpreted the *Dolling-Baker*[306] case to find an implied duty of confidentiality extending to witness statements.[307] Some arbitration institutions provide rules on this matter.[308]

Fourth, arbitration institutions may also be subject to a duty of confidentiality. Here too, national legislations make in principle no provision in this respect. Some institutions, however, explicitly self-impose a duty of confidentiality.[309]

C. What information is confidential?

To say that an arbitration is confidential is as such imprecise, as not necessarily all information related to the procedure must be kept secret. The extent and even the mere existence of the requirement of confidentiality vary depending on the specific procedural aspect in question. The following reviews the four main aspects of the procedure that may be distinguished in this regard.

The first and most obvious aspect of an arbitration that is confidential is the hearings, which most arbitral institutions provide for in their rules, i.e., they exclude persons not involved in the proceedings.[310]

The second aspect relates to information produced in the course of the proceedings. No general consensus rules the question. Some national courts have held that there is no general obligation of confidentiality with regard to such information,[311] while others have

---

304 This is for instance the case in Switzerland: see A. Jolles and M. Canals de Cediel, 'Confidentiality', n. 301 above, p. 100.

305 See, e.g., the Arbitration Rules of the LCIA, art. 30(1); the WIPO Arbitration Rules, art. 73, 74(a), and 75; the Swiss International Arbitration Rules, art. 43; the CIETAC Arbitration Rules, art. 33; the JCAA Commercial Arbitration Rules, r. 40(2).

306 *Dolling-Baker*, n. 289 above.

307 *Hassneh Insurance Co of Israel v. Steuart J. Mew* [1993] 2 Lloyd's Rep. 243 (QB), *at* 246.

308 See the CIETAC Arbitration Rules, art. 33; the Spanish Court of Arbitration New Rules, art. 9; the WIPO Arbitration Rules, art. 74(b); and the Swiss International Arbitration Rules, art. 43, which relates to tribunal-appointed experts.

309 See for instance the CIETAC Arbitration Rules, art. 33; the JCAA Commercial Arbitration Rules, r. 40(2); the SCC Arbitration Rules, art. 9, the Swiss International Arbitration Rules, art. 43; and the WIPO Arbitration Rules, art. 76(a). See also, to some extent, the ICC Rules of Arbitration, Appendix I, art. 6 and the the International Arbitration Rules of the AAA, art. 34.

310 For examples, see n. 299 above.

311 See *United States v. Panhandle Eastern Corp*, 11 FRD 346 (D Del 1998); *Esso*, n. 291 above; and the decision of the Svea Court of Appeal in *A.I. Trade Finance Inc. v. Bulgarian Foreign Trade Bank*, of 30 March 1999, [1999] 4 Mealey's Int'l Arb Rep A-1. See also F. Fracassi, 'Confidentiality and NAFTA Chapter 11 Arbitrations', n. 290 above, pp. 214–215; H. Smit,

found a 'duty of confidentiality [that] attaches to arbitration agreements as a matter of law' and includes 'pleadings, written submissions, and the proofs of witnesses as well as transcripts and notes of the evidence given in the arbitration'.[312] It is the general view of commentators that the documents produced in arbitration proceedings are confidential[313] and this view is reflected in the rules of several arbitration institutions.[314] Against this background of confidentiality, two exceptions emerge. First, it is generally recognized that a court in a subsequent proceeding may order a party to produce documents from an earlier arbitration.[315] Second, a party may disclose evidence introduced in a pending arbitration when doing so to protect a legal right.[316]

The duty of confidentiality may also relate to the arbitral procedure itself. There is, here again, no consensus among national laws and courts on the extent of details that may or may not be disclosed, and even as to whether the mere existence of arbitration proceedings must in principle be kept confidential.[317] Not many institutional rules require parties to keep the details of the existence of arbitral proceedings confidential.[318] In any case, an exception to any such duty of confidentiality is recognized where parties have a legal obligation to disclose the existence of the proceedings, for example to insurers or the stock exchange.[319]

Finally, the aspect of arbitration that is least subject to confidentiality is the award. As a general rule, the publication of an arbitral award is not a breach of a duty of confidentiality,[320] at least if information that could identify the parties is deleted. Publication serves important public interests such as encouraging arbitrators to take greater care in drafting awards, because they will be open to public scrutiny; contributing to the development of the law, including the *lex mercatoria*; and enabling practitioners to cite prior

---

'Breach of Confidentiality as a Ground for Avoidance of the Arbitration Agreement', n. 298 above, p. 567.

312 See *Ali Shipping*, n. 289 above, pp. 651–52. See also A.C. Brown, 'Presumption Meets Reality', n. 293 above, p. 969.

313 C. Müller, 'La confidentialité en arbitrage commercial international: un trompe-l'œil?' (2005) 23 ASA Bull 217, p. 227.

314 See the Arbitration Rules of the LCIA, art. 30(1); the WIPO Arbitration Rules, art. 74 and 76(a); the CIETAC Arbitration Rules, art. 33; the International Arbitration Rules of the AAA, art. 34; and the Spanish Court of Arbitration New Rules, art. 9.

315 A.C. Brown, 'Presumption Meets Reality', n. 293 above, p. 1005.

316 Ibid.

317 C. Müller, 'La confidentialité en arbitrage commercial international: un trompe-l'œil?', n. 313 above, p. 226.

318 See the WIPO Arbitration Rules, art. 73.

319 A.C. Brown, 'Presumption Meets Reality', n. 293 above, p. 1003.

320 Only the New Zealand Arbitration Act 1994 prohibits parties from disclosing any information regarding an arbitral award: see J. Rosell, 'Global Development: Confidentiality and Arbitration', n. 294 above, p. 19 and A.C. Brown, 'Presumption Meets Reality', n. 293 above, p. 1012.

decisions, thus ensuring a consistent application and development of the law.[321] Unlike national laws, most institutional rules make publication subject to the parties' consent.[322]

[321] *Fouchard Gaillard Goldman on International Commercial Arbitration*, n. 241 above, para. 384.
[322] See the International Arbitration Rules of the AAA, art. 27(4); the Arbitration Rules of the LCIA, art. 30; the UNCITRAL Arbitration Rules, art. 32(5); the Swiss International Arbitration Rules, art. 43; and the WIPO Arbitration Rules, art. 75 and 76(a).

CHAPTER 5

PRACTICE GUIDELINES

The preceding chapters have discussed a number of technologies that may be used in relation to arbitration proceedings, explaining how they operate, what their advantages and disadvantages are, in which situations they may best be resorted to, and how they should be used, both from a technical and legal perspective. Drawing on such discussions, this chapter presents guidelines, meant as a convenient reference tool in practice. It is organized based on the main situations in which a practitioner might face questions related to the use of IT in arbitration.

This chapter begins with a review of the most frequent concerns practitioners have with regard to the irruption of IT use in arbitral proceedings, and it suggests, where possible, simple responses to these concerns. The second section sets forth guidelines on the use of e-mails. Indeed, although e-mailing has become an ordinary means of communication for the vast majority of practitioners, the social rules or best practices governing its use are hardly well settled compared to other means of communication. This has the consequence that many slip-ups, resulting in embarrassment if not serious losses in efficiency, could be avoided by defining usage rules. The third section addresses videoconferencing, proposing guidelines for, first, deciding whether a real-life situation is open to videoconferencing; second, preparing a conference to be held through a video linkup; and third, selecting a videoconferencing system. Finally, this chapter provides guidelines to be used to define a protocol for the use of information technology, i.e., a definition of which technologies should be used in which aspects of an arbitration.

I. FREQUENT CONCERNS AND RESPONSES

As in many other areas, a striking difference exists between what the market offers in terms of legal IT capabilities and the extent of their actual use. In the vast majority of cases, this difference can be explained by concerns of potential users. However, these concerns have often already been satisfactorily addressed by either the market, best practices or simply general understanding, essentially in the form of specific ways in which technology should be used, but these responses remain on many occasions unrecognized, misunderstood, or underrated. The issues themselves are frequently overrated too. Hence, this section sets out to discuss, in a practice-oriented fashion, the most frequent concerns of legal practitioners in relation to the use of electronic communication technologies in arbitral proceedings.

Most legal practitioners, when advised to implement some IT solution in their practice, voice the following concerns:

- first, electronic communications create a particularly important risk of security breaches;
- second, technology is unreliable and usually breaks down at the most inconvenient time;
- third, faking identities is relatively easy on the Internet and consequently it may be difficult to trust the authenticity of a message; and
- fourth, professionals have their working habits and are afraid that changing them to adapt to IT may decrease their productivity.

These considerations form, in turn, the substance of the following paragraphs, which seek to identify the origin of the concerns, to assess their true meaning and put them into perspective, and to suggest solutions.

A. Security

Here is an example of the typical attitude of a lawyer towards technology. Many law schools are equipped with shared printers, which are located in rooms that are oftentimes not locked and thus easily accessible to students. Some professors, when preparing their exams with the help of their assistants, insist on the fact that the exams are not sent by e-mail among them, convinced as they are that students could easily intercept the message; rather, the files are transmitted on floppy disks or USB keys. But then, sometimes, the draft exams are printed out and left sitting on the shared printers for several hours or even half a day, free to be picked up by whomever passes by.

Here is another such example. Some law firms forbid their practitioners to save any file on their desk computers or on the local server, insisting instead that they use the firm's virtual private network, i.e., an encrypted remote computer network, for fear of hackers intruding into one of the local computers or servers. Hacking into the firm's files on this network would indeed be truly difficult. But most practitioners need to take files with them, to work on at home or while traveling. On such occasions, it is not infrequent for a lawyer to download all the files pertaining to a case onto a laptop, which is usually not access-protected, and is sometimes even left in a gym locker, beneath a chair in a bar, or in a car in a public parking lot, all places where thefts are common.

Here is a third example, which does not relate specifically to lawyers: many reports on consumer behavior on the Net show that one of the greatest concerns of online consumers is a misuse of their credit card number – this is even one of the current main obstacles to the development of e-commerce. But in the offline world, people give their credit card numbers away frequently in totally unprotected situations without a second thought (in shabby restaurants on remote Greek islands, to pick an example at random – it always takes much thought to pick wisely at random).

In sum, most people are more concerned about security in cyberspace than in the 'real world'. There are several explanations. On the one hand, most people are confused by the apparent complexity of computers, which seem to 'behave' in unpredictable ways and are thereby associated with risk and the sense of lacking control. On the other hand, common knowledge about computer security is much lower than the general understanding of security in the 'real world', because concerns relating to the latter have been around for much longer. In addition, this lack of knowledge and this sense of lacking control are fueled by two more factors. First, hacking is a feat (in computer science, a standard term for a successful security breach is actually 'exploit'), while breaking into a house or stealing a laptop in a parking lot is nothing to write home about. News items and movies featuring hacking exploits reinforce the idea that electronic communications, but also electronic data storage, are fundamentally insecure. Second, the Internet security industry has become one of the most successful IT-related sectors, making it economically important for Internet users' security concerns to remain.

Concretely, such security concerns may be considered to relate to two main aspects: the transmission of information (which corresponds to the risk of interception) and its storage (related to the risk of intrusion).

1. Interception

From a technical point of view, two main situations pertaining to data interception must be distinguished, because they involve partly different technologies and techniques: e-mail interception on the one hand, and Web-based information transmissions (i.e., Internet surfing) on the other.

a. E-mail interception

It is often considered that a standard, unencrypted e-mail is not more secure than a postcard. In a sense, this is technically correct, as all those who have the e-mail in their 'hands' are in principle able to read its contents. It should not, however, be misunderstood to mean that anyone could intercept any e-mail communication. This would be exaggerated to the point of being wrong, although it is what many people believe. The reality is that an e-mail can basically only be intercepted at two points, the two points where people have the e-mail in the 'hands': nodes and the end users' computers.

Nodes

The first possible point of interception of e-mails is the nodes through which an e-mail transits (or rather, in technical parlance, the 'supernodes', which are the parts of a computer network that actively route data). All e-mails that are not purely internal to a corporate network travel through a relatively high number of nodes such as servers, systems, and network devices, which all constitute possible points of interception. Some of these nodes, but not all, are indicated in the header of each e-mail – more precisely in the full version of the header, as most e-mail programs hide this information by default for convenience. Roughly simplified, these nodes play a role equivalent to mailmen and all other persons handling mail in the postal system. An unencrypted e-mail passing through these nodes is similar to a postcard going through the postal system: for everyone having access to one of these nodes, an e-mail is as easily readable as a postcard, using a simple hacker technique called packet sniffing.

The question that arises then is whether these persons are interested in actually taking advantage of their ability to intercept the e-mail to which they have access. To answer it, one should first think about what these nodes actually consist of, in terms not of technical devices, but of organizations or individuals. There are four main types of such nodes:

- *Internet Service Providers (ISP)*: the entity providing access to the Internet (and related services such as domain name registration and hosting) has particularly easy access to the information that travels through its system. There was indeed a case in 1999, largely reported in newspapers at the time, of a San Francisco ISP that intercepted e-mails of one of its customers, namely Amazon.com, and transmitted them to a competitor.
- *E-mail providers*: traditionally, most people's e-mail address is provided by their ISP, but with the growing number of e-mail addresses each person uses and the development of attractive substitute e-mail providers, this tends to be less true. This offers a new point of interception, because these e-mail providers have access to the data that transits through their systems, in a similar fashion as ISPs.
- *Corporate networks*: e-mails sent from an office travel across the corporate network. Sometimes the network itself plays the role of an ISP, but not necessarily; if it does not, the e-mail goes first through the network and then through the servers of the ISP. In any event, a message may be intercepted within the network by system administrators and security officers, for example, but also by other employees who manage to break into the system. Breaking into the system from a computer directly connected to the corporate network may in fact be relatively easy, depending on the security measures implemented by the system administrators. Sometimes it is sufficient to run a simple program, called a packet sniffer, on one's own computer to intercept e-mail traffic. It may be added that hotel or conference center networks, or the systems of an Internet café, are generally even less secure than a corporate network.
- *Local loop*: most Internet traffic travels through a shared physical set of wires, also used for telephone services and possibly cable television. Such wires may be tapped, though such an action is obviously much more complicated than e-mail snooping at one of the other nodes mentioned above.

As to the likelihood that e-mail interception indeed occurs, in principle most of these nodes are commercial enterprises, which have a strong interest in respecting the privacy of the e-mails that transit through their system. Corporate networks also have a strong incentive not to interfere and not to allow interference in communications. Nevertheless, renegade employees may for instance act in retaliation against their employer – such actions have occurred in the past.

In addition, most governments now have the capabilities to intervene at one of these nodes, and it has happened many times that the 'cyberpolice' in repressive countries have arrested political dissidents on the basis of an intercepted e-mail. If these capabilities are considered in light of the fact that governments sometimes go as far as kidnapping arbitrators in order to influence the outcome of an arbitration procedure, it becomes sensible to consider security measures when e-mails are sent to and from problematic countries.[323]

End users' computers

The second possible point of interception of an e-mail is the sender and recipient's computers. Interception can be either manual (by far the most frequent occurrence) or by way of software.

Intrusion by software consists of installing, on the targeted computer, bugging software which surreptitiously monitors the user. Such software, generally called spyware, typically operates by what is called 'keystroke logging', i.e., it records and transmits all or specific keystrokes. Such installation can be achieved by two ways. First, it may be done by physically sitting in front of the computer in question and, using a disk or USB drive, copying the bugging software onto the computer's hard disk, possibly booting from an external disk in order to circumvent access protections. Second, a keylogger may be transmitted electronically, for example as a Trojan horse or a virus, which may be contained in an e-mail attachment. The keylogger then installs itself on the targeted computer. The FBI famously used a keylogger transmitted as a Trojan horse (specially customized in order to elude usual protection software) to obtain an access code of a person who was transmitting sensitive information in encrypted form, which the FBI could not otherwise read. As a confirmation of the ease of breaking into the sender and recipient's computer, a team of researchers from the University of California, Berkeley, recently showed how a ten-dollar piece of electronic equipment could be used to sniff out any form of data entry using a keyboard, simply by recording the sounds keystrokes make.[324]

Manual intrusion means stealing a login and password in order to log into the computer's usual resources (e-mail server, shared disk). This may be achieved either from afar or by physically breaking into the room containing the computer and finding, for instance, a post-it under the keyboard or in a drawer with the login and password. A hardware keylogger may also be used, i.e., a device connected to the keyboard cable which logs keystrokes.

---

323 On such security measures, see Section I.A.D. Encrypting and digitally signing e-mail, p. 158 below and Section 4. In practice: setting up encrypted and digitally-signed e-mail, p. 163 below.

324 See L. Zhuang, F. Zhou, and J. D. Tygar, 'Keyboard Acoustic Emanations Revisited' <www.cs.berkeley.edu/%7Etygar/papers/Keyboard_Acoustic_Emanations_Revisited/preprint.-pdf> (Berkeley, University of California, November 2005).

Assessment and responses

In sum, there certainly are security threats, but it seems rather clear that the likelihood of e-mail interception is rather low, comparable to the risk of interception of paper correspondence. In this context, one should recall that no correspondence is perfectly secure, not even in the real world and that it therefore seems unreasonable to worry excessively about the security of electronic communications. In other words, the previous paragraphs are not meant to increase the security paranoia that often exists in relation to electronic environments, but merely to explain where the main risks arise. These main risks, identified above, call for the following three types of security measures.

(a) The most basic and obvious set of measures is the implementation of the same security solutions as those used for physical documents. Concretely, this means protecting the physical access to one's personal computer, which should be considered to be an inherently confidential object. A laptop should typically not be left in a gym locker or beneath a chair in a bar.

(b) Standard computer user safety recommendations provide a second set of measures to reduce security risks. Such recommendations include for instance:

- Not to open any e-mail attachment if the sender is unknown, because this may launch an application installing spyware or a virus, which may contain a keylogger.
- To ensure that all computers one uses are equipped with high quality and up-to-date anti-virus and anti-spyware tools.
- If possible, to avoid using software products that have a high number of known security loopholes or that are targeted by virus and spyware producers, such as Microsoft applications (Microsoft Outlook, in particular, can easily be replaced by other applications, which are more secure and just as powerful). The vast majority of spyware and viruses are designed to take advantage of Microsoft security loopholes, because anti-Microsoft behavior is prevalent among virus and spyware writers.
- To dedicate professional computers exclusively to professional use, as deceptive applications are often downloaded in the context of peer-to-peer file swapping or while visiting not strictly professional websites.
- All these recommendations only truly make sense if they are followed by all the users of a specific computer, which leads to the additional recommendation to strictly monitor access to the computer in question. Do your children, for instance, sometimes use one of the computers you also use for work? This computer may be the floodgate to infecting your other computers as you transfer files from this computer to them.

(c) If more security is desired, one may resort to the following solutions:

- Protect documents with password-restricted access: many word processors provide a function allowing the encryption of a document and password-restricted access to it. A document can then be sent without concerns for security, regardless of the trans-

mission channel. The password should then be conveyed separately over another channel, which is considered more secure – telephone, fax, registered letter, etc. In Microsoft Word, for instance, this function is turned on at 'File / Save as / Tools / General options'. Pdf documents can also be password-protected, for instance using Adobe Acrobat Professional, which features a command 'Document / Protection', which offers many document protection functions. Other pdf editors, some of which are available for free (e.g., PDFCreator), achieve very similar results.
- Use encrypted e-mails, which may be acquired quite easily and installed for free.[325]

b. Web-based transmissions interception

Web-based transmissions may, just as e-mails, be intercepted at any node, and in particular by anyone within the same local network (hotel, corporate network, etc.). But such transmissions are usually protected by encryption, in situations where sensitive information is being transmitted, using the Secure Sockets Layer protocol (SSL). SSL, introduced in 1994, is the main protocol used to encrypt, and thus protect from interception, communications over the Internet between a server and a user. In principle, SSL could constitute a security layer for almost any communication protocol used to transmit data over the Internet, including the Simple Mail Transfer Protocol (or smtp) used for e-mails. In practice however, it is most frequently used in relation to the submission of confidential information by the user in the context of Internet browsing. In this case, SSL is used with the standard Web-browsing protocol called the HyperText Transmission Protocol (http) to form https, the more complete protocol used to secure Web pages for applications such as e-commerce when data like credit card numbers are submitted. One may recognize a secure Web page by the fact that its address begins with 'https' instead of 'http' and that a padlock icon is displayed at the bottom of the page.

When a Web page is SSL-secure, this means that the user's browser will encrypt the data (resorting to encryption of up to 256 bit, which is currently considered to be unbreakable) using a code provided by the server (called a public key). It is incumbent upon website builders to provide for such security measures. The user cannot do much but verify that no sensitive information is transmitted to a website whose address does not begin with 'https'.

Other instances of use are file uploading and downloading from distant servers, creating Virtual Private Networks or VPNs (private and secure communications networks built into the public network that is the Internet), and also interactions between an e-mail program and the server it is using (the retrieval and sending of e-mails is secure between the user's computer and the e-mail server).

---

325 See Section II.D. Encrypting and digitally signing e-mail, p. 158 below and Section II.D.4. In practice: setting up encrypted and digitally-signed e-mail, p. 163 below.

In addition to securing communications with a server to prevent eavesdropping, SSL also authenticates the website to which one submits information, or more precisely the server of the website. This authentication helps prevent fake websites from easily harvesting confidential information that a trusting user would submit. This authentication takes the form of an SSL certificate, which can be viewed by double-clicking on the padlock displayed at the bottom of the browser's window. Such a certificate looks like this:

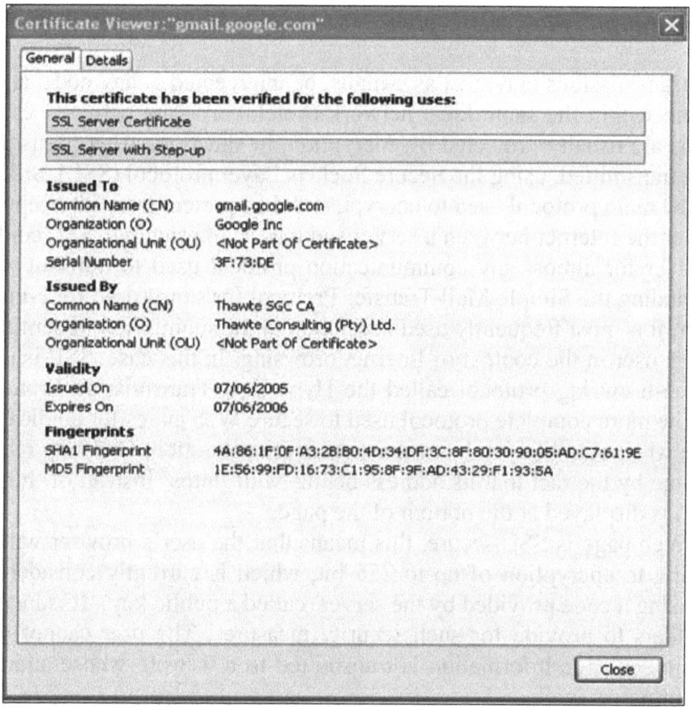

Figure 27. Google SSL certificate

When a certificate authenticates a website, it proves that the site belongs to whom it says it belongs. For this purpose, the certificate contains information about the certificate holder (Google Inc. in the example above), the certificate issuer (Thawte in the instance above), and the certificate itself, in relation to the periods of its validity for instance.

Most certificates are issued by trusted third parties and must be paid for. However, it is also possible to create one's own certificate and to 'self-sign' it. Such a self-signed SSL certificate provides the same technical protection against interception, i.e., it encrypts the communications in the same way as a third-party certificate would. Of course, it does not authenticate the website in a trustworthy manner. In most browsers, self-signed certificates trigger a warning message indicating that the certificate was not recognized, but most people are not stopped by such a message, just as they are not stopped by a window warning that a third-party certificate has expired. Self-signed certificates are sometimes used for websites that are essentially for Internet traffic within a corporation, typically for the site of a company's webmail.

2. Intrusion

The protection against intrusion into data storage systems (of which e-mail servers are one instance) and other applications is in principle a matter for professional system administrators. The diversity of hacking strategies and security mechanisms that have been developed in response to them is too great and changes too quickly to be presented here. Nevertheless, it may be useful to briefly point out the two basic technical properties that are used to secure access to systems and applications: authentication and accounting.

a. Authentication

Authentication is in essence the process by which a user provides information that is in principle only available to him to identify himself to the system. The most common authentication mechanism on the Internet today is simply to log into a system using a username and password. Under some circumstances however, passwords may be stolen as they are transmitted across networks, and badly chosen passwords can be guessed. There are other, stronger authentication systems. The following outlines the functioning, advantages, and issues of the three main types of authentication systems, namely passwords, access tokens, and biometric systems (i.e., systems relying on fingerprint or retina scans).

Passwords

Many computer science studies, conducted at different times during the last decades, have consistently shown that approximately 40 to 50 per cent of user-chosen passwords can be readily guessed.[326] This ease of guessing password is the consequence of two factors: first, people often badly choose their passwords, typically favoring obvious ones because they are easier to remember and, second, there are many effective currently available instruments for cracking password protection.

Examples of badly chosen passwords are typically:[327]

---

[326] See 'Password' entry on Wikipedia, paragraph 'Likelihood that a password can be guessed' and entry 'Password cracking', paragraph 'Dictionary attack'.

[327] See further, ibid.

- Those constituted of less than seven characters, as current computers are fast enough to try all combinations of that length – provided the password program allows such highly repeated trials.
- Those constituted of personal information (name of family member or friend, birthday, place of birth, preferred holiday destination, maiden name, licence plate number, phone number, login name, etc.), as they can be guessed.
- Those frequently used for their extreme convenience of use, such as 'password', a blank entry, a row of letters from the keyboard, etc.
- Those constituted of words that can be found in a list, typically in a dictionary, as a computer can automatically go through all entries of an electronic dictionary – provided, again, that the password program allows such highly repeated trials.
- A default password that come with a computer security program, as lists of such passwords may be found on the Net.[328]
- Those created by a password generator, because such generators use routines, making the results predictable.

Other common security flaws related to passwords are for instance to write down passwords in order to store them in a convenient place – some people even save lists of passwords on their computers.

Based on the above, the following password policy is recommended:

- Favor password programs that do not allow many tries without a long period between trials.
- Use at least 8 characters combining letters, numbers, and special characters, which together form a phrase without meaning.
- Change passwords frequently.

Access token

An access token is a security device that normally attaches to a COM port of a computer (USB or serial port, for instance) which, when used in conjunction with appropriate software or hardware, allows authorized access to a given system running on the computer in question. The most common examples include smart cards and smart card readers.

A smart card is a plastic card normally the size and shape of a traditional credit card, but including a microprocessor and a user interface. A smart card communicates with a computer through a smart card reader. Information stored on the chip of the card is difficult to duplicate or disrupt, unlike the information stored on magnetic stripe cards. However, it should be noted that they are not secure against laboratory attacks. The cost of a card depends on the chip's capacity and its capabilities.

An access token can also be a small device producing new temporary passwords at regular intervals (every few minutes, for instance), in synchronicity with the system run-

[328] See for instance the impressive list at <www.phenoelit.de/dpl/dpl.html>.

ning on the computer to which access is sought. Thus, to access the system on the computer, it is necessary to provide the login ID as well as the password produced at that precise moment by the external device. The level of protection of such a device is quite high since the password changes at short time intervals. An intruder will need the login ID, the access token, and the password to the access token. A variation thereof is a device, usually in a form similar to a calculator, which generates a password on the basis of a number given for each new login by the website, following a complex and unidentifiable algorithm.

Biometrics
Biometrics is an increasingly important method of authentication.[329] The primary areas of biometric technology are:

- face recognition;
- fingerprints;
- hand geometry;
- iris recognition;
- palm prints;
- retina pattern;
- signature;
- voice.

Other areas for authentication are currently being researched and include body odors (the chemical pattern created by human body smell), ear shape (the shape and structure of the ear), as well as keystroke dynamics (individual human typing rhythms and characteristics).

Such devices may give the impression that they are more adapted to Mission Impossible movies than to ordinary legal procedures, but in reality they have become easy to acquire, install and use. The more common biometric technologies can nowadays be run on devices costing approximately USD 100.

b. Accounting

Accounting (also called 'logging') is the process of monitoring and tracking the operations of a given system and the behavior of the users of such systems. Such processes are used, for instance, to verify if someone is trying to break into a system or to misuse it. Accounting can for instance reveal unusual usage patterns, which may indicate that a

---

[329] For examples, see ib-IS (iButton - Biometric Integration System) <db.maxim-ic.com/ibutton/-solutions/product.cfm?ID=341> and Ruggedized Biometric Readers <db.maxim-ic.com/ibutton/solutions/product.cfm?ID=430>.

password has been stolen, that attackers have found vulnerability in a system, or that a previously well-behaved user (for instance an employee who has just learnt that he was laid off) has had a change of heart.

Hence, an essential component of a secure application is a thorough monitoring and tracking mechanism, i.e., one that automatically provides detailed information about the following elements:

- attempts to compromise the security of the system (for example attempts to log in by guessing passwords);
- successful intrusions by hackers, misuse and abuse of the system by legitimate users or cheaters; and
- if possible, an automated check of the log files and automated reporting of suspicious activities.

For users who are not professionals but would like to take some security measures themselves, an accessible way is to acquire intrusion detection software such as Tripwire.[330] Such systems monitor changes in the software installed on a server and set off an alarm if it is being tampered with.

3. Infection

The risk of infection, i.e., for a computer or an entire network to be affected by a virus or a Trojan horse, constitutes a serious threat. It is a threat both to confidentiality, because those technologies are frequently used to access protected data,[331] and to the storage of data, in the sense that such data may be exposed to destruction by infection. When infection occurs, it is usually due to a lack of security. Hence, the following reviews the main forms of infection, explains in a few words how the related technologies operate, and suggests simple solutions to reduce the risk of infection.

a. Viruses

A virus is a program, i.e., text instructing a computer to perform given actions, that infects a computer. It is well known that viruses are the source of major problems and can cause huge financial losses. In recent years, famous viruses have made the headlines for causing major problems to the business community. Recent surveys state that only 83 per cent of Internet users use an anti-virus application, and of those, only 73 per cent update it regularly, which means than just slightly more than 60 per cent of Internet users are

---

[330] See <www.tripwire.com>.

[331] See paragraph End users' computers, p. 135 above.

correctly protected against viruses.[332] This is a significant issue if one considers that viruses caused some USD 55 billion in losses to companies in 2003, admittedly one of the worst recent years in terms of virus matters.[333]

A virus can affect a computer in different ways, such as removing files, altering its content, reconfiguring or overwhelming a system, or displaying a graphic content and blocking all other form of access to the computer. It has the ability to copy itself into a system without specific instructions in that respect from the user or the operating system. There are different ways in which that duplication can take place, the most important of which being simple scripts (i.e., very small programs) run when loading a Web page, reading an e-mail, or opening a file created by ordinary applications. Nowadays the most common and dangerous types of virus are the mass mailing viruses that access a user's address book and e-mail themselves to the contacts contained in it using the same e-mail system, thus causing recipients to believe that the e-mail is safe. Viruses can be activated in different ways: just by executing the application, or automatically on a certain date, or with a certain event.

In most situations, three main rules should be followed to strongly reduce the risk of infection by viruses:

- Do not execute or open any file whose origin or name is unexpected.
- Run a regularly updated anti-virus program.
- Activate a firewall (which is typically achieved, in Windows XP, by following the path Start / Network connections / Connection to local network / Right-click on Properties / Advanced / Settings).

Macro viruses, however, deserve special consideration. A macro is a script set to automate repetitive actions in certain programs, in particular word processors, spreadsheets, and datasheets. Typical legitimate actions that a macro executes are formatting, performing advanced 'search and replace' tasks in text files, or linking cells in spreadsheets. Typical illegitimate actions that a macro executes are, unfortunately, viruses. A Microsoft Word user should be aware that this application is very vulnerable to viruses, since its macro language is very simple (which is otherwise an advantage for the end user) and the application is used by an extremely large number of people throughout the world.

The main advisable security measures for macro viruses could be summarized as follows:

- A radical solution is to require all correspondents to send only documents in rtf format. Indeed, in principle, rtf files do not contain macros and they can be read and

---

332 See, e.g., A. Kandra and A. Brandt, 'The Great American Privacy Makeover', PCWorld Magazine <www.pcworld.com/reviews/article/0,aid,112468,pg,1,00.asp>, November 2003, p. 3.

333 See Reuters, 'PC viruses spawn $55 billion loss in 2003' <news.zdnet.com/2100-1009_22-5142144.html>, 16 January 2004.

created by any word processor, following a very simple procedure (Save as / set 'File type' to rtf). Generally, rtf files are much less likely to contain a virus. But they are only *less likely* to do so; it is not at all impossible for them to contain a macro virus. Indeed, some such viruses disguise a doc file as a rtf file; hence the sender would think he had created a secure rtf file, while the document is in fact an infected doc file. The only way to ascertain that a given file is indeed an rtf document is to open it with the Notepad application as an ascii text. If it is a real rtf file, its first line will start with '\rtf'. A supplemental problem with rtf files is that they do not save all the formatting elements a doc file contains. Hence, conversion to rtf may seriously alter the presentation of the contents of a file.

- Another solution, less demanding for correspondents, is to open doc files with a viewer, such as the Notepad application just mentioned. Such viewers typically do not activate macros yet allow displaying the document's contents. This solution requires no special action on the part of the correspondents. However, here again, the drawback is formatting, as the document viewer may not show the contents of the document in exactly the format in which it was saved.
- A partial solution, which has no disadvantages but does not provide perfect security against macro viruses, is to systematically refuse to activate macros when prompted to do so by the word processor. It does not provide perfect protection because word processors may fail to prompt the user and activate macros without warning.
- In any event, an up-to-date anti-virus program should always be run.

In sum, what seems the most advisable and practicable is to comply strictly with the last two proposals (do not activate macros when prompted to do so and run an up-to-date anti-virus), and to implement the other two solutions (using a document viewer and requesting rtf files) only in situations implying serious security risks, such as being sent unexpected documents or if harm can be expected from a given sender. In addition, one should remember to always make regular backups. This at least limits the amount of information that a virus can destroy permanently.

b. Trojan horses

A Trojan horse, in computer science parlance, is akin to a virus, but it does not have, in principle, the ability to replicate and thus to spread itself. In addition, it is not hidden: just as the real Greeks' Trojan horse of the Trojan wars, it looks like a legitimate, useful or at least harmless device, but in reality its purpose is malicious. Trojan horses are usually set up as a useful program performing some desired function, which is there only to serve as a camouflage for the real, malevolent function of the program. These malicious functions typically, but not necessarily, consist of spying, and more precisely of 'packet sniffing'.

A packet sniffer, in the sense used here, taps into the data stream in and out of a computer. All or part of this data may then be decoded and reconstructed into files, or it may more simply (and often more efficiently) be scanned for passwords. The main problem with a packet or password sniffer is the difficulty of detecting it since it does not change anything on the user's system; it just logs. It might be manually detected, though, by experimented technicians, as the presence of a sniffer might be revealed by a higher number of logs. But no programs currently exist to protect a system against sniffers. The only method to fight against this menace is to modify passwords frequently and to be sure that they always travel through an SSL-encrypted network.

B. Breakdowns

Another frequently expressed concern is that technology may cease to work precisely at the moment when it is needed the most. Here the concern often matches concrete complaints based on personal experience: who indeed has not experienced a computer, a network access, a printer, or more simply a photocopier crashing or breaking shortly before an important deadline? And it is true: technological systems break down, time and again, no matter how careful one is.

Many reports, published in newspapers, in scientific articles or in books on management,[334] carried out in different countries and in different business sectors, consistently show that, all in all, five to ten per cent of the global time of work is lost due to problems with technology and computers in particular. This unproductive time, which is in principle more than compensated by efficiency advantages gained through technology, is of course not only due to technical failures (it can also be caused by a user's inability to make a specific application work, or the waiting time for a connection or a printer), but no doubt these amount to a significant part thereof.

In addition, the heavier the reliance on technology, or in other words the more important the computer resources used, the higher the chances of a breakdown, as the technology is more in demand and the user is more likely to make mistakes when accomplishing technically complex tasks.

Nevertheless, this is a not an issue without a solution. The three following types of measures may significantly reduce the concerns related to a possible technical failure at the worst time.

Redundancy

One night in 1986, power plant operators in the Ukraine turned off the main cooling system of a nuclear reactor. Their aim was to test the plant's safety systems, and more precisely to verify how well the backup cooling system worked. It turned out the backup system did not work, but the engineers had turned off the main system in such a way that it could not be quickly reactivated. The coolant overheated and the reactor rapidly became unstable. As safety regulations had been grossly ignored that night in the town of Pripyat, where the Chernobyl station was located, the reactor's power spiraled out of

[334] See for instance, among many references, L. Bellenger and M.-J. Couchaere, *Plus efficace et moins stressé* (Issy-les-Moulineaux, ESF, 2004).

control. The reactor's core melted, releasing radiation that spread across the former Soviet Union, Europe and Eastern North America. What was arguably the worst engineering catastrophe in history occurred because the plant had ceased to operate under a fault-tolerant design once Chernobyl's main cooling system had been shut down. A fault-tolerant design is one in which the important equipment is redundant, i.e. duplicate. For instance, airplanes have most of their technical equipment in duplicate (and often actually in triplicate), because a technical deficiency must not affect their flying capabilities. Cars have spare tires, because punctures are inevitable. IT systems should follow the same principle.

Technical failures and breakdowns are actually an issue of availability, and the usual solution to availability issues is to have another system ready to fulfill the task that the defective system should have handled. All the important parts of technical equipment should have backups. Specifically, this means that one should always have, if relying on technology for certain actions, another computer available, preferably a spare that resembles the original as much as possible. A typical way of organizing this is to acquire two identical computers, one for usual use and one for backup, and to make regularly (for instance every few days) an electronic image of everything contained on the 'main' computer's hard disk. Programs such as Acronis TrueImage[335] or Norton Ghost[336] can do this with a single mouse click and in only a few minutes. This image may then be uploaded onto the backup computer, again within only a few minutes, to create a clone of the first computer.

In addition, all important files should preferably also be accessible from two sources, for instance from a shared hard disk and from a personal disk. In professional data storage environments, the shared hard disk, usually accessed over a virtual private network, is backed up every day and is also accessible in another way, for instance over the Web.

Dedication

Using a computer for many different tasks may require installing different software. And programs sometimes conflict, especially if an error occurs during the installation process, preventing the originally installed programs from operating as they did before. Using a computer for different purposes may also require particular configurations, which the user may not know how to cancel when reverting to the original purpose of the machine. Some of the most intrusive forms of applications in this regard are sophisticated computer games and file-sharing programs, but they are not the only ones.

Consequently, it is advisable to dedicate the computers to be used for arbitration to specific purposes. This implies, above all, that the computer should be used only for strictly professional matters. This includes monitoring access to the computer, avoiding for instance that one's children use it. This also implies carefully checking all data imported to this computer, for example if it comes from a source that cannot be trusted

---

[335] See <www.acronis.com>.

[336] See <www.symantec.com>.

completely; this is often the case of home computers, which are usually not professionally managed. Preferably, the data should first be submitted to a virus check on the professional computer or network. One of the most common ways to limit the damaging effect of other users' imprudent actions is to restrict administrator access to the computer, which has the effect of preventing any new application from being installed without the intervention of the administrator.

Testing

Most legal practitioners believe that a computer program, if it is of good quality, should work on the first try, regardless of its complexity and the circumstances. But such an approach to technology is bound to disappoint: it is close to impossible to create software that is completely error-free. Even the best technology developed by the best computer engineers has bugs. And the tiniest of inaccuracies in the code can produce the most dramatic of consequences. Here is a famous example.

July 12th, 1962, 0520 A.M., Cape Canaveral, Florida. NASA is about to send off the first flight of its gigantic Mariner program, which is to be series of unmanned exploratory travels to our neighboring planets, Venus, Mars and Mercury. For the first time in history, a spacecraft is about to fly by another planet. After years spent imagining all possible causes of failure and taking preventive measures, the spacecraft is finally deemed ready. The signal is given, and Mariner 1 takes off majestically. But after a few minutes, it goes into an unscheduled yaw-lift; it veers from its course. It is now headed towards an unavoidable crash, likely to occur in an inhabited area. The flight supervisor has no choice: he pushes the button that will destroy the object of years of obsessive work and dedication. Mariner 1 explodes in mid-air.

What happened? A bug. A tiny error in the computer code. A hyphen was missing in an equation. The best engineers in the world had produced a marvel of technology, but it ended in a fireball because of a single wrong character in a script of gargantuan dimensions.

One thing that should strike the reader is that we lawyers are not used to such error sensitivity and the unpredictability that follows, and thus do not expect it elsewhere. The text of this book – which has been proofread many more times than any legal brief – certainly contains several errors that each would have led any spacecraft to destruction, but that do not in the least affect the quality of legal writing.

The only effective response to technology's error sensitivity and unpredictability is testing. Technology, however amazing, should be tested beforehand in a simulation of the real event. It is obviously not feasible to launch a spacecraft just to see if it works before doing it for real – otherwise NASA would have done it. But one can hold a videoconferencing session to make sure it operates correctly before holding the actual conference. So many factors play a role in technical systems – and this is even more the case with complex technologies such as case management websites and videoconferencing systems – that smooth operations are only a matter of probability, not of certainty. Hence it is highly advisable to take the time, however precious it may be, to test a technology before the actual event. In other words, in the language of Chapter 1, one cannot stress enough the importance of first mastering it, then using it.[337] And once a system works, it should be tampered with as little as possible, it should be dedicated to that specific usage, and it should be created in duplicate.

C. Authentication

One more example drawn from daily life at the University of Geneva: in early summer 2004, a few days before an important final examination, one of the assistants of the professor who was giving the exam received an e-mail saying:

> 'I've a last-minute doubt regarding one question of the exam. As I'm not at home at the moment, I don't have the list of questions with me. Would you be so kind and send it to me again?'

The message was signed with the professor's initials and it was sent from an e-mail address in the form of

> [first name].[last name]@bluewin.ch

Bluewin, it may be specified, is the domain name of a common (and thus unsurprising) commercial e-mail provider in Switzerland.

The assistant prepared the reply, attached the file containing the examination questions, moved the mouse cursor to the 'send' button, prepared to click, and stopped, struck by a sudden suspicion. She picked up the phone and called the professor who was the alleged sender of the message. The professor denied having any question about the examination, having an e-mail address with this provider and having sent any e-mail at all to the assistant during the last hours, let alone having misplaced the list of examination questions. No doubt the real sender of the message, who was of course a student trying to find out the exam questions in advance, was more of a clever technician than a good lawyer…

The saying 'On the Internet, nobody knows you're a dog' captures this issue quite nicely. And indeed, identity theft is one of the main concerns of commercial actors on the Internet.[338] By extension, many lawyers feel a general uneasiness about the issue of authenticating the real sender of a message.

---

[337] See Chapter 1, Section IV.B. Lack of experience: IT as a trump card?, p. 22 above.

[338] ID theft is the use of personal information such as name, credit card number, or any other personal data without the authorization of the concerned person to commit fraud or any other crimes. One may think that ID theft is a rare offense. But in reality, it costs banks approximately USD 1 billion per year: B. Sullivan, 'ID theft costs banks $1 billion a year', MSNBC <msnbc.-msn.com/id/3078480>, 26 March 2003.

Nevertheless, by and large, the issue is overrated. The following seeks to put it into perspective. To do so, it first specifies the issue – it has two different dimensions, which on some occasions require different solutions – and then sets out possible solutions, which are presented in order of increasing complexity.

1. THE ISSUE

The issue of authentication, in a broad sense, corresponds to two questions that may be asked by the recipient of a message. The first question is:

> 'Can I be sure the sender of this message is the person he says he is?'

This is important in the situation where information is requested, expressly or implicitly, by the sender of the message. This is authentication in its strict sense.

The second question is:

> 'Can I be sure the sender of this message will not deny having sent it, as it bears no manuscript signature?'

This is of significance in the situation where the message carries consequences that may be negative for the sender (waiving a right, for instance). This question relates in fact to what is technically called non-repudiation.[339] On this matter, one should bear in mind that the general legal principle is that the burden of proving that a given sender has sent a specific message lies with the person who claims to be entitled to a right or course of action on the basis of this message.

Considered from the perspective of a message's sender, and not its recipient as was done in the preceding, both questions also correspond to the situation where a message is misattributed to someone, i.e., a message is attributed to a given sender, who in fact did not send the message in question. Finally, non-repudiation also has its counterpart for the sender, who may wish to ascertain that the recipient of a message will not subsequently deny having received it.

2. SOLUTIONS

One may suggest the following concrete and simple solutions for avoiding, or at least lessening, issues of authentication and non-repudiation, both from the point of view of the recipient and the sender:

---

[339] See, for example, G.L. Grant, *Understanding Digital Signatures: Establishing Trust over the Internet and other Networks* (New York, McGraw-Hill, 1998), p. 14.

- Make a *quick phone call* if there is any suspicion whatsoever. This will greatly reduce the risk that fraud is taking place and that a technical defect has occurred during the transmission of information. Both authentication and non-repudiation are thus ensured, although this solution does not produce strong evidence that a message has indeed been sent or received (as it can be denied that the telephone call took place). If evidence is needed, the same action should be undertaken, but by fax.
- Consistently use the *same e-mail address*. As the example above suggests, creating an e-mail account with a fake name is easy. Using the same address – and not one from the office, another one from home (possibly with two different e-mail programs) and a third one when traveling (for instance using a webmail system such as Hotmail) – obliges a fraudster to make an intrusion into your e-mail account in order to pass himself or herself off as you, which is significantly more difficult than creating a fake e-mail account. In addition, when a new e-mail address needs to be created, for instance because of spam volumes, the new address should be communicated to your contacts using the old e-mail account, not the new one.
- *Change the password* of your e-mail account regularly, and watch who knows your password. This reduces the risk of identity theft, i.e., that someone uses your e-mail account to access confidential information or to commit any other fraud. This recommendation is particularly important if the same password is used for different logins or situations.
- *Acknowledge receipt* of a message, if it is not otherwise replied to. Not only is this basic good manners (as e-mails still sometimes get lost as a result of technical deficiencies or e-mail overload and ensuing difficulties with their management), it also allows non-repudiation of receipt – particularly so if the recommendations of the preceding paragraphs are respected, as they ensure the identity of the acknowledging person. In this sense, it is a service done to the sender. If all the persons involved in a process systematically follow this procedure, it can be expected to create an atmosphere of trust and it will be more difficult to allege non-receipt. It must be specified that currently the most widely deployed e-mail protocols do not allow for the automatic non-repudiation of e-mails, i.e., non-repudiation without the recipient's collaboration. Only if specific protocols and e-mail programs are used can one prove the notification of an e-mail without the cooperation of the recipient. Hence, if non-repudiation by the recipient without his or her cooperation is considered particularly important and registered letters cannot be used, one may suggest the following solutions. First, the rules of procedure in an arbitration could provide that a specific e-mail program allowing non-repudiation must be downloaded and installed on the parties' computers and used for all communications with the arbitral tribunal. Second, the arbitral tribunal might send e-mails that only invite the parties to consult their case status on the website used for the arbitration, on which the documents to be notified would be posted. The website would be password-protected and could thus

record the parties' logins. The parties would then be notified at the time they consult the documents or the message on the Web.

- For particularly important documents, *use a password* for opening the file,[340] a password that only the true sender and intended recipient know. This password should be transmitted through a different channel, for instance over the phone. Password protection authenticates the sender and provides for non-repudiation of sending (and it constitutes quite strong evidence thereof). In addition, such password protection obviously also achieves its primary goal, i.e., that only the intended recipient is able to read the document.
- The most complete solution, which is more complex to implement, is to use *digital signatures* with public-key encryption. Such digital signatures provide the best guarantees of authentication, which often go beyond the level of certainty that is actually required in practice. Digital signatures are addressed in further detail below.[341]

D. WORKING HABITS

The most fundamental obstacle of all to the use of information technology in arbitration, as in most other business contexts, is working habits. One must admit that working with electronic documents might jar with several aspects of the working habits of the majority of senior lawyers, who constitute the main population in the field of arbitration. Younger generations (born in the seventies and later), who grew up with computers, often have an easier contact with computers. Nevertheless, even these younger people have usually been trained to work with books, articles, memos, and other paper documents spread out on a desk, notes scribbled on notepads, files organized in hanging folders and ring binders, papers piled in stacks, etc.

The problem is that no matter how big one's screen, it will always be smaller than most desks and it will always be in two dimensions. Consequently, the number of documents that can be displayed at one time is less than on a desk; the vast majority of people actually prefer to have only one document displayed at a time, which occupies the entire screen, as the two-dimensional layout of a screen makes it more difficult to concentrate on one window than it is to focus on one paper document even on a relatively full desk. Hence, many people find that, as long as one works with a relatively limited number of documents and files at a time, they are closer at hand on a real desk than on a virtual desktop and that it is easier to keep an overview of paper documents than of electronic ones.

---

[340] On protecting word-processing documents with a password, see paragraph End users' computers, p. 135 above.

[341] See Section II.D. Encrypting and digitally signing e-mail, p. 158 below and Section II.D.4. In practice: setting up encrypted and digitally-signed e-mail, p. 163 below.

Moreover, reading on a screen takes some getting used to, especially for longer texts; it requires a different kind of concentration from that needed to read a book, and it is not taught in school. Inexperienced on-screen readers typically read 25 per cent slower from a computer monitor than from print. On-screen reading is also usually associated with increased eye strain and fatigue – an effect that can however largely be reduced by certain actions, such as consciously blinking and regularly focusing one's eyes on distant objects. (It must also be pointed out that the alleged long-term eyesight deterioration due to intensive on-screen reading is nothing but pointless urban legend; it is simply a medical impossibility.)

In addition, many users make a very common mistake in the use of computers, i.e., they put their e-mail software on automatic e-mail check at very short intervals, sometimes even every minute, and have incoming messages accompanied by a pop-up or sound alert. It is a mistake because it reduces concentration and thus efficiency, thereby precisely achieving the opposite result than the one sought. Any management manual will confirm that such behavior seriously distracts the user, as any task requires a given period of time to obtain full attention and effectiveness – it may be specified that this period is longer if the task is more complex, amounting to approximately 20 minutes for intellectually complex tasks.

These differences between working with computers and working on a real desk have created a reluctance to spend the time needed to acquire the necessary skills and to change working habits. Many lawyers print out e-mails in order to read them like a letter – ironically, this is even true for some of the most long-standing experts in the field of IT and the law. Some even admit to being almost totally unable to use a computer and having a secretary as a human interface between them and the machine. At the other end of the scale, arbitrators coming to a hearing with nothing but their laptops are still considered 'impressive', which means that they still are the exception.

So the question: why change? Why learn to use the best of IT in legal practice? The answer is grounded in a basic management principle: the most important tasks are those that have the highest 'multiplying effect', as management theorists call it. This is the capacity of a project to allow or trigger other projects, i.e., to be a catalyst for improving the work process of an individual or an organization as a whole. Some obvious examples include selecting and recruiting a skilled workforce, learning a language, and drafting an action plan. Acquiring IT skills falls into the same category.

Hence, as one such 'impressive' arbitrator using only a laptop during arbitration hearings suggested, it would be useful for all lawyers to acquire at least the following basic skills:[342]

- Typing: many applications teaching how to type quickly are currently on the market. Basically, they teach by a repetition of exercises. At the beginning of the course they

342 So Albert van den Berg, during a presentation made at Use of IT in Arbitration – The State of the Art and the Future, ASA Conference, Berne, 5 September 2003.

explain how to place one's fingers properly. Thereafter, they go through exercises requiring the user to strike given keys, in increasingly complex and quick sequences. Typing skills may be improved tremendously by the use of such applications. It should be remembered that a major part of most lawyers' work consists of typing and that a very large part of interactions with a computer consist of text input. In other words, the time invested in learning to type quickly is in principle paid off a great many times by the time gained later on.

- Learning in depth some basic applications, such as Microsoft Word, PowerPoint, and Adobe Acrobat.
- Moreover, and it cannot be stressed often enough: do not keep your e-mail on automatic-checking mode with short intervals between e-mail checks. An incoming message may easily put an end to one's concentration, which must then be rebuilt. Retrieving e-mails once or twice a day should be enough. But this requires that one not allow other people to get used to and thus expect extremely prompt e-mail answers; similarly, one should not expect it from other people. Urgent requests should be accompanied by a phone call.
- Finally, it is useful to spend some time forcing oneself not to print everything out but to read lengthy texts on a screen, as well as to work on a file involving numerous documents while resisting the temptation to use paper copies of the documents.

II. E-MAILING

Electronic mail has become one of the principal means of private and professional communication. However, although the use of e-mails has become as natural to many people as placing a phone call, and despite the fact that about one billion people today possess an e-mail address, e-mail use is still very much marked by unfortunate practices. A likely reason is that the technology provides for much more diversified uses than the telephone and that the social norms or standards (which fundamentally constitute best practices) do not yet exist for e-mail to the same extent as they do for other forms of correspondence.

Hence, the following suggests some basic practical recommendations for the day-to-day use of e-mails, which are based on guidelines generally accepted by entities that have taken a position on this subject.

A. Sending e-mail

When sending e-mail, the main concerns are the information sent and the addressee. When considering writing an e-mail, it may be useful to consider five of the classical journalist's questions: What? Who? How? When? Why?

What information is to be sent?
One should consider the kind and size of information to be sent, which includes, when forwarding an e-mail, if it is really useful or indeed advisable to forward the history or not. It may also be recalled that e-mail should never be used to send a password or bank account information, and unnecessary attachments should be deleted.

It is important to be cautious when writing e-mails, especially if the content can prejudice the sender (incriminating e-mails), since in some cases the sender can be legally compelled to disclose his or her electronic messages. And in this context it must be remember that removing an e-mail from a computer or e-mail account may not remove it from the server, nor, to a certain extent, from the hard disk of the computer on which it was stored.[343] An e-mail can be recovered in many situations which are plainly counter-intuitive.

To whom are you addressing the mail?
It is important to use the carbon copy ('cc') and blind carbon copy ('bcc') options correctly and to check to whom the e-mail is sent, in particular when using the option 'reply to all', as one may not wish to reply to all the addressees on sensitive topics. Furthermore, when using the carbon copy option, privacy issues may arise if copying to one's own client (since it discloses his or her address) or to the opposing party's client without an express consent.[344]

Also, an e-mail should be sent only to people who really need it, in order to avoid the proliferation of e-mails, which do encumber one's mailbox.

How is the information sent?
At this stage, a prudent user should consider if, regarding the type of information at hand, it is appropriate to use e-mail rather than other means of communication. Once the possibility of using e-mail has been accepted, one should write it using preferably the ascii format (rather than html). When attaching documents, it is in principle advisable not to use proprietary or unusual formats, but rather rtf, pdf, or even html. In the subject line, the sender should also write a descriptive title to allow easy identification; for this purpose, a common system of nomenclature is very helpful. If an encryption system is available, one should consider using it to send encrypted e-mails, keeping in mind that the recipient must be equipped with an encryption key ring to be able to read it.[345]

When is the e-mail sent?
Here the user must consider if the moment at which he or she intends to send the information is appropriate or whether it may be preferable to send it later for any strategic

[343] See further Chapter 4, Section II. Confidentiality issues, p. 122 above.
[344] See for instance the advice in this regard of the Auckland District Law Society, 'Electronic Mail. Guidance for Practitioners' <www.adls.org.nz/profession/guidelines/guide1.asp>.
[345] See further Section II.D. Encrypting and digitally signing e-mail, p. 158 below and Section II.D.4. In practice: setting up encrypted and digitally-signed e-mail, p. 163 below.

reason. Once the e-mail has been sent, it cannot be undone. Sending an e-mail is such an easy task that users frequently do it heedlessly.

Why is the e-mail sent?
The purpose of the e-mail has to be considered, since it can determine the language used – if no answer is expected, the e-mail may specify that it is for information purposes only. The intended purpose of the e-mail obviously also determines whether it is really necessary to send it.

Other precautions
Some general precautions may also be recommended:

- Only important e-mails should be marked as such.
- Add a disclaimer, if only for the psychological effect it has.
- Consistently use the same e-mail address for the same addressee.

B. Receiving e-mail

As noted above, e-mail is one of the main conductors of viruses. Thus, one should be very cautious when opening e-mails. Some advice may be repeated here:

- One should be suspicious when an unexpected e-mail requests the recipient to do something, such as follow a url link. The most common and effective way of transmitting a virus by e-mail is by asking its recipient to click on a url address or to open a file with the extension .exe or .doc – the latter, as explained above, may contain macros.
- Moreover, with the advent of html mail, a system can be infected just by opening an e-mail message. And if the mail client has a preview pane that shows the contents of a message before the mail has actually been opened, then one does not even have to open the message to be infected! This risk is due to the fact that modern e-mail programs, those running on most current computers, can display much more than just plain text documents. The current crop of e-mail programs display colored backgrounds, graphics, and special text fonts. To achieve this, the programs must accept and run little programs, called 'scripts', embedded within the e-mail. Scripts may request a computer to download data from a website, and such data may be a virus. Most of these types of e-mail viruses are rather benign, but a few of them are designed to wreck serious havoc. As a protection, it is suggested to turn off all references to ActiveX, Javascript or any other special effects. It may finally be noted that most of the viruses transmitted by e-mail have so far been specifically created to target flaws in Microsoft Outlook and Outlook Express.
- Never reply to an e-mail requesting passwords or bank account information. Sometimes these e-mails use the pretense that the recipient's bank has changed its system and needs this data. Naturally, such a request does not come from the bank. Sending

such fake messages is called 'phishing'; it is one of the main sources of identity theft on the Net.

C. Keeping Track of Hidden Information: Metadata

Metadata, as the name suggests, is information about information. A very common example of metadata is the information provided by Microsoft Word when the 'track changes' option is activated, since it allows the user to know who wrote or removed what information, when he or she did it, etc.

Metadata can consist of different types of information, and typically the following:

- the user's name and initials;
- the company name;
- the name of the computer;
- the name of the server or the hard disk where the document was saved;
- the name of other persons participating in editing the document;
- the name of previous document authors;
- documents revisions and versions;
- template information;
- hidden text; and
- comments.[346]

Metadata is very useful when multiple authors work on the same document since it allows them to know what information has been changed since the last version. However, managing metadata is critical because it can disclose information that was not intended to be shared, possibly resulting in exceedingly embarrassing situations. Here is one famous example.

On February 5th, 2003, Secretary of State Colin Powell gave a well-remembered address to a plenary session of the United Nations Security Council, in which he made the case for military action in Iraq. One of the important documents Colin Powell used to prepare his speech, and to which he referred during his address to substantiate his claim, was a dossier published by 10, Downing Street. But soon afterwards, a journalist and a lecturer in politics, here at Cambridge University, discovered not only that the dossier had been plagiarized from a U.S. researcher on Iraq, but more importantly that it had been edited, doubtlessly to be 'improved', by several Foreign Office and Downing Street officials who had strictly no legitimacy to interfere with the report. How did the journalist and the academic discover this? Thanks to metadata hidden in the Word document that

---

346 F.C. Rice, 'Protecting Personal Data in your Word Documents' <msdn.microsoft.com/library/-default.asp?url=/library/en-us/dnword2k2/html/odc_ProtectWord.asp>.

contained the dossier. The metadata revealed on whose computer the file had been opened, modified, and saved.

Metadata may typically be generated in the following situations:

- When the user creates a new document from a template, as the template copies all metadata to the new document.
- When the user displays the data entry dialog, adds or selects information, and accepts it.
- When the user saves a document, the directory in which the document is saved may have a metadata file that may be inserted into the document.
- User details, time and date stamps are also frequently stored as metadata.
- When the user edits a document, with the track changes function turned on and the show changes function turned off.

Metadata can be transferred by sending documents via e-mail, sharing files or creating new documents from existing templates. This contrasts with the difficulty of removing metadata, since it requires that every person working on the same document turn the 'track changes' function off and remove information included in the 'properties' section. Applications are available, however, that automatically reveal and erase metadata in Word documents and e-mail, protecting sensitive information while allowing compliance with audit requirements. iScrub is one example.

The solution to the potential problems metadata may cause is not to stop using certain applications, but to pay attention to what is added, removed and amended, and to have an appropriate policy in place including tools to protect against unintended information disclosures. A very good solution when a document is not expected to be modified is to convert it into pdf or html format. (The Blair government learned the lesson, and their next report on Iraq was released in pdf format.) More precisely, the following recommendations can be made on the basis of the foregoing paragraphs.

Create clean documents

As previously said, a newly created document can include metadata if the document is merely a modified version of an existing document saved under a new name. Thus it is advisable to disconnect a document from its past life by copying the old document into a new shell created with a new template.

Consider the recipient of each document

A good policy should distinguish among documents that are internal, documents to be shared with cooperators, and documents to be shared with adversaries. To gain efficiency some companies may use information about a client for a document template. However it can be undesirable for this information or the relationship between the company and the client to be disclosed, and it is therefore necessary to 'publish' the document as described below.

Publish documents
The expression 'publish a document' means cleaning it up as if it had to be published (in a more professional manner than Downing Street's dossier on Iraq), thus removing comments and making sure that no unwanted information or undesired change remains in the document. 'Publish' is the electronic equivalent of the instructions to verify that there are no marks, notes or comments on the document before copying it for distribution.

Other precautions
- The 'fast saves' function in MS Word should not be used.
- The 'save version' function in MS Word should not be used. Use instead the 'comment' function.
- Create templates for different documents and for different purposes and/or addressees.
- Generally speaking, before transmitting a document, clean it up following a checklist or have software do it for you, or convert it into a format containing metadata which is more easily verifiable (pdf or html, for instance).

D. ENCRYPTING AND DIGITALLY SIGNING E-MAIL

Imagine you are in a country whose government you do not trust and you need to exchange e-mails with your secretary or team in an arbitration involving that government. Or one of the recipients of your e-mails relating to an arbitration is located in one such country, be this person a witness, an expert, a party, a member of a team of counsel, an arbitrator, or a secretary. In such a case, but also if you simply have special security concerns, extra security measures may be required. The most obvious measure is the use of encrypted and digitally signed e-mails.

E-mail encryption and digital signatures are very closely linked: both rely on asymmetric key cryptography. E-mail encryption, which consists of making messages unreadable by third parties, involves this form of cryptography insofar as only one person is able to decrypt, and thus read, a message that anyone can encrypt. Digital signatures, conversely, consist of creating a sort of code that only the signatory could have created; it involves cryptography in the sense that only one person, the one who is authenticated by the signature, is able to encrypt a specific part of a message, which may then be decrypted by anyone. It may be noted that the encrypted part in this situation is not a part of the body of the message, which remains readable in plain text without decryption.

The system of asymmetric key cryptography (also called public key cryptography) involves a pair of keys or ciphers: one public, one private. These two keys, which take the form of algorithms, correspond to each other, and to no other key. Together, they constitute what is sometimes called a key ring. The private key is a type of secret code. The public key is an open code, a counterpart of the secret one.

The private key is used to decrypt data encrypted using the public key (in the context of e-mail encryption) and to encrypt data that can then be decrypted by the public key (in the context of digital signatures).

The public key is used to encrypt data that can only be decrypted by the secret code (e-mail encryption) and to decrypt data that could only have been encrypted using the secret key (verification of a digital signature). These functions are further detailed below.

1. PRIVATE AND CONFIDENTIAL E-MAILS: ENCRYPTION

In the context of e-mail encryption, the public key is used as a padlock, and the private key is the only key that opens the padlock. Here is how it works: the public key transforms the text of the message into a cipher text. This cipher text can then only be decrypted using the corresponding private key, which only one recipient holds.

An encrypted message looks like this:

From: Gabrielle Kaufmann-Kohler <gabrielle.kaufmann@droit.unige.ch>
Subject: IT & arbitration
To: Thomas Schultz <ts395@cam.ac.uk>

-----BEGIN PGP MESSAGE-----

Version: GnuPG v1.2.1 (MingW32)

Comment: GnuPT 2.7.2

hQIOA2zmrj9w1bMoEAf/aWsz7AD5oKDJfPr2vWq9HcWlY4xFkBf9Zz+xNIEKoXeNGVXsNzh
j7ls4yD1pIHtHFIZ3KEAIQGOjDAWMCDZGgbpAR6EbK3v1mkWN6cHEcNUJAi+8xGcADQyp
fYVLHCywEQ7sq2yvHTtZ7xbxDh1NKSyttrlrxLOGYZNOpv9W+mu2CYiSykHJMDPHvDylOXL
/siY9tgvFOJAXJnmOBtM7L/HxEXUAJ5Uy60rOmQkhe8/Qj4hA1Y6KHgXsfMf1+ko2M9NUxP
OevZq5DJRfZXqA03xg72cm77IAsJu7j/nCT+klV4DR+4OH2ZRnU0jPgwiLrG8niQ++ucCjgV
2YLFwxAf9GIm3dxBGcKBOPoBsgfmGx5Thi58hsHYW2+LR/yR4yiJEigo3nacKReFeN+9ERX
N9FTkVecmcrKzTSINMWbSbO+slo8k05UOuqa2P7OLf0ymBjazzcI9xp7K398rbCGrN2LqjK2
c7/HQTj3ZQifHA2uH5vamPFJOO1vDz1/kZYvhOfFelxwztdFLFwQnfVDZYqsnjJVE3dnXOk/4j
ln8Tkf8mPrhRGEH9HuK2kdyJMY4KnE3enVhE/EzbXlpQOIdW6kLFJeYjB+w1j2RD5/aoamN
ez37qa9KyfqCf++hpRFIqUaf1bCqJdj6uLsIEOovoxOla7Xo+s6bV26s6wYISMEwvCyNXoallp
AqNuESbx+KVk7ny9nmY8C1uV8S6QTmWs37JZkHIAhY==cWfm

-----END PGP MESSAGE-----

Once the message is decrypted using the appropriate private key, the cipher text simply becomes plain text, readable as any other text. If the text cannot be decrypted, this means that either the wrong public key was used for encryption or the wrong private key is being used for decryption, the latter implying in principle that the message has arrived in the wrong hands.

Users would in principle apply for a pair of keys or a 'key ring', keep the private one secret and distribute the public one through websites called 'keyservers' or by e-mail. This is what made asymmetric key encryption such a breakthrough: there is no need to transmit the private key to decrypt messages, only the public key, used for encrypting messages, travels across networks on which it can be intercepted.

To send an encrypted e-mail to someone, one may either ask this person to send his or her public key, or try to download it from a keyserver – in any event, this person must own a key ring. This public key is then used to encrypt the message in such a way that only the holder of the private key can read it.

2. Identifying the Sender and Verifying the Authenticity of the Text: Digital Signatures

In the context of digital signatures, the private key is used for signing, the public one for verification. Here is how it works: when applying a private key to a message in order to sign it, the signing program generates a hash value, which is a unique mathematical summary of the content of the message. One hash value can only relate to one specific message. If the message is altered, it will not produce the same hash value. This hash value is then encrypted using the private key and the message is sent. Its recipient then decrypts the hash value using the sender's public key. If the recipient is unable to decrypt the hash value, this means that the public key being used does not match the private key, which indicates that it was not the expected private key that was used to encrypt the hash value and thus to sign the message. Once the hash value is decrypted, the recipient creates a new hash value on the basis of the message received, using the same hash algorithm as the sender. Thereafter, both hash values are compared: if they match, it means that the content of the message was not altered since its signature (i.e., since its 'hashing') and, again, that the signatory of the message did indeed use the corresponding private key.

On this basis, one may say that a digital signature has three functions:

(a) Sender authentication, as only this specific sender's private key could have signed the message.
(b) Non-repudiation of sending, in the sense that the sender cannot deny having sent the message, as only his or her private key could have signed the message.
(c) Data integrity, which means that the content of the message has not been altered since its signature.

Here is what a digitally signed message looks like:

```
Date: Mon, 07 Nov 2005 14:18:20 +0100
From: Thomas Schultz <Thomas.Schultz@droit.unige.ch>
Subject: Contract
To: Gabrielle Kaufmann <gabrielle.kaufmann@droit.unige.ch>

-----BEGIN PGP SIGNED MESSAGE-----

Hash: SHA1


Dear Gabrielle
Please find attached the contract we discussed yesterday.
All the best,
Thomas
```

```
-----BEGIN PGP SIGNATURE-----
Version: GnuPG v1.2.1 (MingW32)
Comment: GnuPT 2.7.2

iD8DBQFDb1NeQQXNCQCKu3sRAnvNAKC4KjsnnKJjEJBHMeXHgrz/5SnC/gCfd98p9cY5x3
QihK6aVcamiJ7i5WQ==UcRV

-----END PGP SIGNATURE-----
```

The confirmation that the message has not been altered and that the sender did indeed use the purported digital signature looks like the following:

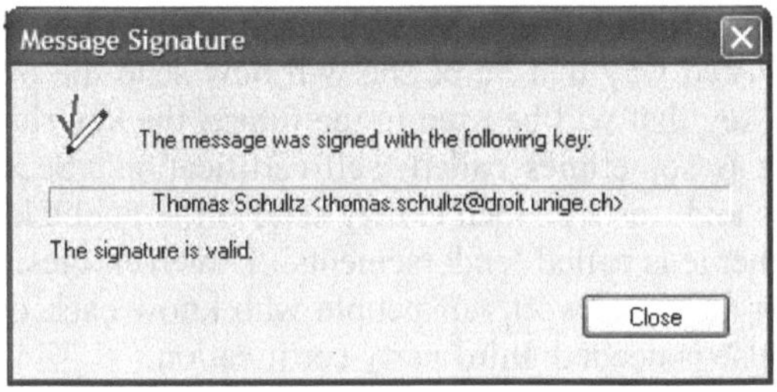

Figure 28. Verification of a digital signature

To digitally sign an e-mail – for which one must own a key ring – one simply applies the private key to the message. The recipient may then check who signed the message and that it has not been altered since it was signed, by checking the message with the public key, which may be found on a keyserver or distributed by e-mail. The question of how and where to obtain the public key to verify a digital signature leads us to the next part, which relates to the question of which key rings one may trust.

3. TRUSTING DIGITAL SIGNATURES AND KEY RINGS IN GENERAL: LINKING CIPHERS TO PEOPLE

A digital signature only proves that a given private key has been used. It provides no guarantee, in and of itself, as to the holder of this key. It only authenticates the key, not the person who uses it. Hence, even if one assumes that the key has not been stolen, how can one know that the holder of a given key is indeed the person he or she claims to be? A private key, in other words, can be the equivalent of a fake ID.

E-mail encryption relies on the use of a public key. But whose public key is used? In principle, if someone wants others to be able to send him or her encrypted messages, this person only needs to publish a public key. Anyone acquiring this public key through a public keyserver – in other words, anyone who knows how digital signatures work – can then send this person secure, encrypted information. Unfortunately, someone else can also create a key ring under a fake name, publish the public key (and thus know the related private key), claim that he or she is the individual bearing the name indicated by the key, and thereby receive at least some of the encrypted messages meant for the individual who does indeed bear the name indicated by the key. This begs the questions: how can one trust the public key? How can one know that a given public key does indeed belong to a given person?

The answer to these two questions is certification, i.e., a confirmation that the key ring and the identity do indeed belong together. This certification can take two forms: either it relies on so-called 'self-certification' or 'endorsements', or a third party provides a 'real' certification.

In the first case, called the 'Web of trust scheme', the certification, in other words the assurance of the identity of the holder of the key, may be based on one of two instances. First, this assurance may follow from a direct contact with a trusted party: if A knows B, and B tells A in a trusted way that he or she will now send the public key, which then identifies the private key that will be used in the future, the key ring may in principle be trusted. This is what is sometimes called 'self-certification'. Second, if A knows and trusts B and B knows and trusts C, then C may send B the public key, which is then forwarded to A. This scheme is called 'endorsements'. However, these two types of 'certification' only work for small networks of people who know each other. For the Internet globally, something else is needed: third-party certification.

The certification of a public key, which may be viewed using a command that varies depending on the e-mail program used, has the following appearance:

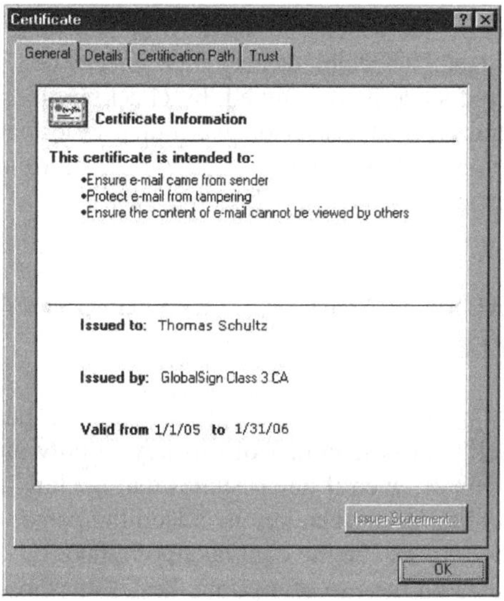

Figure 29. Certification of public key

Third-party certification relies on the idea that a public key (and thus the whole key ring, as the private key necessarily corresponds to the public key) is built into a certificate, which contains information such as the name of the bearer of the key, his address, and so forth, thereby attesting that the public key belongs to the entity noted in the certificate. This public key certificate is then digitally signed by a trusted third party, in principle a certification authority (CA). Such CAs may either be commercial services, run by private companies or governments,[347] or non-profit ventures.[348] The task of such CAs is to check the applicants' true identity and credentials, in other words to establish the correctness of a match between key rings and real individuals or companies. This match is established using methods that vary from one CA to another, but generally rely on a combination of ID cards such as passports or driver's licenses, credit card information, and third party databases and services.

A detailed guide on how to acquire, install and use a pair of keys in order to encrypt e-mails or to digitally sign them is provided in the next section.

4. In Practice: Setting up Encrypted and Digitally-Signed E-mail

This section is organized in two parts. This first part relates to e-mail clients, which are e-mail programs on a computer that download e-mails to the hard disk. The best known programs are Outlook, Lotus Notes, Eudora, Mozilla Thunderbird, or Pegasus Mail. The procedure which needs to be followed in order to set up encrypted and digitally signed e-mails is similar for each program.

The second part below concerns webmails, which are Web-based or browser-based e-mail applications, such as Hotmail and Gmail. In this context, specific instructions are provided in relation to one of the rare webmails that supports encryption and digital signatures, i.e., HushMail.

a. E-mail clients

The first step before sending a secured e-mail is to obtain a digital certificate. There are three possibilities.

First, you can create your own digital certificate using Selfcert.exe. These certificates are considered non-authenticated, however, and a computer will issue a security warning if its security level is set to medium or high. To create a self-certificate, the following steps should be followed:

- Launch the file called Selfcert.exe – if you cannot find it, use the search tool in the Start menu.

---

[347] For a worldwide list of CAs, see J.A. Avellan, 'Certification Authorities, CA Initiatives and Authentication Products and Services', <www.qmw.ac.uk/~tl6345/ca.htm>.

[348] See for instance <www.cacert.org>.

- Once you find it, double click on it and the window reproduced in Figure 30 below will appear.
- Enter the name of your certificate.

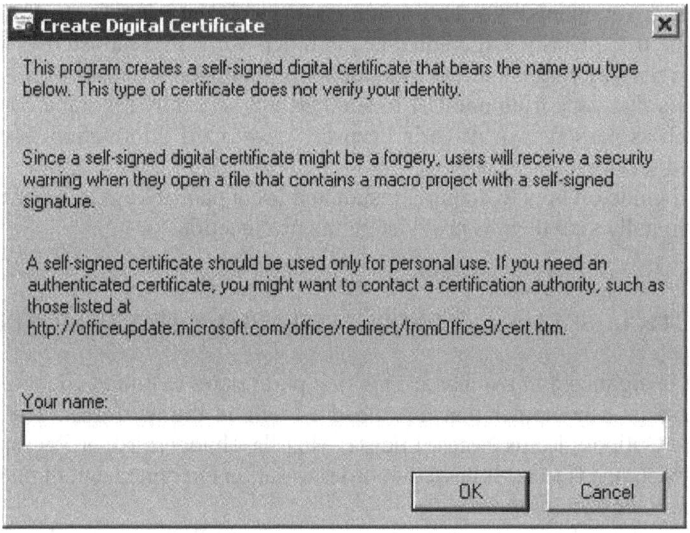

Figure 30. 'Selfcert' window – creating a self-certificate

Second, you can also obtain a certificate from a commercial authority. There are a number of authorities which provide this service: VeriSign; AOL; Securesign; SecureNet; and others. These certificates must be paid for, and the price varies greatly depending on the duration and trustworthiness of the certificate. To get a digital certificate, you will be asked to submit a request providing information about your company. It will then be necessary to install the certificate.

Third, you can obtain an internal certification if your company has its own administrator acting as certification authority for your company.

Once you have a digital certificate you can write your e-mail. Before sending it, it will be necessary to modify the security parameters. To do this click on the 'Options' bar, as shown in Figure 31 on the next page.

Then click to modify the security parameters. The window reproduced in Figure 32 on the next page will appear.

Select the different options to encrypt the attachments and to add a digital signature. If you wish to receive an acknowledgment of receipt, also select this option.

Then, click on security parameters to modify them in case the one appearing is not the correct one. In the following window, you will have the option of choosing the certificates for the digital signature and for the encryption.

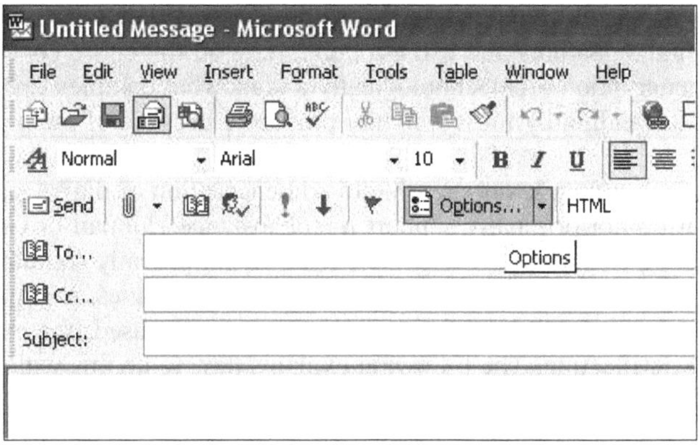

Figure 31. Setting security parameters in MS Outlook

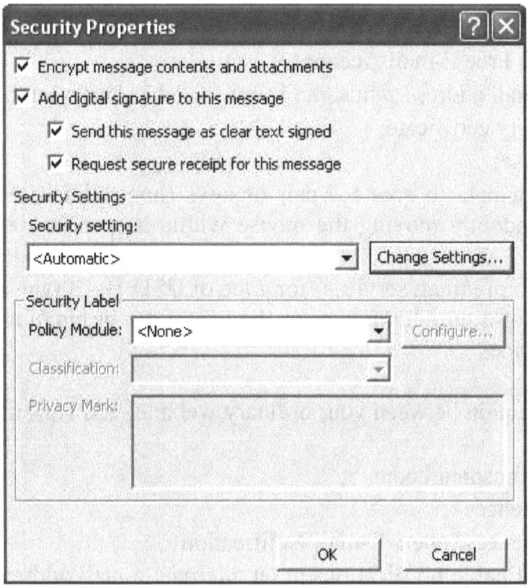

Figure 32. Setting encryption options and adding a digital signature

Once you have completed these steps, you may proceed to send the e-mail as usual.

b. Webmails

Most webmails, i.e., most websites providing access to e-mails, do not support sophisticated security technologies such as e-mail encryption and digital signatures. The reason is that the process of encoding the message – using a private key on a specific part of the message for digital signatures and using a public key on the entire contents of the message for e-mail encryption – is technologically a somewhat complex operation, which is considered too demanding by most webmail providers because of the high volume of e-mails they process.

Moreover, it is in principle not possible to add encryption or digital signature features to webmails that do not originally support it (for instance Hotmail or Gmail). Hence, if one insists on using webmail instead of an e-mail client, the only solution is to create an account with a webmail provider that supports such technologies, and maybe to set up a connection between the new webmail and the one usually used, for example an automated reception notification. The following explains how to do this with such a webmail provider, i.e., Hushmail.

Starting out

The first step is to create an account with Hushmail:

- go to <www.hushmail.com>;
- click on <Create Free E-mail Account>;
- choose your e-mail address @hushmail.com (or other Hushmail domains);
- accept the security certificate;
- enter a passphrase;
- generate random data to create a pair of keys (one public, one private), which is achieved by randomly moving the mouse within a specific field prompted by the website;
- either upgrade to premium services (for a fee of USD 10–20; the advantage is primarily the absence of a time limitation for the use of the webmail and storage space) or use the free services.

Next, create a connection between your ordinary webmail and Hushmail:

- log in to <www.hushmail.com>;
- click on <Preferences>;
- click on <Preferences Index>E-mail Notification>;
- check the box ‘Enable notifications at an alternate e-mail address when you receive mail at this address’;
- enter the e-mail address corresponding to your ordinary webmail, which will receive an alert if you have received an encrypted or digitally-signed e-mail on your Hushmail account.

Encrypted mail

To send encrypted e-mails, you will in principle need to ask your recipient to upload his or her public key to Hushmail’s keyserver. An easier alternative, but not as satisfactory, is to enter a secret question and answer – the recipient will have to provide the secret answer in order to decrypt the message. To do this, simply click on <Compose>Message Options>. Reverting to the first solution, in order to upload the public key to Hushmail's keyserver, the recipient should follow these steps, as described by Hushmail:[349]

- export his or her public key in text format;
- go to <www.hushtools.com>Key Management>Advanced>Upload a public key>;
- paste the public key in text form in the box indicated;
- the website then requires associating the uploaded key with an e-mail address.

For you to be sent encrypted e-mails, the sender will simply need to download your public key from Hushmail's keyserver, which for recent versions of encryption software means following these steps:[350]

- right-click the PGP icon in the system tray;
- select <Options>Servers>New>PGP Keyserver LDAP>;
- enter 'keys.hush.com' in the <Name> field, and click OK.

Digital signatures

To send digitally signed messages:

- the sender simply needs to click on <Compose>Message Options>Sign Message>;
- the recipient will then need to go to <www.hushtools.com> in order to verify the authenticity of the signature. This also allows users to check the integrity of the message (i.e., that it has not been tampered with).

For you to receive digitally signed messages, the sender will need to upload his or her public key to Hushmail's keyserver, following these steps:[351]

- export his or her public key in text format;
- go to <www.hushtools.com>Key Management>Advanced>Upload a public key>;
- paste the public key in text form in the box indicated;
- the website then requires users to associate the uploaded key with an e-mail address.

---

[349] See <www.hushmail.com>Support>Using PGP with Hushmail>.

[350] For a more complete description, including older encryption software, see <https://www.hushmail.com/help.php?subloc=pgp&l=154>.

[351] See <www.hushmail.com>Support>Using PGP with Hushmail>.

III. VIDEOCONFERENCING

Chapter 2 suggested when generally videoconferencing technologies could be beneficially resorted to, which categories of situations are most open to it and what advantages a video linkup may have in such circumstances. It also sketched out how such systems operate from a technical point of view and consequently what equipment they require; Chapter 2 further reported on an experiment whose goal was to assess the reactions – both enthusiasm and reservations – that most lawyers would be likely to have faced with such technologies. In other words, it sought to provide the necessary information to decide upon the advisability of resorting to videoconferencing.

It did not, however, venture far into practical detail about how these technologies should be used, about how videoconferencing sessions should be prepared and conducted. This is the main topic of the present section. But before this is specifically addressed, the following reviews, for the sake of practical convenience, some general recommendations on whether or not, on a concrete situation, videoconferencing is an advisable resource.

A. To videoconference or not to videoconference

Practitioners periodically come up to me and ask the following question: 'My client requested my opinion', they say, 'on whether we should not take advantage for the upcoming arbitration of the latest communication technologies and save time and costs through the use of a video linkup. What do you think?' The only correct answer is unfortunately very lawyer-like: 'It depends'. What exactly it depends on forms the substance of the following recommendations. These recommendations are thus made to help evaluate if, in a concrete situation, a video linkup would provide the required advantages and whether these advantages would outweigh the inherent disadvantages of not holding an in-person meeting. They also suggest some concrete actions that can contribute to increasing the advantages of videoconferencing and decreasing its downsides.

Prior experience

When dealing with parties or arbitrators who are inexperienced with videoconferencing generally, and preferably also if they are inexperienced with the specific platform or technology intended to be used, one should preferably schedule a videoconferencing session that can be replaced by a telephone conference if a problem occurs.

A hearing necessarily requiring image transmission should not be scheduled in the form of a videoconference if the parties do not have sufficient experience with the technologies being used. In other words, with inexperienced participants, one should start with particularly simple situations that could also be dealt with satisfactorily by a telephone conference.

Moreover, a test session should be scheduled as much in advance as possible unless participants have already used the specific platform with exactly the same computer they will be using during the session. It for instance occasionally happens that, although the technology used is quite simple and robust, some participants cannot connect to the platform because of oversensitive security measures (for example firewalls on different levels, some of which cannot be deactivated by the user but require the assistance of a systems administrator) or cannot install the necessary application on their computer because of conflicting software. Another typical issue is the possible disturbing 'echo' caused by one of the parties using loudspeakers instead of the expected headsets (this is called a Larsen effect in sound engineering, i.e., an acoustic loop between a microphone and a loudspeaker, which creates an endless circle of amplifications of the same sound; it is purposefully used by many heavy metal bands – an indication of how pleasant such a sound is).

In addition to holding such a test session, it would be useful to provide the participants with an interactive demo before the first use, so that they can practice and become comfortable with the technology. Finally, if the budget allows it, it may often be prudent to involve a secretary in charge of manipulating the software, to allow the participants to focus on the meeting, and not on how the technology works.

Prior meetings of the participants

To increase the sense of reality and to allow at least for some 'vibes' between the participants, videoconferencing should only be resorted to, whenever possible and especially in larger cases that in any event entail several meetings, after all the participants have met at least once in person.

This reduces the effect of 'dehumanization' of the communications, as the participants can more easily associate the image they hear and the voice they hear with a real person whose personality they know at least a little.

Expected antagonistic character of the meeting

Videoconferencing should preferably not be used in situations of conflict or when the assessment of the other participants' states of mind is particularly important (e.g., some key witness hearings). In such situations, the disadvantages of not meeting face-to-face would be particularly important.

On some occasions however, it will simply not be realistic to hold an in-person meeting; hence, this is only a recommendation, and not a strict rule.

Document presentation

As to the selection of the appropriate videoconferencing platform, consideration should be given to the availability of document presentation and sharing facilities, including the possibility of pointing at specific parts of documents, highlighting sections of the text, and if possible sharing other applications. These features largely contribute to the overall benefits of videoconferencing, allowing participants to show exhibits during hearings and to work collectively, during procedural meetings or deliberations, on a document that is instantly updated before the eyes of all participants.

Regarding the presentation of documents, it must be said that most document presentation and sharing technologies will become rather difficult to handle if a large number of documents are used (if a figure must be suggested, one may roughly assess the critical limit at some 30 documents). Hence, the more numerous the documents expected to be viewed during the meeting, the less convenient a virtual meeting will become.

Connection speed
On the technical front, the most frequently encountered problem, which makes a videoconferencing session practically impossible, is the lack of Internet bandwidth. An ordinary broadband connection is currently not necessarily sufficient for multipoint conferencing.

The main issue in this regard is that the connection speed indicated by a computer or by an access provider is in principle the maximal speed that can be reached, but this maximal speed is only rarely attained in actual fact.

The only real way to ascertain the definite speed of a connection is to try it out, in a test session resembling as much as possible the actual intended meeting, including the time of day, as this may give an approximate idea of the number of people who may be sharing a connection at a given time.

Using a videoconferencing system relying on dedicated lines is another solution, though it in principle entails much higher costs and more specific equipment. Even if such technology is used, one should not dispense of a trial session.

Even if the most recent and high-end equipment is acquired, the connection speed may still be insufficient because of the pipe into a city or a region, i.e., the general cables connecting a city or a region to the rest of the global network, which may constitute a real bottleneck for information transmission.[352]

B. Setting up a Videoconferencing Session

As was suggested many times throughout this book, working with IT involves some technical and legal concerns that should be managed before any problem arises. This can be done by scheduling the videoconference in advance and taking some preventive actions. The following considers some such actions. Meeting these guidelines, it must be specified, is not a guarantee that no problems will arise, since technology is unpredictable, but rather a way to minimize the risks of such problems occurring.

Scheduling the meeting
As a basic rule of thumb, and urgent situations excepted, one may suggest that a videoconference session should be scheduled at least two weeks to a month in advance. This will allow the parties and the arbitrators the opportunity to examine any technical problems in advance and to solve them in time.

[352] For further technical explanations of all these issues, see Chapter 2, Section II.A. Videoconferencing technologies, p. 35 above and Chapter 2, Section II.D. Caveats, p. 59 above.

At the time of scheduling the videoconferencing session, decisions should be taken on the following aspects:

- Date, time, and anticipated duration of the videoconference.
- Purpose of the videoconference.
- Number of terminal stations and their location.
- Technology to be used. If the participants are not yet equipped with a videoconferencing system, they should for instance decide if they want to invest in the acquisition of equipment (software and hardware) or if it is preferable to resort to a videoconference services provider to organize the online meeting. The second option has the advantage of efficacy and efficiency, as these providers have at their disposal tested rooms and equipments, and the disadvantage of costs, as this kind of service may be quite expensive.[353]
- Participants at each station, including whether an observer of the opposite party or of the arbitral tribunal may be present. On the day of the conference a formal and recorded statement should be required from the parties confirming that there are no other persons in the room. A procedure should also be determined to verify the identity of the participants, if they are not known by both parties, including witnesses and experts: such a procedure could for example consist of showing IDs to the camera or as scanned documents, or of personal identification by a trustworthy and known third party.
- Arrangement of the participants in relation to the camera and audio equipment. Due to the limited angle of webcams, it may be recommended to use a second one placed in the corner of the room showing the whole room, if hearing the individual in question requires certainty that no person is secretly in the room, for instance when hearing witnesses or experts.
- Support material such as physical blackboards (if no electronic blackboard feature is included in the videoconferencing software) and any other materials or documents should be available in each conference room. If any such material is expected to be used frequently it would also be useful to have a camera dedicated to it, in order to avoid having to redirect the camera each time.
- Identification of the files, documents, and notes that may be available at each station, especially to witnesses and experts testifying by videoconference.
- In the event of a broken connection to a participant, the procedure to contact the remaining participants.
- Fallback solutions. These may for instance consist of resorting to a reserve conferencing equipment, with duplicate computers and conferencing hardware, and possibly an entire duplicate videoconferencing platform. Simpler solutions may comprise an

[353] See further Chapter 1, Section II.A.2. Dedicated videoconferencing, p. 36 above.

audio linkup (i.e., telephone conferencing) instead of a visual linkup. Dates for a postponed meeting should also be contemplated.

- Presence or availability of technicians.
- If desired, the means of recording the videoconference and the availability of the records to the parties and the arbitrators.
- Preparatory actions to be undertaken ahead of the videoconference, such as test sessions, and their timing. Before the conference, at least one test phase should be carried out to ensure that things will work as expected and that the risks of breakdown are mastered.[354]

Test session
The test session should take place some one or two weeks before the online meeting. The purpose of this second phase is to evaluate the quality and reliability of the infrastructure in place. It basically consists of a short test run, including the following elements:

- Connecting all the required hardware.
- Logging into the platform.
- Exchanging a few words.
- Maybe showing a few safe documents.
- Verifying that all terminals, systems and peripherals are well configured and work correctly.

This test must be done sufficiently in advance to allow technicians to replace any inadequate piece of equipment and to solve any technical issue. During this test, the arbitral tribunal and the parties should familiarize themselves with the general controls, functions, and peripherals necessary to log in, communicate, show documents, and use any other function provided by the platform. This is also the time to acquire missing pieces of hardware or maybe licenses to use the platform

Preparing the actual meeting
Just before the conference, it is advisable that the arbitral tribunal and all other participants are in place long enough in advance to be able to receive any technical instructions from the technicians. A few minutes could also be helpful for participants to find their bearings and to toggle on and off the different components to ascertain that they work correctly and that the sound and image transmission can be disconnected if some participants wish to confer privately (the arbitrators among themselves, or a party and its counsel, for example).

[354] Further on test phases, see, for example, E. Schäfer, 'Videoconferencing in arbitration' (2003) 14-1 ICC Bull 35.

The actual meeting
During the videoconference, the following further element should be considered:

- Light: to have a good quality image, the light source, preferably artificial, should be placed behind the camera.
- Corporal expression: it is necessary to avoid quick movements as the transmission rate (the number of images per second) is lower in even the best videoconferencing systems than, for instance, on television. Quick movements may thus seem jerky.

C. EXAMPLES OF VIDEOCONFERENCING SOFTWARE

This section provides a series of summary descriptions of various videoconferencing technologies. These descriptions are not meant to be complete presentations; their purpose is merely to provide an overview of different technologies and services, to provide a general understanding of these tools and to constitute a first reference for parties, arbitrators, or arbitral institutions contemplating the use of a specific ad hoc videoconferencing application. All of the platforms reviewed in the following work with standard IP videoconferencing equipment, i.e., a webcam and a headset. What this section does not discuss, however, is dedicated videoconferencing systems and stand-alone all-in-one hardware and software equipment. Such systems, as was already submitted in Chapter 2,[355] are best left to professional companies, i.e., to either videoconferencing solution suppliers, such as Tandberg, Polycom, or Cisco, or to professional videoconferencing service providers, as for example Demorum.

1. CLICKTOMEET

ClickToMeet is a very professional videoconferencing application, featuring many useful functions.[356] It has been used, inter alia, by the US and Dutch militaries, NASA, a variety of US federal government and Chinese district programs, and schools in the London area.[357] On the downside, however, it requires installing locally, i.e., on the computer on every user, a program that will handle communication with the central servers, from which all transmissions are dispatched to the different participants. This program unfortunately interferes quite strongly with other applications and it may thus take some time to solve all the issues it creates, before the system can run properly. But once the system is up and running, it is very user friendly and powerful. Another drawback of this other-

[355] Ibid.
[356] See <www.clicktomeet.com>.
[357] See <www.clicktomeet.com/eng/government/programs.htm> and <www.clicktomeet.com/eng/-solutions>.

wise very satisfactory system is an apparently unavoidable audio lag, even when used on high-speed connections.

As this application was used for the Geneva experiment and has thus been described in detail in Chapter 2,[358] it is sufficient to repeat here its main characteristics, which are the following:

- Multipoint videoconferencing with up to 500 concurrent users, of which up to 16 can be shown at the same time on the screen. (It must be specified that, above ten concurrent users, particularly fast computers must be used, but this is in principle true for all videoconferencing applications).
- Document presentation.
- Mouse movement tracking.
- Application and desktop sharing.
- Works only with Windows operating systems.
- The costs of ClickToMeet may only be obtained by direct enquiry with the company and depend on too many factors to be reproduced here; as a very rough estimate, it comes with a four zero price tag, though in the lower range of that category of figures.

2. Macromedia Breeze

Breeze is particularly robust, flexible, fast, and intuitively user-friendly videoconferencing application. Its main features are:

- Multipoint videoconferencing with no maximal number of concurrent active participants.
- Text chat.
- White board.
- Document presentation, with an overlay feature, for annotations on documents without changing their original content.
- File sharing.
- Application and desktop sharing.
- Possibility of combining audioconferences and videoconferences.
- Supports Windows as well as Apple Macintosh operating systems.
- Clear list of attendees.
- Administrator of the platform (for instance the chair of the arbitral tribunal) has good control over all participants.

---

[358] See Chapter 2, Section II.B.3. The Technology, p. 44 above.

- Only requires the installation, on the computer of every participant, of a small application (Macromedia Flash) which is already integrated in 98 per cent of all Web browsers. This installation takes usually less than a minute. Hence, the risk of conflicting software is largely reduced.
- Costs: either USD 0.32 per minute and user, or USD 750 per month for ten participants.

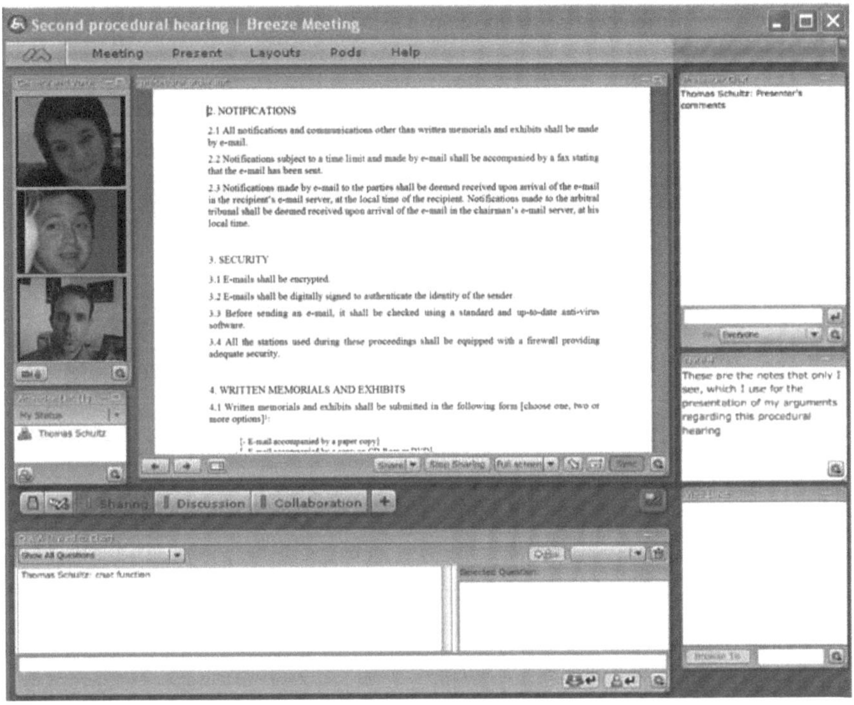

Figure 33. Breeze videoconferencing interface

3. MEGAMEETING

The 'enterprise' version of the Megameeting videoconferencing system features the following elements:[359]

[359] See <www.megameeting.com>.

- Multipoint videoconferencing allowing up to 13 people to participate actively (sending and receiving image and sound), with an apparently unlimited number of 'spectators'.
- Sharing applications, documents and desktops among participants, including remote desktop control.
- Security via RTMP/RTMPT/RTMPS.
- Compatibility between Windows, LINUX and Mac operating systems.
- Browser-based software (i.e., it does not require downloading any software).
- Costs are a one-time account setup fee of USD 8,500.

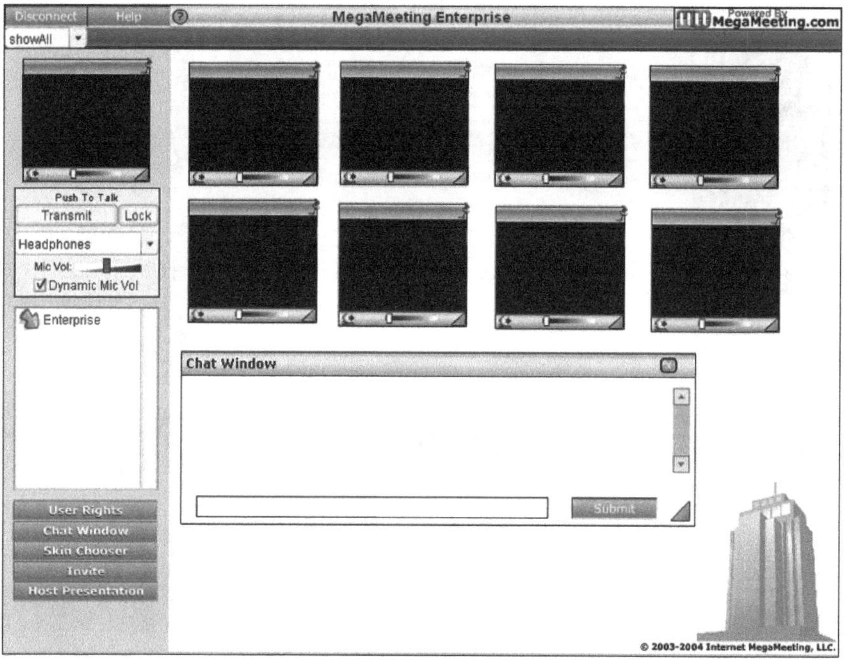

Figure 34. Megameeting videoconferencing interface

4. IVISIT

iVisit is a multipoint (i.e., multi-user) videoconferencing application developed by the inventor of IP videoconferencing, Tim Dorcey. It is a very popular application, with over three million installations so far. One of its most distinctive features is that it is totally compatible with Windows and Apple Macintosh. Its other main features are the following:[360]

- Videoconferencing allowing up to 16 persons to participate at the same time in a private videoconference room (or only point-to-point communications, i.e., two participants only, in the free version of the program).
- Sharing desks and files with the other participants.
- Co-browsing of the Internet.
- Other functions such as recording sessions, chatting, and an address book.
- The price for access to participate in multipoint videoconferencing sessions (involving eight to 16 participants) starts at USD 50 per year and per participant. Additional control and reliability, using an in-house server, starts at USD 1,600 per year for an unlimited number of accesses to multipoint sessions.

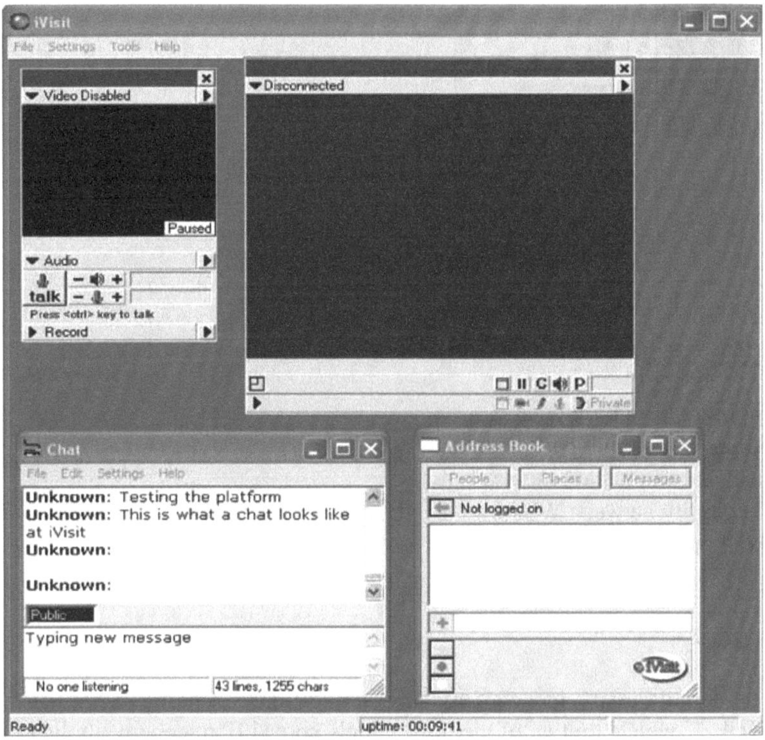

Figure 35. iVisit videoconferencing interface

[360] See <www.ivisit.com>.

5. EARTHLINK VIDEOCONFERENCING SOFTWARE

Earthlink is a free client/server videoconferencing system allowing multiple participants to take part in a videoconference.[361]

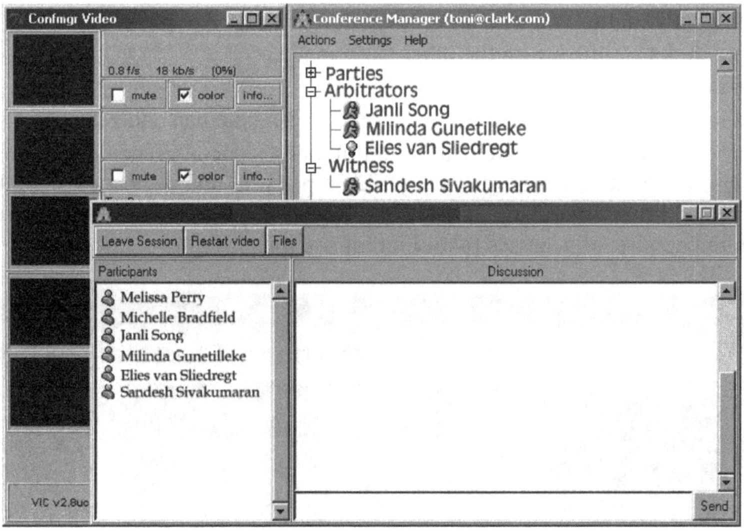

Figure 36. Earthlink videoconferencing interface

In its current version, its main features are:

- Multipoint videoconferencing.
- File transfers to other participants.
- Private chat and instant messaging.
- Compatibility between Windows, LINUX and Mac OS X.
- Firewall protection.

6. FESTOON

Festoon is a multipoint videoconferencing application[362] running on Skype[363] and on Google Talk,[364] which are two of the most widely spread IP telephony applications. With

[361] See <www.research.earthlink.net/confmgr>.
[362] See <www.festooninc.com>.
[363] See <www.skype.com>.

more than 3.7 million downloads of the program since its creation, it is one of the most popular videoconferencing systems.[365] It works as a simple plug-in installed on top of Skype or Google Talk, which allows users to add images to the traditional Skype or Google Talk audioconferences.

Figure 37. Festoon videoconferencing interface

The main characteristics of Festoon are:

- Videoconferencing, allowing up to eight people to be shown in video windows at the same time.
- In total, 200 people can join a session only to watch and listen (i.e., 'spectators' in a 'one-to-many' conference).
- Application sharing and desktop sharing (everything any user sees on his or her screen can be broadcast to the others in real time).
- Works with computers of little power (i.e., starting at 800 MHz processors, where the standard today is above 2,000 MHz).
- Secure transmissions (128 SSL encryption).

---

[364] See <www.google.com/talk>.

[365] See 'Worldwide instant messenger users united in video calls' <www.festooninc.com/news_-1205.asp>, 22 December 2005.

- Does not work with Apple Macintosh computers.
- Free to download and to run.

7. Windows NetMeeting

Windows NetMeeting is one of the most rudimentary, and thus user-friendly, videoconferencing applications available. It can only transmit image to and receive image from one other station, i.e., NetMeeting allows only for point-to-point videoconferencing involving two users or user groups. The quality of the image being transmitted is, in addition, relatively low. It nevertheless has the advantage of being extremely easy to install, as it comes pre-installed with most recent version of Windows or may otherwise be downloaded for free; it may thus be used for instance if a point-to-point videoconferencing session needs to be scheduled on very short notice. Its use is free.

NetMeeting offers the following features:

- Point-to-point videoconferencing, in which participants only need appropriate video, sound and voice hardware. Calls are placed mainly through the MSN Messenger Service.
- Text-chatting, which can be used to send written messages to other participants during a conference.
- Whiteboard presentations, including real-time drawings, enabling one participant to show images to the other.
- Sharing applications and transferring files, which can be very useful to create a joint document.
- 'Remote Desktop Sharing', allowing control over one computer from another.

To install NetMeeting, one should follow these steps:[366]

- In the Start menu, select Run.
- Type 'Conf.exe' and hit return.
- The NetMeeting Wizard will launch and ask you to supply information such as your name, e-mail address, and geographical location, and will then create a shortcut on the desktop or in the Quick Launch bar.

---

366 For further technical instructions of use, see, for example, the description provided by MeetingByWire, <www.meetingbywire.com/XPNetMeeting.htm>. See also the fact sheet established by Nova Southeastern University, <www.nova.edu/techtrain/apptrain/netmeeting>.

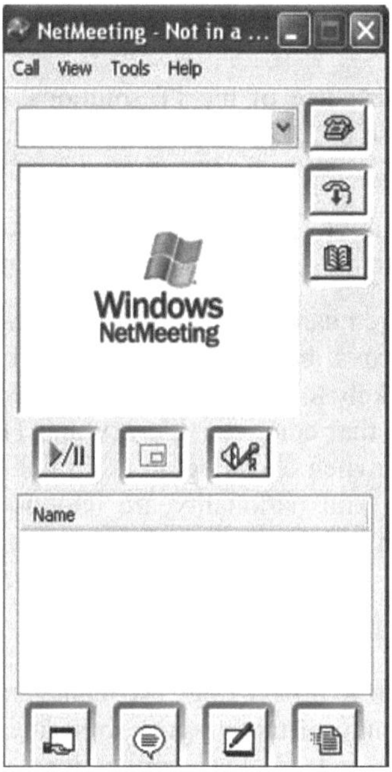

Figure 38. NetMeeting videoconferencing interface

IV. DEFINING A COMMUNICATIONS PROTOCOL

Different aspects of an arbitration procedure correspond to different types of communications, which require or allow for specific technologies. If extensive recourse to IT solutions is planned, it is advisable to define in advance which type of communications will be handled in which way and by which technology. This is the purpose of a communications protocol, i.e., an agreement or a decision of the arbitral tribunal – in principle embodied in a procedural order – on aspects of the procedure such as the technical organization of the submission of documents (briefs and documentary evidence) and exhibits in other forms; on the form all or some hearings will take; and on all other forms of communication exchanges between the arbitrators, the parties, and possibly external participants such as witnesses or experts.

Organized according to the main types of communications usually taking place in arbitral proceedings, this section provides recommendations for the most frequently used technologies. But before doing so, it addresses the question of who decides on the use of IT in arbitration.

A. The use of IT: who decides, when and how?

Prior to entering into the substance of the IT solutions, a threshold question most be posed: who decides on the use of IT in arbitration? In theory, the answer is the same as for any procedural matter:

> The parties decide if and how IT should be used in arbitration, if they agree, and, if they do not agree, it is up to the arbitrators to decide on these matters.

In practice, the answer is more nuanced. Even if the parties agree, it would be preferable to secure the arbitrators' approval before making a final choice. Forcing an IT option on an unwilling arbitrator is unlikely to favor the smooth conduct of the proceedings.

It may further be recalled that computer literacy and IT considerations should never become the prevailing issues when choosing an arbitrator. Other factors, such as expertise, experience, availability, and nationality are undoubtedly more important for the management of the arbitration and the quality of the outcome.

On this basis, the practical answer to the threshold question may be further elaborated on the basis of the three following hypotheses:

- If the parties wish to resort to an existing case management website such as WebFile, NetCase or ECAF, they may certainly agree so in advance without first seeking the arbitral tribunal's consent. Indeed, these applications, ready-made and user-friendly, are likely to become common practice and arbitrators should agree to use them.
- If the parties wish to use other institutional procedural rules on the use of IT, they may state so in general terms, but should leave the actual implementation to be discussed with and, if need be, determined by the tribunal.
- If the parties wish to use IT means without reference to specific rules, they may state so, for example by providing that hearings may be held by videoconference or that submissions may be filed electronically and that specifications will be agreed upon or decided by the tribunal at the outset of the proceedings.

As to the form in which the decision on and about the use of IT may be reached, the following situations are the most likely:

- The parties may consider the different uses of IT and its practicability and make joint or separate proposals to the tribunal.
- In response to proposals, or if no proposals are forthcoming, the tribunal may also review the available options and make suggestions of its own initiative, usually by submitting a draft procedural order providing for IT solutions to be discussed at an initial procedural hearing.

The following sections must be read bearing these clarifications in mind.

B. Submissions (briefs, memorials, applications) and documentary evidence

The parties and the arbitrators should examine different methods of sending documents, such as by courier, fax, e-mail with or without attachments, on diskettes, or on CD-Roms. These data carriers should be labeled with contents, author, intended recipient, date, and the compression software used if applicable. The size of a document and the availability of document compression systems should also be taken into consideration in choosing one method or another.

Generally, it is impractical to send and receive very long documents such as memorials with or without exhibits by e-mail. Hence, it is preferable to provide that such documents will be communicated on a CD-Rom, with or without a paper version depending on the wishes and habits of the tribunal members, counsel, and party representatives.

When using electronic methods, the parties should also think about the format of the document and whether to use doc, pdf or rtf formatting, and maybe specific software for word processing and spreadsheets. It is recommended to use either pdf or rtf format.[367]

If parties intend to use electronic means as their primary method for filing documents, they should define an alternative backup method for sending them, such as courier or fax, in the event of difficulties with the electronic means. A safe solution is to send a hard copy of the most important documents by post or special courier after they have been sent electronically. That solution has the disadvantage, however, of defeating the cost efficiency that electronic communications may otherwise achieve.

The parties should also decide on other aspects of document submission, such as:

- preparing a database of documents, including the allocation of costs for creating this database;
- labelling and identifying files and physical data carriers such as diskettes and CD-Roms;
- acknowledging the receipt of an e-mail and its attached document – every so often an e-mail reaches the addressee but the attachment cannot be opened; and
- checking for viruses (possibly specifying the anti-virus software to be used) before sending a document.

Security is another important issue that should be discussed by all parties, including the methods for authentication and non-repudiation, and encryption technologies. When deciding on such items, the parties should specify the procedure to be followed. They can also define a certain protection technology to be used against internal and external security threats, in order to prevent documents from being intercepted.

---

[367] See Section I.A.3.a Viruses, p. 142 above; Section II.A. Sending e-mail, p. 153 above; and Section II.C. Keeping track of hidden information: metadata, p. 156 above.

C. Other communications

Any other communications, whether from the parties to the tribunal, between the parties with a copy to the tribunal, or from the tribunal to the parties, can generally be handled by e-mail (or fax). All explanations given with respect to e-mails apply to these other communications as well.

D. Hearings

To prepare hearings adequately, the parties and arbitrators should first agree on which situations call for which type of meeting:

- in person;
- videoconferencing; or
- teleconferencing.

If teleconferencing or videoconferencing is to be used, all required documents should be made available to the participants, which may for instance be achieved by a case management system, by the file-sharing application of the videoconferencing software, by e-mail if the number of documents is limited, or on a CD-Rom or another physical data carrier if recourse to IT is to be kept to a minimum or some of the data require software different from the one agreed by the parties (such software can then be included on the data carrier). This data carrier should be sent by registered mail specifying the compression system used.

If videoconferencing is used for hearings, a number of specific recommendations should be followed.[368] These include providing a list of the persons who will attend the conference; the situation of the cameras (location, angle, rooms in which they are installed); the identity of all persons who are in the same room as the participants; the authentication of the identity of the participants who are not known by another trustworthy participant; the documents to be shown; etc.

E. Deliberations between arbitrators

The arbitrators are free to decide how they intend to organize their deliberations and in which form they will hold them. This being said, the parties and the arbitrators may wish to address specific provisions regarding the treatment of confidential documents if deliberations or the drafting of the award are carried out electronically. In this case, the parties

[368] See further Section III.B. Setting up a videoconferencing session, p. 170 above.

and the arbitrators should agree on a protocol for protecting against interception – password-protected documents, encryption, etc.[369]

F. Form and Notification of the Award

The fundamental rule as regards the notification of the award is that it should always be sent in paper form. For the sake of convenience an advance copy may be sent in electronic format. But the still uncertain status of the validity of awards in electronic form suggests that the absence of paper may lead to difficulties at the stage of enforcement or recognition, and it thus requires a notification in paper form.[370] As this safety measure is easy to implement and does not generate any significant cost, it should always be respected, even if the idea that arbitral proceedings may be carried out entirely online would seem, as such, to be an attractive prospect.

---

[369] See Section I.A. Security, p. 132 above.

[370] On these issues, see J. Arsic, 'International Commercial Arbitration on the Internet – Has the Future Come Too Early?' (1997) 14 J Int Arb 209, p. 217; M.E. Schneider and C. Kuner, 'Dispute Resolution in International Electronic Commerce' (1997) 14 J Int Arb 5, p. 24; and G. Kaufmann-Kohler and T. Schultz, *Online Dispute Resolution: Challenges for Contemporary Justice* (The Hague, Kluwer Law International, 2004), pp. 216–223.

CHAPTER 6

DRAFTING SUGGESTIONS

Choosing the most appropriate technology for one's projects and determining how it should be used on the basis of legal, practical, and technical criteria is only half the journey to actual IT usage. The second half of the journey is providing for such usage in legal terms. The greatest challenge in this respect is to set out clear and predictable rules without being too restrictive. Hence, this chapter sets forth drafting recommendations and samples for the two main vehicles used to provide for the use of IT: arbitration agreements and procedural orders. In the context of arbitration agreements, a brief remark is also made with regard to institutional rules of procedure, to which an arbitration agreement may refer. For the sake of practical convenience, this chapter then also provides sample forms to be used by the parties, either to propose the use of specific technologies during the procedure or to report a technical problem to the other party and the arbitral tribunal.

I. ARBITRATION AGREEMENTS

Parties wishing to provide for the use of IT during the proceedings, either before or after a dispute has arisen, may do so by inserting a specific clause to this effect in their arbitration agreement. This clause can either contain in itself the provision that IT will be used, or it can simply state that certain institutional procedural rules will be applied, which include provisions regarding IT. The purpose of the following is to discuss how such arbitration agreements may best be drafted.

A. In general

At the outset of this section, it may already be noted that the gist of drafting an arbitration agreement providing for IT usage is that it should include no detailed provisions on the technologies to be used. If included at all, technical provisions should be termed as broadly as possible (i.e., using terms such as 'electronic document management', 'electronic document transmission', 'videoconferencing'), because the available technologies change rapidly and the dispute may emerge a long time after the agreement has been signed.

It may also be specified, at this level of general considerations, that if the arbitration agreement refers to institutional rules of procedure containing provisions regarding the use of IT, reference should only be made to rules that do not contain detailed provisions on technology. The reason for this recommendation is the difficulty of foreseeing all possible purposes of technology. Consequently, only general statements should be contained in such institutional procedural rules. For instance, one may think of 'formats that are standard in the international legal community', with examples like 'doc, rtf, jpg, bmp', or 'formats that can easily be read and produced by all parties'. The final decision on specific IT solutions in this matter, provided by the institutional rules of procedure, should always remain within the discretion of the arbitral tribunal exercised in consultation with the parties.

These general recommendations are further specified in the following, which makes a distinction between pre-dispute and post-dispute agreements.

B. Pre-dispute Arbitration Agreement

Generally speaking, pre-dispute arbitration agreements providing for IT usage should be termed as broadly as possible. The main reason for this is that the available IT tools may change quite radically between the time an arbitration agreement is signed and the start of the proceedings. It should in principle be sufficient to mention the parties' intent to resort to IT.

In this respect, one should distinguish between an arbitration clause providing for arbitration administered by an institution offering IT services, such as the ICC, the AAA, or WIPO, and arbitration by an institution making no such services available or ad hoc arbitration. In the former case, reference should be made to the services offered by the institution chosen, more precisely to the pertinent rules of the institution. If such rules offer several alternatives, it will most often be preferable not to make a definitive choice at the time of entering into the contract. Moreover, the parties should avoid specifying the procedural rules and IT services as they stand at the time of the conclusion of the contract. Indeed, technologies that are outdated at the time they come into play may do more harm than good.

If the arbitration clause provides for ad hoc arbitration or arbitration under the auspices of an institution which offers no IT services, it may make sense to provide for a duty to consider the use of IT and to negotiate its implementation at the outset of the proceedings. The wording of such a provision could be as follows:

> In the event of any dispute arising out of or in connection with the present contract, the parties agree to refer such dispute to arbitration by […]. In relation to such arbitral proceedings, the parties agree to discuss and consider resorting to electronic means of communication.

B. Post-dispute Arbitration Agreement

Post-dispute arbitration agreements providing for IT usage may be more precise than pre-dispute agreements. Nevertheless, arbitral proceedings may have a long duration and a door should be left open in case technology evolves significantly during the proceedings and a new instrument becomes more appropriate.

Here again a distinction must be made between arbitrations administered by an institution offering IT services and other arbitrations. In the first case, the parties may of course agree to resort to the IT procedural rules of a specific institution (ICC, AAA, WIPO). In such event, it is in principle advisable to use the standard clause proposed by the institution.

If the parties choose ad hoc arbitration or other institutional arbitrations, they may provide for IT usage in their agreement. However, the provision should not give detailed specifications. These should only be determined after consultation with the members of the arbitral tribunal, as it would not make sense to provide for solutions with which the arbitrator is not willing to work. Hence, the following wording may be appropriate:

> The parties agree to use IT means of communication for submissions, including exhibits, and other communications. They also agree to hold hearings by videoconference whenever appropriate. They shall request the tribunal to give appropriate instructions after communication with the parties.

II. PROCEDURAL ORDER

The drafting of a procedural order will frequently be the cornerstone of the issue regarding if, when, and how electronic communication technologies are to be used. What will in principle set IT usage in motion is the procedural order handed down by the arbitrators, be it preceded or not by specific instructions from the parties. This section first suggests some recommendations as to what should be taken into consideration when drafting a procedural order. It then provides a sample procedural order, which may be adapted to concrete cases.

A. COMMENTS

The procedural order by the arbitral tribunal on the IT solutions that will be used should be rendered, as much as possible, after having sought the parties' agreement, during a preparatory meeting or during the terms of reference phase in an ICC arbitration. Such a decision should address in particular:

- The exchange of electronic documents: whether documents will be exchanged as e-mail attachments, through a case management website, or using a physical carrier (DVD/CD).
- Admissible file formats. Standard format transmission should always be used (doc, rtf, pdf, jpg, bmp, etc.), to avoid forcing a party to install proprietary software in order to read the file. In addition, one should use formats that do not carry metadata (information about the author of the document, on which computer it was modified,

tracked changes, etc.) and that do not execute scripts (very small applications executed by the computer, generally Microsoft Word macros but possibly viruses). Concretely, this means that the rtf format should preferably be used, rather than doc. Conversion of a doc document to rtf is simply achieved by selecting rtf when doing a 'save as', in any word processor.

- Available fonts. Unavailable fonts on a computer may significantly change the layout and pagination of a Word document.
- File naming and classification system. This is particularly important if a case management system is used, to which all participants upload documents.
- Scanning documents not available in electronic format. The rules should specify whether it is possible or not, whether it should be done using text recognition software (which always has some inaccuracies) or not (by saving the scanned document in an image format, thereby preventing the use of the search function and making editing much more difficult).
- Fallback strategies. In case a given technology does not work properly, the rules should provide which other IT solution will replace it, or whether offline solutions should be used instead, etc. For instance, when scheduling a videoconference, one should keep in mind that technical breakdowns occasionally occur. Some such breakdowns cannot be minimized by having backup equipment available, simply because it can be difficult to provide backups for certain equipment, such as the central servers of the Internet service provider. In such situations, it should for instance be decided in advance if a videoconferencing session that cannot be completed can be replaced by a telephone conference or if it should be rescheduled, etc.
- Videoconferences should be scheduled to last a half day at most; like teleconferences, such sessions require much more concentration than face-to-face meetings and are therefore tiresome.
- Costs allocation for the acquisition and use of IT tools.
- An express provision that the arbitral tribunal may amend such rules.

B. Sample Procedural Order

The procedural order suggested in the following can either be issued as a separate ruling or incorporated into a first, broader procedural order dealing with the relevant matters of procedure.

Language in brackets signals comments, suggested additions or alternative provisions; it is to be adapted by the arbitral tribunal to the case at hand.

ARBITRATION _________ ____[DATE]___

[Party A]

v.

[Party B]

PROCEDURAL ORDER N. __

The Arbitral Tribunal, having consulted with the parties, directs that the following procedural rules on the use of IT shall apply to these arbitration proceedings.

1. DETAILS OF PARTIES AND ARBITRATORS

1.1 Claimant

Recipient 1: Name_________________	Recipient 2: Name___________________
Address________________	Address__________________
______________________	________________________
______________________	________________________
Phone_________________	Phone___________________
Fax___________________	Fax_____________________
E-mail________________	E-mail__________________

1.2 Respondent

Recipient 1: Name_________________	Recipient 2: Name___________________
Address________________	Address__________________
______________________	________________________
______________________	________________________
Phone_________________	Phone___________________
Fax___________________	Fax_____________________
E-mail________________	E-mail__________________

1.3 Arbitral tribunal

Chair:
Name________________
Address______________
____
____
Phone________________
Fax__________________
E-mail________________

Arbitrator appointed by Claimant:

Name________________
Address______________
____
____
Phone________________
Fax__________________
E-mail________________

Arbitrator appointed by Respondent:

Name________________
Address______________
____
____
Phone________________
Fax__________________
E-mail________________

2. NOTIFICATIONS

2.1 All notifications and communications other than written memorials, exhibits and awards shall be made by e-mail.

2.2 Notifications subject to a time limit and made by e-mail shall be accompanied, simultaneously and in any case before the expiration of the time limit, by a fax stating that the e-mail has been sent. The fax shall contain a copy of the cover e-mail, printed out so as to show the precise date and time at which it was sent.

2.3 Notifications made by e-mail to the parties shall be deemed received upon arrival of the e-mail in the recipient's e-mail server, at the local time of the recipient. Notifications made to the arbitral tribunal shall be deemed received upon arrival of the e-mail in the chair's e-mail server, at his or her local time.

3. SECURITY

3.1 Throughout the proceedings, the parties and the tribunal shall use standard anti-virus software and firewalls; they undertake to keep these technical means regularly updated.

[3.2 E-mails shall be digitally signed to authenticate the identity of the sender.]

[3.3 E-mails shall be encrypted, according to technical specifications to be agreed upon.]

4. TECHNICAL PROBLEMS

4.1 In the event of a technical problem, all participants in the proceedings, i.e., the parties, the arbitrators, experts and witnesses, shall use the appended incident form to report the issue.

4.2 The incident form shall be sent immediately after the technical problem has been detected.

4.3. The incident form shall be sent to the participant with whom the communication failed (typically from the addressee to the sender in case of poor reception of the communication, and from the sender to the addressee in the event of an inability to transmit the intended files), with a copy to the other party (if not the main addressee), the arbitral tribunal (if not the main addressee), and the arbitration institution.

4.4. The incident form shall be sent using the most reliable available means of communication, e.g., fax.

5. WRITTEN MEMORIALS AND EXHIBITS

5.1 Written memorials and exhibits shall be submitted in the following form [choose one, two or more options; a distinction may also be made between memorials (e.g., by e-mail and CD-Rom) and exhibits (e.g., only on CD-Rom)]:

[- E-mail accompanied by a paper copy]
[- E-mail accompanied by a copy on CD-Rom or DVD-Rom]
[- CD-Rom or DVD-Rom]
[- In paper copy]

5.2 All submissions mentioned in Paragraph 5.1 shall be sent at the latest on the last day of the time limit. Submissions in paper or on electronic carrier (e.g., CD-Rom or DVD-Rom) shall be sent by special courier.

5.3 All submissions sent by e-mail shall be subject to the provisions of Section 3 above. Submissions made by e-mail accompanied by a copy on paper or electronic carrier (e.g., CD-Rom or DVD-Rom) shall be deemed received at the time of arrival of the e-mail in the recipient's e-mail server, at the local time of the recipient.

5.4 All documents to be transmitted that are not available electronically shall be scanned and saved in pdf format with text recognition if the document is composed of text.

5.5 In addition to the virus check of e-mails under Section 3 above, the parties shall check for viruses, using standard and up-to-date software, any written submission or document that is intended to be attached to an e-mail or to be saved on a CD-Rom or DVD-Rom, diskette, USB drive, or any other physical data carrier.

5.6 Files shall be named according to the following formula:

XY.000.------------.DDMMYYYY.***

Where:

- XY is the abbreviation of the sender, according to the following acronyms:

  - CL is the claimant
  - RD is the respondent
  - CH is the chair of the arbitral tribunal
  - AC is the arbitrator appointed by the claimant
  - AR is the arbitrator appointed by the respondent
  - AT is the arbitral tribunal as a whole
  - SE is the secretariat of the arbitration institution

- 000 is the abbreviation of the nature of the document, according to the following acronyms:

  - MEM: memorial
  - DEV: documentary evidence
  - OEV: oral evidence (transcript or audio recording)
  - AWA: award
  - POR: procedural order
  - NOC: notice and communication
  - OTH: other

- ------------ is a short description of the document

- DDMMYYYY is the date of production of the document

- *** is the format of the document

6. HEARINGS, WITNESSES, AND EXPERTS

6.1 This section shall apply to any hearing or portion of hearing to be held by videoconference.

6.2 At the request of either party or on its own motion, the tribunal may direct that a videoconference be held for:

- Procedural sessions.
- [Oral arguments on jurisdiction or on the merits.]
- [The hearing of witnesses of fact.]
- [The hearing of expert witnesses.]
- [Any other purpose, at the arbitral tribunal's discretion.]

6.3 Except in urgent situations, such as the scheduling of a hearing on interim measures, the tribunal shall give the parties at least [one month] [two weeks] advance notice.

6.4 When ordering the videoconference, the tribunal shall address the following elements:

- Date, time, and anticipated duration of the videoconference.
- Purpose of the videoconference.
- Identification of terminal stations.
- Technology to be used.
- Participants at each station, including whether an observer of the opposite party or of the arbitral tribunal may be present.
- Identification of the files, documents, and notes that may be available at each station, especially to witnesses and experts testifying by videoconference.
- Preparatory actions to be undertaken ahead of the videoconference, such as test sessions, and their timing.
- In the event a participant's connection is broken, the procedure for contacting the remaining participants.

6.5 At least one week before the scheduled videoconference, the tribunal and the parties shall run a test to evaluate the infrastructure and the capabilities of the network.

6.6 During the videoconference, the participants [or the witness] shall always be in view of the camera. [One camera shall be placed so as to provide a view of the entire room.]

6.7 Participants shall identify themselves by showing a piece of identification to the camera. The tribunal may request other forms of identification.

6.8 A technician shall be present [available] at every station, and his identity shall be communicated to the tribunal at least three days before the videoconference.

6.9 The videoconferences shall be recorded (image and sound).

6.10 In case of failure of the videoconferencing system, the tribunal shall reschedule the videoconference or take any other appropriate measure.

7. Award

7.1 Awards shall be notified to the parties in paper form, by registered mail or special courier.

7.2 The tribunal, at its discretion, may circulate an electronic copy of the award to the parties as soon as, but not before, each party has received the award in paper form; the time of reception shall be certified by the special courier used to notify the award. The award in electronic form shall be for purposes of convenience only. It shall not constitute the original award and it shall have strictly no procedural consequence whatsoever; the original award is the award sent in paper form. The sending of the electronic copy of the award shall not constitute notification of the award; only the award in paper form shall form the object of the notification.

8. Cost allocation

Each party shall provisionally bear the costs that it incurs to comply with this order. The parties shall advance in equal shares the costs incurred by the tribunal to comply with this order. The tribunal shall make a final cost allocation in the award, taking into account all relevant circumstances.

9. Exceptions and revision of these rules

9.1 Upon a reasoned request, the tribunal may authorize a party to transmit a notification, communication, memorial or exhibit in a format or using a program different than those provided for herein. Subject to contrary directions from the tribunal, the party so authorized shall provide the other parties and the tribunal with all necessary hardware, software and technical support at its own expense.

9.2 The arbitral tribunal may proceed to revise, amend and complete these rules at any time during the procedure. [Upon request of a party or on its own motion, the tribunal may in particular, after consultation with parties, provide for the use of new technologies.]

9.3. Once a year, the arbitral tribunal and the representatives of the parties shall engage in consultation on the matter of possible revisions of these rules, to adapt them to the evolution of the relevant technologies.

Place and date

Signatures

III. INITIATION FORM

A. Comments

The form provided below is to be used by a party – or, with a few minor changes, by an arbitrator – wishing to resort to IT solutions during the future proceedings and thus wishing to initiate discussions on the use of technology. More precisely, it would usually be used by one party to propose the use of electronic communication means to the other party and to the arbitral tribunal, with a mention of preferences for specific technologies. The form is thus meant as a basis for negotiations between the parties. The idea is that once the proposing party has filled in the form, it should be sent to the other party, jointly with a blank copy, so that the addressee can in turn fill in the fields. This will allow a good evaluation of the technical capabilities of the parties and help focus their attention on the aspects of IT usage that they may want to define in advance.

The arbitral tribunal must in principle abide by the IT agreement of the parties and use the technologies specified therein. Nevertheless, it is certainly not advisable to force any technological tool on unwilling arbitrators who are unlearned in technical matters; it would only result in disruptions of the procedure and the very purpose of IT usage may well be defeated.

Hence, if the IT agreement between the parties is concluded before the arbitrators are appointed, computer literacy should be taken into consideration when selecting the arbitral tribunal – although it may be recalled that it should never be the prevailing criteria.[371] If the arbitrators are selected for the parties by an appointing authority, this authority should be informed of the parties' wish to resort to IT to an extent exceeding ordinary IT usage.

If, conversely, the IT agreement between the parties is concluded after the arbitral tribunal has been appointed, it is strongly recommended to engage in consultation with the arbitrators to obtain their approval before making a final choice on the technologies to be used.

With regard to the contents of this initiation form, two remarks should be made. First, with respect to Paragraph 2.3, the second solution (providing that the award shall be sent first in paper form and later, upon reception of the paper copy, in electronic form) is meant to strictly exclude all issues that might arise in the time between the reception of the electronic copy and the reception of the paper copy.

Second, with respect to Paragraph 3.3.b, standard actions undertaken prior to a videoconferencing session, which may be listed under this paragraph, are: determination of date and time, terminal stations, and participants, followed by testing.

---

[371] See Chapter 5, Section IV.A. The Use of IT: who decides, when and how?, p. 182 above.

It must be said, finally, that this form as well as the following one, and the following one in particular, are inspired by those of the ICC, as published in the 2004 Special Supplement on 'Using Technology to Resolve Business Disputes' to the ICC International Court of Arbitration Bulletin. However, the forms provided here are largely simplified compared to those of the ICC (especially this one), so as to be accessible to persons who are not IT specialists; it is believed, indeed, that, in the current state of IT usage in arbitration and the general computer literacy of most practitioners, user friendliness and simplicity should clearly prevail over technical comprehensiveness.

B. SAMPLE INITIATION FORM

Case________________________

Reference____________________

Date________________________

Participant initiating IT usage____________________

Contact details:

Participant initiating IT usage ________________________
____
____

Technician in charge ________________________
____
____

This initiation form is being sent to the following persons and/or entities:

Name________________________	Name________________________
Address______________________	Address______________________
____________________________	____________________________
____________________________	____________________________
____________________________	____________________________
Phone________________________	Phone ______________________
Fax__________________________	Fax ________________________
E-mail_______________________	E-mail ______________________
Name________________________	Name________________________
Address______________________	Address______________________
____________________________	____________________________

______________________	______________________
______________________	______________________
Phone______________	Phone ______________
Fax________________	Fax ______________
E-mail______________	E-mail ______________

1. INTRODUCTORY REMARKS

1.1 The IT suggestions contained in this form cover (select applicable):

a. Technologies to be used for communications (Section 2 below):

- ☐ Communication technologies for written memorials and exhibits
- ☐ Communication technologies for other, general communications
- ☐ Communication of the award

b. Specifications regarding the use of such technologies, with respect to (Section 3 below):

- ☐ Format of electronic documents
- ☐ Naming of electronic documents
- ☐ Videoconferencing

1.2 In the event of a technical problem, the parties agree:

- ☐ To use the incident form appended to the present form
- ☐ To resort to ad hoc methods to report and resolve technical issues

2. TECHNOLOGIES TO BE USED FOR COMMUNICATIONS

2.1 We propose that all written memorials and exhibits be exchanged by:

- ☐ Standard e-mail
- ☐ Secure e-mail (encrypted and digitally signed)
- ☐ Using the following case management website:
- ☐ On a CD-Rom

- ☐ On a DVD

- ☐ All transmissions in one of the formats listed above must be accompanied by a paper copy, sent on the same day as the electronic copy.
- ☐ All transmissions in one of the formats listed above must be accompanied by a notification by fax providing that the electronic copy has been sent.

2.2 We propose that all notifications and communications, including procedural orders, other than written memorials and exhibits be made by:

- ☐ Standard e-mail
- ☐ Secure e-mail (encrypted and digitally signed)
- ☐ Using the following case management website:
- ☐ On a CD-Rom
- ☐ On a DVD-Rom

- ☐ All transmissions in one of the formats listed above must be accompanied by a paper copy, sent on the same day as the electronic copy.
- ☐ All transmissions in one of the formats listed above must be accompanied by a notification by fax providing that the electronic copy has been sent.

2.3 With regard to the arbitral award, we propose that:

- ☐ The arbitral tribunal forward an electronic copy of the award to the parties as soon as it is made. Such award shall be for informational purposes only. It shall not constitute the original award and it shall have strictly no procedural consequence whatsoever; the original award shall be sent in paper form. The sending of the electronic copy of the award shall not constitute notification of the award; only the award in paper form shall form the object of the notification.
- ☐ The arbitral tribunal forward an electronic copy of the award to the parties as soon as, but not before, each party has received the award in paper form; the time of reception shall be certified by the special courier used to notify the award. The award in electronic form shall be for convenience purposes only. It shall not constitute the original award and it shall have strictly no procedural consequence whatsoever; the original award is the award sent in paper form. The sending of the electronic copy of the award shall not constitute notification of the award; only the award in paper form shall form the object of the notification.

3. TECHNICAL SPECIFICATIONS

3.1 Format of electronic documents

We propose the use of the following formats for electronic documents:

Type of document	*Format*
Text documents	☐ DOC ☐ RTF ☐ PDF
Spreadsheets	☐ XLS
Images	☐ JPEG ☐ GIF ☐ BMP
Sound	☐ MP3 ☐ WAV ☐ AIFF ☐ WMA
Video	☐ AVI ☐ MPEG ☐ MOV ☐ DivX

3.2 Naming of electronic documents

We propose the following system to name documents:

XY.000.------------.DDMMYYYY.***

Where:

- XY is the abbreviation of the sender, according to the following acronyms:

  - CL is the claimant
  - RD is the respondent
  - CH is the chair of the arbitral tribunal

- AC is the arbitrator appointed by the claimant
- AR is the arbitrator appointed by the respondent
- AT is the arbitral tribunal as a whole
- SE is the secretariat of the arbitration institution

- 000 is the abbreviation of the nature of the document, according to the following acronyms:

  - MEM: memorial
  - DEV: documentary evidence
  - OEV: oral evidence (transcript or audio recording)
  - AWA: award
  - POR: procedural order
  - NOC: notice and communication
  - OTH: other

- ------------ is a short description of the document

- DDMMYYYY is the date of production of the document

- *** is the format of the document

3.3 Videoconferencing

a. We propose the use of the following videoconferencing system:

Name of system: ____
Approximate costs (in addition to equipment):____________________________
Equipment required:____
More information available at:____________________________________

☐ We have tested the system and certify that we have the equipment necessary to use it.

b. The preparation of videoconferencing sessions shall in principle, except specific agreement by both parties, follow these steps:

Action	Time before conference

IV. INCIDENT FORM

A. Comments

The form presented in this section is to be employed in case of a technical deficiency. It may be used by any participant in an arbitration – the parties, the arbitrators, possibly the arbitration institution as well as experts and witnesses. It may also be used for communications addressed to any of these participants, i.e., communications to the arbitral tribunal, communications between the parties, etc.

The form will probably be used mainly by the addressee of an electronic communication. The addressee would typically report of the poor reception of the communication or lack thereof. For example, a participant may not be able to open or unzip an attachment to an e-mail, download a document posted on a case management website, or play the recording of a videoconferencing session on his computer. In this case, the incident form is sent to the sender of the electronic communication in question, with copies to the arbitral tribunal (or the other party, if the tribunal was the addressee) and, if applicable, to the arbitration institution.

In addition, the form may also be used by the sender of an electronic communication, who realizes that his or her communications are not reaching their addressee. Typically, a sender may receive notice that his or her e-mails bounce, i.e., that they cannot reach the addressee because the mailbox is full, or the e-mail is too large, or the addressee's system misidentifies the message as spam. A case management website, which may for instance be used to upload written memorials, may also temporarily be out of order for reasons beyond the control of any participant involved. In this case, the form is sent to the addressee of the electronic communication in question, with copies to the arbitral tribunal (or the other party, if the tribunal was the addressee) and, if applicable, to the arbitration institution. This form may be sent, for instance, by fax, if no electronic means of communication guarantees proper reception at that moment.

The arbitral tribunal then decides whether specific action should be taken, including how the electronic communication should be re-sent and if the applicable timelines should be extended. The decision on the extension of the timeline would for instance depend on the following elements: whether the sender has conformed to the specifications regarding format and technology provided by the procedural order; the reason, if it can be established, of the transmission failure; possible safety measures taken by the sender, such as prior tests; and the cooperation of the addressee in solving the issue. In any event, the timelines applicable to procedural stages following the procedural stage in which the incident has occurred should never be extended for a longer period than the time between the notification of the incident and the *bona fide* restoration of a successful transmission – otherwise, the recipient would be tempted to wait for a long time before alleging improper reception of an electronic communication.

In this context, it may briefly be mentioned that at least two reasons may prevent e-mail communications from reaching the addressee, possibly without any automated notification of failure. The first reason relates to the size of the e-mail, together with its attachments: if the size of the e-mail is larger than what is guaranteed by the ISP of the sender, the e-mail is simply marked as 'sent' but never reaches the addressee, and, depending on the policy of the ISP, it may be the case that no error message is produced by the system. In such a case, the sender has no way of knowing, other than contacting the recipient, if the message has indeed reached the addressee's servers. The second reason materializes when the ISP of the sender has been put onto a list of ISPs that do not sufficiently combat spam originating from their clients. In this case, the ISPs of some recipients simply delete all e-mails originating from a sender using such a blacklisted ISP, without any notification, neither to the sender nor to the recipient. In 2005, the ISP of a prominent international law firm in Geneva was put onto such a list, with the result that all communications from employees of this firm to recipients of certain organizations (the identity of which was unpredictable for all but IT specialists), including Geneva University, simply vanished into thin air without anyone being alerted.

B. Sample incident form

Case__________________________

Reference______________________

Date__________________________

Participant initiating IT usage______________________

Contact details:

Participant initiating IT usage ___________________________

Technician in charge ___________________________

This initiation form is being sent to the following persons and/or entities:

Name__________________________	Name________________________
Address________________________	Address______________________
Phone_________________________	Phone ______________________
Fax___________________________	Fax ______________________
E-mail_________________________	E-mail ______________________

Name__________________________	Name________________________
Address________________________	Address______________________

____________________	____________________
____________________	____________________
Phone____________________	Phone ____________________
Fax____________________	Fax ____________________
E-mail____________________	E-mail ____________________

DESCRIPTION OF THE INCIDENT

A. Date of the incident____________________

B. Time of the incident____________________

C. Person who detected the incident____________________

D. Areas concerned by the incident

1. Technologies used for:

- ☐ Communication of written memorials and exhibits
- ☐ Communication of other, general communications
- ☐ Communication of the award

2. More specifically, the issue relates to:

- ☐ Sending of electronic documents
- ☐ Format of electronic documents
- ☐ Naming of electronic documents
- ☐ Videoconferencing
- ☐ Other____________________

E. Detailed description of the incident

____
____
____
____
____
____
____

F. Suspected origin of the incident:

G. Proposed solution:

CHAPTER 7

CHECKLISTS, REMINDERS, AND CHARTS

This chapter is meant as the most hands-on part of the book; it reviews and synthesizes much of the contents of the preceding chapters into a few simple lists and tables. More precisely, this chapter has two purposes. On the one hand, it seeks to remind the practitioner of the main questions that should be posed either when planning for IT usage or when actually resorting to such technologies. On the other hand, it seeks to provide, in the form of charts, an easily accessible overview of the main practical and legal aspects of IT usage in arbitration. It must be recalled, however, that by nature such checklists, reminders, and charts cannot be exhaustive, and consequently other relevant parts of this book should also be referred to, as indicated in the following.

This chapter is organized in four parts. First, it provides general reminders that essentially relate to all forms of IT usage. It then reviews the main elements that should be kept in mind in relation to the use of e-mails, in particular which precautions should be taken in sending and receiving e-mails. Third, it suggests steps to follow when planning for and organizing a videoconference. Finally, it provides charts on the most important aspects of the use of IT in arbitration.

I. MAIN TASKS

General recommendations

(1) Take time to plan for and organize IT usage, especially if it involves a technology that participants are not familiar with. For instance, a videoconferencing session should never be scheduled without providing for time to test the equipment and remedy any unsatisfactory aspects.[372]
(2) Before using a new technology, take time to experiment and play with it, as not having mastered it may constitute a significant disadvantage and waste of time.[373]
(3) Have IT support available at all times, in case of technical deficiencies – a risk that can never be totally eliminated.
(4) Have back-up solutions available.[374]
(5) Seek simplicity: keep IT solutions as simple as possible.[375]

[372] See Chapter 5, Section III.B. Setting up a videoconferencing sessions, p. 170 above.
[373] See Chapter 1, Section IV.B. Lack of experience: IT as a trump card?, p. 22 above.
[374] See Chapter 5, Section I.B. Breakdowns, p. 145 above.

The parties should

(1) Consider the respective advantages of resorting either to institutionalized IT services such as those of the ICC, AAA, or WIPO,[376] which require less time investment, or implementing ad hoc IT solutions, which may be tailored more precisely to the needs of the case and the parties.
(2) Use very broad technical provisions in pre-dispute arbitration agreements.[377]
(3) Use broad technical provisions in post-dispute arbitration agreements.[378]
(4) Do not bind an as yet unknown tribunal to specific IT solutions.

The tribunal should

(1) Consult with counsel and render a procedural order on the use of IT, which should cover:[379]
  (a) Exchange of electronic documents.
  (b) Admissible file formats.
  (c) Available fonts.
  (d) File naming and classification system.
  (e) Scanning documents not available electronically.
  (f) Breakdown management.
  (g) Videoconferencing.
  (h) Costs allocation for the acquisition and use of IT tools.
  (i) Revision of technical rules if needed.
(2) When ordering the selection of a given technology, provide a clear description of the process in a complete and easily understandable manner.
(3) Always conduct the proceedings ensuring that the use of IT does not deprive a party of:
  (a) A real opportunity to present its allegations of facts, submit legal arguments, and tender pertinent evidence on relevant facts.[380]
  (a) A real opportunity to rebut the opponent's case, which implies equal access to the record and that the arbitral tribunal does not have ex parte communications with any party.[381]
(4) Do not select or use a given technology in a way that would put one party at a substantial disadvantage.[382]

375 See Chapter 1, Section IV.A. Creeping featurism: the more IT, the better?, p. 21 above.
376 See Chapter 3, Section I. State of practice, p. 75 above.
377 See Chapter 6, Section I. Arbitration agreements, p. 187 above.
378 Ibid.
379 For a proposal of procedural order, see Chapter 6, Section II. Procedural order, p. 189 above.
380 See Chapter 4, Section I.A. The right to be heard, p.108 above.
381 See Chapter 4, Section I.B. Adversary proceedings, p. 114 above.
382 See Chapter 4, Section I.C. Equal treatment, p. 116 above.

II. E-MAILING

Sending e-mails

(1) Give the e-mail a descriptive title.
(2) Mark an e-mail as important only if it really is.
(3) Preferably use text format rather than html.
(4) Use a final signature indicating phone numbers to call in case of technical problems.
(5) Check language once again.
(6) Double-check the addressee(s), also in cc and bcc fields.
(7) Prefer rtf or pdf format for attachments.
(8) Remove unnecessary attachments.[383]
(9) Check for the existence of metadata in attachments (i.e., check if the option 'Track changes' is on, check information in the 'File/Properties' section, and maybe use a meta-data remover).[384]
(10) Check attachments for viruses, if not automatic.[385]
(11) Protect confidential files sent as attachments with a password.
(12) Consider using a digital signature.[386]
(13) Consider using encrypted e-mails.[387]

Receiving e-mails

(1) Use the preview option if available.
(2) Do not open any suspicious attachment of any e-mail – for instance be cautious when following a url address or opening an '.exe' or even a doc file, as they may contain viruses.
(3) Classify e-mail efficiently.
(4) Always acknowledge receipt.[388]

[383] On all the above, see Chapter 5, Section II.A. Sending e-mail, p. 153 above.
[384] See Chapter 5, Section II.C. Keeping track of hidden information: metadata, p. 156 above.
[385] See Chapter 5, Section I.A.3. Infection, p. 142 above.
[386] See Chapter 5, Section II.D. Encrypting and digitally signing e-mails, p. 158 above.
[387] Ibid.
[388] On all recommendations, see Chapter 5, Section II.B. Receiving e-mail, p. 155 above.

III. VIDEOCONFERENCING

A. GENERAL REMINDERS

Videoconferencing is *not a perfect substitute* for in-person interactions, as it does not transmit all elements of non-verbal communication. For example, it may take users a few minutes to get used to the lack of normal eye contact during a hearing that may make it more difficult to direct attention clearly. Unexperienced participants should be informed of this beforehand.[389]

Sufficient broadcast quality (i.e., sufficient line speed and CPU power) must always be provided, as low-quality image transmissions will make it difficult to establish an interpersonal rapport and may cause frustration and be counter-productive. What constitutes sufficient broadcast quality depends on the videoconferencing platform being used, but as a general rule one may recommend opting for 400–500Kbps for both sending and receiving and, for CPU, at least a Pentium III and preferably a Pentium IV.[390]

B. VIDEOCONFERENCE OR IN-PERSON MEETING?

The advisability of meeting by way of videoconferencing rather than in person depends on a variety of factors, including the following.

Factors to consider in relation to videoconferencing

(1) General cost and time constraints; (2) Geographical distance between the parties; (3) Availability of the participants; (4) Contents of the meeting.

For detailed explanations of these elements, the reader is referred to their earlier discussion above.[391] For present purposes, it will suffice to give a summary overview of the situations in which it seems a priori advisable or not to consider videoconferencing.[392]

---

[389] See Chapter 2, Section II.C.1 Assessing videoconferencing, p. 51 above.

[390] See Chapter 2, Section II.D.1.b. Image quality, p. 61 above and Chapter 5, Section III.A. paragraph Connection speed, p. 170 above.

[391] See Chapter 2, Section II.C.1.b. Videoconferencing v. in-person meetings, p. 52 above and Chapter 5, Section III.A. To videoconference or not to videoconference, p. 168 above.

[392] For a more detailed discussion of these issues, see ibid.

Situations or factors calling for videoconferencing

(1) Hearing a witness who cannot be physically present at the hearing.
(2) Allowing an arbitrator or counsel who cannot attend in person (for example because of a flight cancellation) to participate rather than having to postpone the hearing.
(3) Evaluating and preparing a witness.
(4) Long distances separate the parties and the dispute is of low value.
(5) The collective drafting or editing of a document whose contents are not sensitive enough to require the presence of all drafters (certain contracts, for instance).
(6) Finalizing the terms of reference and procedural calendar or dealing with other procedural issues with the parties when an in-person meeting is not possible or not desirable.
(7) Deliberations among the arbitrators.
(8) Meetings among co-counsel.
(9) Hearings in certain expedited proceedings.
(10) Hearings on interim measures.

Situations or factors against videoconferencing

(1) Perceiving the state of mind of the participant(s) is important (for instance examination of a crucial witness suspected of hiding facts).
(2) A very large number of documents is to be used.
(3) The situation requires visual perception and the parties are absolutely inexperienced with videoconferencing technology and cannot provide sufficient guarantees in relation to the preparation of such a conference.
(4) The parties and the arbitrators have never met and it appears desirable for them to have an opportunity to meet in person, especially at the early stage of the arbitration.

Some situations may at the same time call for videoconferencing because of one factor and oppose it as a result of another factor – for example hearing a witness whose state of mind needs to be precisely assessed but who cannot travel to an in-person meeting without causing major delays in a time-driven procedure. In such situations, a part of the solution follows from other factors, the most important of which being the experience of the participants with videoconferencing, as it for instance becomes easier with experience to assess a state of mind through this technology.

C. Preparing a Videoconference

A videoconference takes time to prepare. The exact required duration will depend on the contents of the hearing and on the experience of the participants with the technology. For experienced participants, i.e., for persons who have already used the same technology on the same computers and the same Internet lines several times, setting up a videoconference may not require any more preparation than organizing a teleconference. As a rule of thumb, for inexperienced parties, one may suggest the following timelines.[393]

About 30 15 days before the scheduled conference, determine:

(1) Date, time, and duration.
(2) Technology to be used.
(3) Number of terminal stations and their location.
(4) Number of participants in each conference room.
(5) Procedure to determine the identity of the participants.
(6) Physical position of the equipment in relation to the participants.
(7) Presence of observers in each conference room.
(8) Documents available at each station, especially to witnesses and experts.
(9) Presence and availability of technicians.
(10)Alternatives in case of communication disruption.
(11)Whether and how the videoconference should be recorded.
(12)Preparatory actions to be undertaken before the videoconference, such as test sessions, and their timing.

One week before the conference, run a test, which involves:

(1) Connecting the required hardware.
(2) Launching the application and logging into the server.
(3) Exchanging a few words to test the audio capacity of the system (time lag, clarity, volume, sound disruptions).
(4) Showing irrelevant documents.

One hour before the conference:

(1) Have a technician ready and at hand.
(2) Launch the application and connect to the server.
(3) Toggle in and out of the components.
(4) Check lighting (should be behind the camera and bright enough).
(5) Mute microphone in order not to be overheard during the preparation for the conference and turn camera to show an irrelevant image, while waiting for the other participants to connect.
(6) Possibly upload to a private part of the server the documents that will be shown during the conference.

---

[393] See Chapter 5, Section III.B. Setting up a videoconferencing sessions, p. 170 above.

During the conference:

(1) Avoid quick movements.
(2) Be disciplined and wait for one's turn to speak.

VI. CHARTS FOR IT USAGE

A. PRACTICAL ASPECTS

1. ADVANTAGES OF TECHNOLOGIES

In what respect is recourse to the following technologies beneficial?

	Economic efficiency	*Speed*	*Effectiveness of process*	*Convenience*
Case management website	Document handling (reproduction, storage, and shipment) and seamless workflow (simplification of formalities, standardization, and automation)	Shipping; transmission of documents in general		Location-independent accessibility of documents; centralized archiving; portability of file; search functions
Videoconferencing	Traveling (out-of-pocket expenses and lost working time)	Traveling; availability of participants; time for realization of tasks; time between tasks	Hearing otherwise unavailable witnesses; richer communication than in teleconferencing	
Live notes		Immediate accessibility of transcript	Improved possibilities of cross-examination of witnesses or experts	Immediate accessibility of transcript; hyperlinking of transcript to evidence or video recording for facilitated retrieval of information
ODR provider	Economies of scale	Ready-to-go IT platforms		Experienced provider of IT services for dispute resolution

2. General technical measures

Global assessment of some usual technical measures.

	Economic efficiency	*Speed*	*Convenience*	*Reliability*	*Security*
Prior tests		---	---	+++++	
Redundant equipment	--			++++	
Dedicated equipment	--		--	+++	+
Encryption			-	-	++++
Passwords on documents					+++
Digital signatures			-	-	++++
Metadata removing software		-			+++
Antivirus				++	

3. Videoconferencing

Advisability of holding a videoconferencing session.

	Very high	*High*	*Under certain circumstances*	*Low*	*Very low*
A telephone conference call would also be appropriate	No disadvantage				
Travel costs disproportionate with regard to the disputed amounts		Consider importance of person heard			
Travel costs disproportionate with regard to the expected benefits of the meeting		Consider interpersonal rapport			

Serious problem of availability of an arbitrator, a counsel, a witness			Preferable to postponing meeting?		
No in-person hearing expected at all during the arbitration				Parties and arbitrators should meet at least once	
Hearing expected to last for more then two hours				More difficult to keep focus online	
Confidentiality is of utmost importance					Video necessarily allows recording
Deliberations and procedural meeting between the arbitrators	No disadvantage				
Meeting with co-counsel	No disadvantage				
Hearing for urgent interim relief	Better than no hearing at all				
Procedural hearing, e.g., drafting or reviewing the terms of reference or mission statement		If participants have met before	If participants have not met before		
Hearing witness or expert	If witness or expert unable to travel	If witness or expert is shy / inexperienced		If witness or expert is a good speaker	
Assessing or preparing witness		If witness credibility is not in question		If witness credibility is in question	
Expedited arbitration		May be the only realistic option			
Arbitration involving large distances between the participants and low amounts in dispute	May be the only realistic option				
	Very high	*High*	*Under certain circumstances*	*Low*	*Very low*

B. Legal aspects

1. Due process at risk

Main situations in which due process is likely to be jeopardized by the use of technology.

	Real opportunity to present the case	*Sufficient opportunity to present the case*	*Oral hearing*	*Adversary proceedings*	*Equal treatment*
Complexity of technology	X		(maybe)	(maybe)	X
Technical glitches	(maybe)		(maybe)	X	X
Speed (over-simplification of proceedings)	(maybe)	X	X		

2. Oral hearings

Existence and extent of a right to be heard orally under the major European arbitration laws and the UNCITRAL Model Law.

	Switzerland	*England*	*Germany*	*France*	*Italy*	*Netherlands*	*Belgium*	*Sweden*	*UNCITRAL*
Oral hearing does not have to be held, unless the parties have agreed otherwise	X	X							
Oral hearing does not have to be held, unless a party requests it					X	X			
Oral hearing must be held, unless the parties have agreed otherwise			X	X			X	X	X

3. Confidentiality

Reference to provisions included in procedural rules of arbitration institutions.

	International Arbitration Rules of the AAA	*ICC Rules of Arbitration*	*WIPO Arbitration Rules*	*Arbitration Rules of the LCIA*	*Swiss International Arbitration Rules*	*CIETAC Arbitration Rules*	*JCAA Commercial Arbitration Rules,*	*SCC Arbitration Rules*
Arbitrators	art. 34		art. 76(a)	art. 30(2)	art. 43	art. 33	r. 40(2)	art. 20(3)
Parties			art. 73; 74(a); 75	art. 30(1)	art. 43	art. 33	r. 40(2)	
Witnesses / Experts			art. 74(b)		art. 43	art. 33		
Arbitration institution	art. 34	app. 1, art. 6	art. 76(a)		art. 43	art. 33	r. 40(2)	art. 9
Hearings	art. 20(4)	art. 21(3); app. II, art. 1	art. 53(c)	art. 19(4)		art. 33		art. 20(3)
Information produced in proceedings	art. 34	app. II, art. 1(3)-(6)	art. 74; 76(a)	art. 30(1)	art. 43	art. 33		
Existence of the arbitral procedure			art. 73					
Publication of the award	art. 27(4)		art. 75; 76(a)	art. 30	art. 43			

BIBLIOGRAPHY

ABEL R.L., 'Western Courts in Non-Western Settings: Patterns of Court use in Colonial and Neo-Colonial Africa' in *The Imposition of Law*, S.B. Burman et B.E. Harell-Bond (eds) (New York, Academic Press, 1979).

American Bar Association Task Force on Electronic Commerce and Alternative Dispute Resolution and Shidler Center for Law, Commerce and Technology, University of Washington, 'Addressing Disputes in Electronic Commerce : Final Recommendations and Report' (2002) 58 Bus Law 415.

ARSIC J., 'International Commercial Arbitration on the Internet – Has the Future Come Too Early?' (1997) 14 J Int Arb 209.

Auckland District Law Society, 'Electronic Mail. Guidance for Practitioners' <www.-adls.org.nz/profession/guidelines/guide1.asp>.

AVELLAN J.A., 'Certification Authorities, CA Initiatives and Authentication Products and Services', <www.qmw.ac.uk/~tl6345/ca.htm>.

BELLENGER L. and COUCHAERE M.-J., *Plus efficace et moins stressé* (Issy-les-Moulineaux, ESF, 2004).

BERGER K.P., *Internationale Wirtschaftsschiedsgerichtsbarkeit* (Berlin, de Gruyter, 1992).

BERNARDINI P., National report: Italy, in *International Handbook on Commercial Arbitration*, Suppl. 31 of September 2000, J. Paulsson (ed.) (The Hague, Kluwer Law International).

BRANDL M. and others, 'IP Telephony Cookbook', University of Bremen, <www.informatik.uni-bremen.de/~prelle/terena/Cookbook.pdf>, 9 March 2004.

BRENNAN S.E., 'How conversation is shaped by visual and spoken evidence' in *World Situated Language Use: Psycholinguistic, Linguistic and Computational Perspectives on Bridging the Product and Action Traditions*, J. Trueswell and M. Tanenhaus (eds) (Cambridge MA, MIT Press, 2005).

BROWN A.C., 'Presumption Meets Reality: An Exploration of the Confidentiality Obligation in International Commercial Arbitration' (2001) 16 Am U Int'l L Rev 969.

BUCHANAN B.G. and HEADRICK T.E., 'Some Speculations About Artificial Intelligence and Legal Reasoning' (1970) 23 Stan L Rev 40.

CACHARD O., 'Electronic Arbitration', module of the UNCTAD Course on Dispute Settlement in International Trade, Investment and Intellectual Property, UNCTAD/EDM/Misc.232/Add.20 <www.unctad.org/en/docs/edmmisc232add20_en.-pdf> (Geneva, United Nations Publications, 2003).

CAPPER P. and SUSSKIND R., *Latent Damage Law – The Expert System. A Study of Computers in Legal Problem Solving* (London, Butterworths, 1988).

CARBONNEAU T.E., *Cases and Materials on The Law and Practice of Arbitration* (2nd edn, Yonkers NY, Juris Publishing, 2000).

CHAPANIS A., OCHSMAN R.B., PARRISH R.N., and WEEKS G.D., 'The effects of four communication modes on the behavior of teams during cooperative problem-solving' (1972) 14 *Human Factors* 487.

CHIASSON E.C., 'Confidentiality and Arbitration' (2000) 58 *Advocate* 417.

CLARK H.H. and BRENNAN S.E., 'Grounding in communication' in *Perspectives on socially shared cognition*, L.B. Resnick, R.M. Levine, and S.D. Teasley (eds) (Washington DC, APA Books, 1991).

COLLINS M., 'Privacy and Confidentiality in Arbitration Proceedings' (1995) 30 Tex Int'l L J 121.

CROWELL J., 'The Electronic Courtroom' (1997) 4 B U J Sci & Tech L 10.

DE BOURNONVILLE P., *Droit judiciaire: l'arbitrage* (Brussels, Larcier, 2000).

E-Arbitration-T, 'Online Arbitration: What Technology can do for Arbitral Institutions', IST-2000-25464/11.5/UBRUN/2048/R/2 <www.e-arbitration-t.com/papersadr/ubrun_se-minar_content.pdf>, 20 January 2003.

FORTIER Y., 'The Occasionally Unwarranted Assumption of Confidentiality' (1999) 15 *Arbitration International* 131.

Fouchard Gaillard Goldman on International Commercial Arbitration, E. Gaillard and J. Savage (eds) (The Hague, Kluwer Law International, 1999).

FRACASSI F., 'Confidentiality and NAFTA Chapter 11 Arbitrations' (2001) 2 Chi J Int'l L 213.

FRIEDMANN L.M., 'Courts Over Time: A Survey of Theories and Research' in *Empirical Theories About Courts*, K.O. Boyum and L. Mather (eds) (New York, Longman, 1983).

FRIEDMAN R.D., 'Remote testimony' (2002) 35 U Mich JL Ref 695.

FRIEDMAN T., *The Lexus and the Olive Tree* (HarperCollins, Glasgow, 2000).

FUSSELL S.R., KRAUT R.E., and SIEGEL J., *Coordination of communication: Effects of shared visual context on collaborative work* (New York, ACM Press, 2000).

GABRIEL H.D., 'The New United States Uniform Electronic Transactions Act: Substantive Provisions, Drafting History and Comparison to the UNCITRAL Model Law on Electronic Commerce' [2000] *Revue de droit uniforme* 651.

GIBBONS L.J., KENNEDY R.M., and GIBBS J.M., 'Cyber-mediation: Computer-mediated Communications Medium Massaging the Message' (2002) 32 N M L Rev 27.

GIRSBERGER D. and SCHRAMM D., 'Cyber Arbitration und prozessuale Fairness' in *Geschäftsplattform Internet IV. Open Source – Multimedia – Online Arbitration*, R.H. Weber, M. Berger, and R. auf der Maur (eds) (Zurich, Schulthess, 2003).

GRANT G.L., *Understanding Digital Signatures: Establishing Trust over the Internet and other Networks* (New York, McGraw-Hill, 1998).

HASCHER D., 'Principes et pratique de procédure dans l'arbitrage commercial international' (1999) 279 *Collected Courses of the Hague Academy of International Law* 50.

HELLAND L., 'Remote Testimony – A Prosecutor's Perspective' (2002) 35 U Mich JL Ref 719.

HÖRNLE J., 'Online Dispute Resolution' in *Bernstein's Handbook of Arbitration and Dispute Resolution Practice*, J. Tackaberry and A. Marriott (eds) (4th edn, London, Sweet and Maxwell, 2003).

HUYS M. and KEUTGEN G., *L'arbitrage en droit belge et international* (Brussels, Bruylant, 1981).

International Chamber of Commerce, Commission on Arbitration, 'Report by the Section on Information Technology on Special IT Requirements in International Arbitration', Doc. 420/21-005, 18 March 2002.

International Chamber of Commerce, Commission on Arbitration, 'Operating Standards for Using IT in Arbitration', [2004] ICC Bull, special supplement on 'Using Technology to Resolve Business Disputes'.

JARROSSON C., 'Les frontières de l'arbitrage' [2001] 1 Rev Arb 5.

JOHNSON R.G., 'Negotiating the Dayton Peace Accords Through Digital Maps', (2000) 8 *Virtual Diplomacy Report Series* <www.usip.org/vdi/vdr/rjohnsonISA99.html>.

JOLLES A. and CANALS DE CEDIEL M., 'Confidentiality' in *International Arbitration in Switzerland*, G. Kaufmann-Kohler and B. Stucki (eds) (The Hague, Kluwer Law International, 2004).

KANDRA A. and BRANDT A., 'The Great American Privacy Makeover', PCWorld Magazine <www.pcworld.com/reviews/article/0,aid,112468,pg,1,00.asp>, November 2003, p. 3.

KARSENTY L., 'Cooperative work and shared visual context: An empirical study of comprehension problems and in side-by-side and remote help dialogues' (1999) 14-3 *Human-Computer Interaction* 283.

KATSH E., 'Adding Trust Systems to Transaction Systems: The Role of Online Dispute Resolution', paper presented at the first Forum on Online Dispute Resolution of the United Nations Economic Commission for Europe, Geneva, 6–7 June 2002, <www.-ombuds.org/un/unece_june2002.doc>.

KATSH E., 'Online Dispute Resolution: Some Implications for the Emergence of Law in Cyberspace' (2006) 10 *Lex Electronica* <www.lex-electronica.org/articles/v10-3/katsh.-pdf>.

KATSH E., 'Online Dispute Resolution: Some Lessons from the E-Commerce Revolution' (2001) 28 N Ky L Rev 810.

KATSH E., 'Online Dispute Resolution: The Next Phase' (2002) 7-2 *Lex Electronica* <www.lex-electronica.org/articles/v7-2/katsh.htm>.

KATSH E., *The Electronic Media and the Transformation of Law* (Oxford, OUP, 1989).

KATSH E., 'The Online Ombuds Office: Adapting Dispute Resolution to Cyberspace' NCAIR Dispute Resolution Conference <mantle.sbs.umass.edu/vmag/katsh.htm>, Washington, 22 May 1996.

KATSH E. and GAITENBY A., 'Introduction: Technology as the "Fourth Party"' in *Online Dispute Resolution (ODR): Technology as the 'Fourth Party' Papers and Proceedings of the 2003 United Nations Forum on ODR*, E. Katsh and D. Choi (eds) (UMass, Amherst and United Nations, Geneva 2003) <www.odr.info/unece2003/pdf/Intro.pdf>.

KATSH E. and RIFKIN J., *Online Dispute Resolution. Resolving Conflicts in Cyberspace* (San Francisco, Jossey-Bass, 2001).

KATSH E., RIFKIN J., and GAITENBY A., 'E-Commerce, E-Disputes, and E-Dispute Resolution: In the Shadow of eBay Law' (2000) 15 Ohio St J on Disp Res 705.

KAUFMANN-KOHLER G., *Arbitration at the Olympics: Issues of Fast-Track Dispute Resolution and Sports Law* (The Hague, Kluwer Law International, 2001).

KAUFMANN-KOHLER G. and SCHULTZ. T., *Online Dispute Resolution: Challenges for Contemporary Justice* (The Hague, Kluwer Law International, 2004).

KAUFMANN-KOHLER G. and SCHULTZ T., with the collaboration of LOUKASS E., BONNIN V., PROTOPSALTOU D., and KIM H., 'The Use of Information Technology in Arbitration' [2005] *JusLetter* <www.weblaw.ch/jusletter/Artikel.asp?ArticleNr=4410&Language=1>.

KESSEDJIAN C., 'Principe de la contradiction et arbitrage' [1995] Rev Arb 381.

KIDD D.L. and DAUGHTREY W., 'Adapting Contract Law to Accommodate Electronic Contracts' (2000) 26 Rutgers Computer & Tech L J 215.

KLANG M., 'Improving Arbitration with Information Technology' in *Proceedings of the 21st Information Systems Research Seminar in Scandinavia (IRIS)*, 'Information Systems Research in Collaboration with Industry', 8–11 August, H.J. Buch and others (ed.), Sæby Søbad, Denmark, Department of Computer Science, Aalborg University.

KRAUSE W., 'Do You Want to Step Outside? An Overview of Online Alternative Dispute Resolution' (2001) 19 J Marshall J Computer & Info L 457.

KRAUT R.E., FUSSELL S.R., BRENNAN S.E., and SIEGEL J., 'Understanding effects of proximity on collaboration: Implications for technologies to support remote collaborative work' in *Distributed work*, P. Hinds and S.B. Kiesler (eds) (Cambridge MA, MIT Press, 2002).

KRAUT R.K., GERGLE D., and FUSSEL S.R., 'The Use of Visual Information in Shared Visual Spaces: Informing the Development of Virtual Co-Presence' in Proceedings of CSCW 2002 <www-2.cs.cmu.edu/~kraut/RKraut.site.files/articles/kraut02-VisualInfoIn-SharedVisualSpaces.pdf>.

KUHN T., *The Structure of Scientific Revolutions* (Chicago, University of Chicago Press, 1970).

LANIER J., 'Virtually There' (2001) 284-4 Scientific American 66.

LEDERER F.I., 'The Road to the Virtual Courtroom? A Consideration of Today's – and Tomorrow's – High-Technology Courtrooms' (1999) 50 SC L Rev 799.

LENOX B.A., 'Personal Jurisdiction in Cyberspace: Teaching the Stream of Commerce Dog New Internet Tricks: Compuserve, Inc. v. Patterson, 89 F.3d 1257 (6th Cir. 1996)' (1997) 22 Dayton L Rev 331.

LEW J.D.M., MISTELIS L.A., and KRÖLL S.M., *Comparative International Commercial Arbitration* (The Hague, Kluwer Law International, 2003).

LEIBOWITZ W.R., 'The Wired World of Marketing Legal Services: There's a New Standard in Netting, Knowing and Keeping Clients' (2001) 27 *Law Practice Management* 28.

LIEBSCHER C., *The Healthy Award – Challenge in International Commercial Arbitration* (The Hague, Kluwer Law International, 2003).

LINSMEAU J., *L'arbitrage volontaire en droit privé belge* (Brussels, Bruylant, 1991).

LOCKRIDGE A., 'The Silent Treatment: Removing the Class Action From the Plaintiff's Toolbox Without Ever Saying a Word' [2003] J Disp Resol 255.

MAILLOT P.-G., 'Using quaternions for coding 3D transformations' in *Graphic Gems*, A.S. Glassner (ed) (Boston, Academic Press, 1990).

MCLUHAN M., *Explorations in Communication* (Boston, Beacon Press, 1960).

MÜLLER C., 'La confidentialité en arbitrage commercial international: un trompe-l'œil?' (2005) 23 ASA Bull 217.

MUSTILL M.J., 'Arbitration: History and Background' (1989) 6 J Int'l Arb 43.

NAUSS EXON S., 'The Internet Meets Obi-Wan Kenobi In The Court Of Next Resort' (2002) 8 B U J Sci & Tech L 1.

PARK SUNOO B., 'Hot Disputes Cool Down in Online Mediation' (2001) 48 Personnel J 3.

PAULSSON J. and RAWDING N., 'The Trouble with Confidentiality' (1995) 11 *Arbitration International* 303.

PERRITT H.H., 'Dispute Resolution in Cyberspace: Demand for New Forms of ADR' (2000) 15 Ohio St J on Disp Resol 675.

PHILIPPE M., 'NetCase: A New ICC Arbitration Facility' in *Using Technology to Resolve Business Disputes*, Special Supplement ICC Bull (Paris, ICC Publishing, 2004), p. 53.

POST D., 'Controlling Cybercopies' [1996] *Legal Times* 44.

POUDRET J.-F. and BESSON S., *Droit comparé de l'arbitrage international* (Zurich, Schulthess, 2002).

PROTOPSALTOU D., SCHULTZ T., and MAGNENAT-THALMANN N., 'Taking the Fourth Party Further? Considering a shared virtual workspace for arbitration' [2006] *Information and Communication Technology Law*, special issue on the virtualization of justice, in press.

RABINOVICH-EINY O., 'Balancing the Scales: The Ford-Firestone Case, the Internet, and the Future Dispute Resolution Landscape' (2004) 6 Yale J of L & Tech 2.

RABURN-REMFRY P., 'Due Process Concerns In Video Production Of Defendants' (1994) 23 Stetson L Rev 805.

RAESCHKE-KESSLER H. and K.P. BERGER, *Recht und Praxis des Schiedsverfahren* (3rd edn, Cologne, RWS, 1999).

REDFERN A. and HUNTER M., *The Law and Practice of Commercial Arbitration* (4th edn, London, Sweet and Maxwell, 2004).

REEB M., *CAS Awards - Sydney 2000. The decisions delivered by the ad hoc Division of the Court of Arbitration for Sport during the 2000 Olympic Games in Sydney* (Lausanne, CAS, 2000).

RHOLL E., 'Web-enabled ADR and extranets', *National Law Journal* <www.nlj.com>, 2 December 2002.

RICE F.C., 'Protecting Personal Data in your Word Documents' <msdn.microsoft.com/-library/default.asp?url=/library/en-us/dnword2k2/html/odc_ProtectWord.asp>.

RIGOZZI A., *L'arbitrage international en matière de sport* (Basle, Helbing & Lichtenhahn, 2005).

ROSELL J., 'Global Development: Confidentiality and Arbitration' (2002) 9 Croat Arbit Yearb 19.

ROTH M.D., 'Laissez-Faire Videoconferencing: Remote Witness Testimony and Adversarial Truth' (2000) 48 UCLA L Rev 185.

SCHÄFER E., 'Der Einsatz von Informationstechnologie in der Handelschiedsgerichtsbarkeit', <www.dis-arb.de/materialien/DIS_Vortr_ITuARB.pdf>, 10 April 2002.

SCHÄFER E., 'Videoconferencing in arbitration' (2003) 14:1 ICC Bull 35.

SCHNEIDER M.E. and KUNER C., 'Dispute Resolution in International Electronic Commerce' (1997) 14 J Int Arb 5.

SCHULTZ T., 'Connecting complaint filing processes to online resolution systems' (2003) 10 *Commercial Law Practitioner* 307.

SCHULTZ T., 'Does online dispute resolution need governmental intervention? The case for architectures of control and trust' (2004) 6 NC J L & Tech 71.

SCHULTZ T., 'eBay: un système juridique en formation' (2005) 22 RDTI 27.

SCHULTZ T., 'Human Rights: A Speed Bump for Arbitral Procedures? An exploration of safeguards in the acceleration of justice' (2006) 9:1 Int A L R 8.

SCHULTZ T., *Réguler le commerce électronique par la résolution des litiges en ligne* (Brussels, Bruylant, 2005).

SCHULTZ T., 'Sailing away from judicial interference: Arbitrating the America's Cup' [2006] 1-2 *International Sports Law Journal*, in press.

SHORT J., WILLIAMS E., and CHRISTIE B., *The Social Psychology of Telecommunications* (London, Wiley, 1976).

SMIT H., 'Breach of Confidentiality as a Ground for Avoidance of the Arbitration Agreement' (2000) 11 Am Rev Int'l Arb 567.

SUSSKIND R., *Essays on law and artificial intelligence* (Oslo, Tano, 1993).

SUSSKIND R., *Expert Systems in Law* (Oxford, OUP, 1987).

SUSSKIND R., 'Hold on to your seats, change is getting faster', *The Times*, 24 January 2006.

SUSSKIND R., *The Future of Law* (Oxford, OUP, 1996).

SUSSKIND R., *Transforming the Law* (Oxford, OUP, 2000).

Tandberg Corp., 'Tandberg and Security', D50172, Rev 3.1, <www.tandbergusa.com/-collateral/white_papers/whitepaper_TANDBERG_Security.pdf>

THIESSEN E.M. and MCMAHON J.P., 'Beyond Win-Win in Cyberspace' (2000) 15 Ohio St J on Disp Resol 643.

VAN DEN BERG A.J., *The New York Convention of 1958: Towards a Uniform Judicial Interpretation* (Deventer, Kluwer Law International, 1981).

VEINOTT E., OLSON J., OLSON G., and FU X., 'Video helps remote work: Speakers who need to negotiate common ground benefit from seeing each other' in *Proceedings of CHI'99* (1999).

YNGVESSON B. and MATHER L., 'Courts, Moots, and the Disputing Process' in *Empirical Theories About Courts*, K.O. Boyum and L. Mather (eds) (New York, Longman, 1983).

WALSH N., 'XML.com: A Technical Introduction to XML' <www.xml.com/pub/a/98/-10/guide0.html>, 3 October 1998.

WHITTAKER S. and O'CONAILL B., 'The role of vision in face-to-face and mediated communication' in *Video-mediated communication*, K. Finn, A. Sellen, and S. Wilbur (eds) (Mahwah NJ, LEA Press, 1997).

WÜHLER N., 'The United Nations Compensation Commission: A new contribution to the process of international claims resolution' (1999) 2 J Int'l Econ L 249.

ZHUANG L., ZHOU F., and TYGAR J.D., 'Keyboard Acoustic Emanations Revisited' <www.cs.berkeley.edu/%7Etygar/papers/Keyboard_Acoustic_Emanations_Revisited/-preprint.pdf> (Berkeley, University of California, November 2005).

LIST OF FIGURES

INDEX

ABOUT THE AUTHOR

Dr Thomas Schultz, currently at Cambridge University, was previously a fellow at the Law School of Geneva University, where he served as the principal researcher for a number of projects on arbitration, information technology and online dispute resolution. On these topics, he has been engaged in work with, and often has provided advisory services to, the United Nations, the Swiss Arbitration Association, the Federation of European Direct Marketing, the America's Cup, and a major Swiss consumer organization.

He is author of two of the most widely respected books on information technology in dispute resolution: *Online Dispute Resolution: Challenges for Contemporary Justice* (with Gabrielle Kaufmann-Kohler, Kluwer Law International, 2004) and *Réguler le commerce électronique par la résolution des litiges en ligne* (Bruylant and L.G.D.J., 2005).

He earned a *summa cum laude* doctorate from Geneva University Law School, a master in laws from the European Academy of Legal Theory in Brussels, and graduated from Geneva University Law School.

Dr Schultz writes and is a frequent speaker in the areas of arbitration, online dispute resolution, cyberspace law and legal theory. His publications earned him, *inter alia*, to be finalist of the Jubilee prize of the Swiss Academy of Humanities and Social Sciences, rewarding the single best research article in all areas of the humanities and the social sciences by a young scholar in Switzerland, for an article on the impact of technology in dispute resolution.